A HISTOR
THE DIOCESE OF C ON

State of Grace

PAMELA SMITH, SSCM, PhD

✝

Blessings to you!

Sister Pamela Smith, SSCM

THE
History
PRESS

Published by The History Press
Charleston, SC
www.historypress.com

Copyright © 2020 by Pamela Smith
All rights reserved

Images courtesy of the Diocese of Charleston Archives and the *Catholic Miscellany*.

First published 2020

Manufactured in the United States

ISBN 9781467145879

Library of Congress Control Number: 2020932101

Contents

Preface

There are many ways to write histories. What has often been termed the "great man theory" of history means that history is written in terms of heads of state who have held office or bishops who have led dioceses. This creates a seamless chronology but also suggests that one person defines an era.

In writing this history of the Diocese of Charleston, it has seemed important to observe chronology in an approximate way but also to proceed thematically. Certain notes and certain themes dominate periods, and always in the background stand thousands and hundreds of thousands of people who not only are affected by history but also make it.

This work, which has been inspired by much reading and considerable travel and consultation around the state, is dedicated to the faithful, those described as "Church"—People of God, Body of Christ and Temple of the Holy Spirit—in the *Catechism of the Catholic Church*. The breath of God moves in and through them, under the leadership of impactful bishops, sterling clergy and religious and laypersons whose gifts so often go unheralded when the life and movement of Church, nation and world are recounted. As the very first bishop of Charleston observed:

> *Our efforts are not those of individuals, nor of disjointed societies; we are members of a body in which there exists but one spirit, and which has but one rule of common action. When one member suffers, all sympathize; when one is invigorated, all rejoice.*[1]

May this bicentennial history honor the very spirited body of our local—that is, statewide—Church.

ACKNOWLEDGEMENTS

D uring the time of my service as director of catechesis and Christian
initiation and then as secretary for education and faith formation,
I logged many miles and made visits to numerous parishes and
schools. I am grateful to all of these for their hospitality and for the view
into their history that accompanied the experience of their dynamic present.
In addition to the people who made the visits hospitable, I am grateful to
directors, staff and/or those overseeing the following locations I have been
privileged to visit before and during my tenure as director of ecumenical and
interreligious affairs:

- The Archives of the Diocese of Charleston, and especially Brian
  Fahey and Melissa Mabry, who were the best resources for fact
  checking and photo procurement.
- The Santa Elena Monument at Parris Island.
- The Santa Elena History Center, Beaufort, South Carolina, with
  its heritage display; its film, *Santa Elena: America's Untold Story*, and
  lectures on excavations of the site at Parris Island provided on March
  24, 2018, by Dr. Lawrence Rowland and John Goldsborough; and
  on Native Americans and connections between the Santa Elena
  settlement and the later colonization of Jamestown offered on April
  6, 2018, by Christopher Hill.
- The motherhouse and heritage room of the Sisters of Charity of Our
  Lady of Mercy, Charleston, and the tour and materials provided by

Sister Anne Francis Campbell, OLM, who also gave the manuscript a thorough reading and offered clarifications and corrections.

- Our Lady of Mercy Community Outreach Center at Johns Island, with the tour and printed materials offered by Erika Plater.
- Mercy Mission in Hardeeville and the tour and background provided by Sister Mary Fran Bassick, DC, supplementing an earlier visit to the mission before its renovation and before the deaths of Sisters Mary Gallagher, RSM, and Lupe Stumpf, RSM.
- Our Lady of the Valley Outreach Center, visited when the Daughters of Charity were managing it.
- The St. Francis Center on St. Helena Island, to which I was introduced when Sisters Sheila Byrne and Stella Breen, OSF, operated it as the Franciscan Center and to which I am now committed as my own community of religious sisters, the Sisters of Saints Cyril and Methodius, have entrusted it to the leadership of Sisters Canice Adams and Marcine Klocko, SSCM.
- The Felician Center in Kingstree, where I learned of its history and service through the hospitality of Sisters Suzanne Dziedzic and Johnna Ciezobka, CSSF.
- The Pee Dee Regional Office of Catholic Charities in Conway, where Michelle Borbely provided much information and insight.
- Mepkin Abbey, which I have visited and at which I have prayed numerous times, even before I ever dreamed of living in South Carolina.
- Springbank Retreat in Kingstree, where I have made private retreats and offered days of recollection on St. Thomas Aquinas and environmental ethics, creation themes in the Bible and poetry as a contemplative discipline.
- The annual Collaboration for Ministry Initiative gatherings for sisters missioned in this diocese, sponsored by the Sisters of Charity of St. Augustine and its foundation, which has afforded an opportunity to meet and learn of sisters active in ministry across the state, and also the Poor Clare community, which is represented each year.
- The various ecumenical gatherings that I have attended and participated in with the Fellowship of South Carolina Bishops (formerly LARCUM), the South Carolina Christian Action Council and the Interfaith Partners of South Carolina.
- The Catholic schools in the Diocese of Charleston, their principals and especially the superintendent, Sandra Leatherwood.

Many of the Charleston diocesan departments, their directors and staff have been excellent resources and have responded promptly to requests for information, statistics or comment. Those who have provided direct service include the following offices:

- Archives and Record Management
- Catechesis and Christian Initiation
- Catholic Charities
- Catholic Schools
- Chancellor
- Diaconate
- Ethnic Ministries
- Family Life
- Hispanic Ministry
- Multimedia and especially the *Catholic Miscellany*, now under the Secretariat of Communications and Public Policy
- Planning and Operations
- Priest Personnel
- Social Ministries
- The Secretariat of Evangelization and Education
- Youth, Young Adult and Campus Ministries

I also have to make special note of Dr. Brian Cudahy, who made it a point to meet with me and share the full manuscript of his recently released book, *From Blackmoor Lane to Capitol Hill*, along with papers he has written about John England. These are listed in the bibliography.

PHOTOS PROVIDED IN THIS text have all been drawn from the Office of Archives, Diocese of Charleston, or the files of the *Catholic Miscellany*, the diocesan newspaper. I am grateful especially to Melissa Mabry and Caroline Lindsey for their eye for suitable photographs and good design. Drawings are believed to have been published in the *Catholic Miscellany*.

INTRODUCTION

When people speak of grace in connection with the South, they tend to go one of two directions. The first is overlaid with charm. It offers vistas of roadways lined with live oaks draped in Spanish moss leading up to old plantations with gallant columns and sweeping staircases. The ideal of gracious living bears vestiges of Tara from *Gone with the Wind*: chamber music, stiff collars, petticoats, southern cooking, slaves in the fields and slaves in the manor house decked out in servants' livery.

The second follows the route of religion. It sings with the strong rhythm of "Amazing Grace," composed by slave trader John Newton, who gave up treating human beings as commodities and cargo when he found Jesus in the mid-eighteenth century. It is that same grace, saving grace, of which John Carroll spoke when he was appointed in 1790 to serve as the first bishop of what he termed "the flourishing commonwealth of the Thirteen American States." He recounted that he "willingly embraced this opportunity which the grace of Almighty God has afforded us to provide those distant regions with the comfort and ministry of a Catholic Bishop."[2] The comfort he anticipated providing was spiritual, but it also had ample material elements, which included stabilizing existing communities of faith, erecting parishes and schools and engaging the civic community. It was left to one of his successors, John England, born in County Cork, Ireland, to shepherd one of the early subdivisions of that first American diocese in 1820. The Roman Congregation of the Propagation of the Faith had recommended him to Pope Pius VII as a man of grace, one "especially outstanding for his piety, prudence, zeal, and faith."[3] He brought to the Carolinas and Georgia, and particularly to Charleston, both senses of grace: refinement of manner and indefatigable care of souls.

As the story of the Diocese of Charleston unfolds, it is clear that the dual nature of grace marks it. There is the grace that the beauty of the region and the splendor of its historic sites exemplify. There is also the grace that sanctifies and imparts an intimacy with the Blessed Trinity and the promise of eternal destiny in their embrace. As the stories told here show, that history is fraught with the tensions of sin and grace, dissolution and creation, slavery and freedom, tragedy and hope. One can justifiably regard the history of the Catholic Diocese of Charleston as a story of the "state of grace" on multiple levels: personal and collective, ecclesiastical and civil.

Chapter 1

Santa Elena, the Spanish Foothold

*Before Jamestown
Before Plymouth,
There was
Santa Elena*

Billboards in and around Beaufort and on interstates and South Carolina's state highways bear this message. So, too, do leaflets in the Tourist Center off Carteret Street, pointing to the little-known Spanish incursion into the sea island that is part of the long-hidden history of Catholicism in South Carolina.

Ribaut Road is named for Jean Ribaut, the Frenchman—a French Huguenot—who started a colony on what is now Parris Island. One of his surprises was what is estimated to have been $1.6 million in Spanish gold, looted from Native Americans there. It may have come from sunken vessels, but it more likely originated with adventurers and explorers who started visiting Santa Elena in the early sixteenth century, decades before Pedro Menéndez de Avilés erected forts and a settlement. By 1566, a year after Ribaut's death in a Spanish-led slaughter, there was Fort San Felipe at Parris Island; by 1577, there was Fort San Marcos. An earlier settlement was called San Miguel de Guadalupe.[4]

It appears that Beaufort's prize and Parris Island's precursor, Santa Elena, changed hands and names a number of times. It was part of La Florida, the Spanish colonial expanse, and there is growing evidence that Santa Elena was its first capital. Some say that Spanish seafarers arrived on the island as early as 1514.[5] Others cite "the first voyage of historical record" as landing at Santa Elena in 1521[6] or slightly earlier, in 1520.[7] The location is still subject to dispute—with current St. Helena Island and Hilton Head Island in South Carolina, Tybee in Georgia and the environs of Winyah Bay, South Carolina, sometimes claimed as the site. But the preponderance of evidence points to Santa Elena having been the sea island off Beaufort, where Marine Corps recruits currently slog through mud, seagrass and fallen branches tangled with bug-infested moss.

Santa Elena was regarded as a jewel. Ribaut, who called it Charlesfort, said (in an older English translation), "There is no fayrer…place."[8] He saw Port Royal Sound (as yet unnamed) as having the potential of a great seaport. When the Spanish held their twenty-one-year settlement from 1566 to 1587, they undoubtedly saw the same panorama of possibility.

For the Diocese of Charleston, not established until 1820, it is historically significant that Santa Elena served a dual purpose: establishing a base for both the Spanish territory in the New World and the propagation of the faith. In 1557, King Philip II of Spain is documented as directing Floridian settlers thus: "That the colonists were not to conquer those nations, nor to do what had been done in the discovery of the Indies, but to settle, and by good example, with good works and with presents, to bring them to a knowledge of our Holy Faith and Catholic Truth."[9]

They were not to behave as brutal conquistadors had and would. Philip directed that Santa Elena be one of two settlements in La Florida, the land full of flowers. Yet simultaneous documents indicate that Pedro Menéndez, the governing officer, was instructed to carry, in his fleet, "'useful' people, food, tools, and weapons in order to supply the crew, and carry out the conquest and colonization of La Florida."[10] Spain's motive was to secure treasure routes from Newfoundland to Mexico and to locate what was expected to be a great inland sea with a potential trade route to the Orient.[11]

Even before Santa Elena was settled, black African slaves showed up on American shores; Spanish explorers had brought them. When Pedro Menéndez first left Spain for the Americas, he had permission from the Spanish royals to bring five hundred slaves to La Florida. The shrouds of history have left chroniclers of his first excursions with some uncertainty as to what extent he actually brought captured Africans to these shores, how he might have treated them, how many may have come or whether he initially brought any at all. What is known is that he wanted Native Americans treated affably. He hoped for their conversion and had planned to send the children of "Indian rulers" to be educated in Havana. Cuba, of course, was part of what was becoming imperial

Spanish America—South America, Central America, Hispaniola and North America (La Florida).[12] There were apparently a number of voyages back and forth, and since the plan to dispatch young Native Americans to Havana seems to have failed, persuasive stories of youths being sent to Spain to be catechized and Europeanized persist.

Pedro Menéndez de Avilés wrested Santa Elena from the French Huguenots in 1565. With his soldiers came Jesuits. In 1566, Menéndez, who had also founded St. Augustine in 1565, thus further populated Spanish holdings in the New World. Spain's claim to North America was seen as the directive of Divine Providence: "The Spanish government believed it had exclusive rights to the continent by the blessing of the Catholic Church"[13] This opinion, not surprisingly, was not shared by France, and it was particularly resisted by the French Huguenots.

MENÉNDEZ

The man who made Santa Elena his capital was the one known as the *adelantado*, the governor. Pedro Menéndez de Avilés was also to be known not long thereafter, by decree of King Philip of Spain, as the "Captain General of the West."[14]

By some accounts, he was a miracle worker, a genius of navigation and combat who time and again overcame seemingly insuperable odds. He was indeed an accomplished seaman who had outwitted pirates as a youth, saved a bride and her bridesmaids from rape and pillage and, in his more mature years, captured Fort Caroline in the Carolinas in the midst of a hurricane. He liked speed and was adept at breaking, or at least bending, rules when it would help get a job done. His loyalty to the king of Spain was nonnegotiable.

Because of his zeal and his methods, other accounts simply judge him a relentless murderer. He led a group of Frenchmen to believe that he was acceding to their requests for mercy. Then he divided them into groups of ten and had his troops behead them. He had the head of Jean Ribaut carried into his fort on a pike. A Floridian inlet he invaded became known as *Matanzas*, the "Place of Slaughters."[15] Menéndez shrugged off these massacres and said that he had given the French Huguenots honorable deaths, given the fact that the order of the day was burning heretics at the stake.

Pedro Menéndez practiced religion, having the chaplain sing the *Te Deum* and say Mass at every settlement and every victory. He named places for the saint of the day: Helen, Augustine and Matthew. At the same time, he was a rabid pursuer of treasure, a man possessed by the spirit of the conquistadors. He was a family man who scoured the coasts of La Florida and Havana in hopes of one day finding his shipwrecked son. He took lifelong risks and endangered hosts of men, but he bothered to spare the lives of a quartet of musicians in the midst of bloody escapades. He was a loyal friend of Philip II of Spain and a captain who had men so loyal they would follow him to the death. Yet he also had discouraged, hungry, cold troops and settlers who deserted him and, on at least one occasion, raised a mutiny.[16] He wanted to evangelize nonbelievers and holders of superstitions, but his relationships with Native Americans were ambivalent—and he apparently brought as yet uncatechized slaves with him.

Menéndez, the *adelantado*, was a driven, complex man, apparently quite unaware of his own contradictions. His biographer insisted that his faith drove him, and he described the spread of religion as part of his "master plan for Florida." It was one that assumed there was a need for "pastoral care…for the colonists and soldiers" but also a responsibility of the "militant Church [to bring] the Gospel to people who, without it, were condemned."[17] It was this man who first brought Catholicism to the sea islands and hoped to lay a foundation for a future of Catholicism in what was eventually to become the Diocese of Charleston.

Religious History

September 1565 is supposed by some to have been the date of the first Catholic Mass celebrated in a North American settlement. But a number of resources focused on explorers' travels presume a time decades earlier. The main reason for contention about this is the fact that Spanish explorers tended to bring priests along on all of their voyages and, when possible, on all of the ships in a flotilla. Monsignor Richard Madden, noted historian of the Diocese of Charleston, cited a landing at Winyah Bay in 1526 as the likeliest date for a first Mass on the mainland and 1540, thanks to the incursions of Ferdinand de Soto, as the likely date for a first Mass in the Piedmont.[18] Then there are the legends of other voyages and voyagers. John Buescher noted that there are stories dating to the time of St. Brendan (circa AD 512) that put Irish monks on American shores. Norsemen told of Eric Gnuppson, a bishop from Iceland then living in Greenland, who went to Vinland or Vineland in 1121.[19]

Central America lays claim to Epiphany 1494 as the time of a first Mass in the present Dominican Republic, a date coinciding with the second voyage of Christopher Columbus. South America cites a celebration of Mass by a Portuguese priest in 1500 at Vera Cruz, Brazil. As far as the continental United States and its commonwealth is concerned, Ponce de León and Vasco Núñez de Balboa are credited with having brought priests along with new colonists to Puerto Rico and the bay of San Miguel in 1509 and 1513, respectively.[20]

Whether or not we can pinpoint the date of the first Mass in the Americas—North, Central or South—it is important to note that Florida and the Carolinas were sites of Eucharistic liturgies in the sixteenth century. Aside from Masses having been celebrated, we can be certain that confessions were heard, marriages were blessed, babies were baptized, the sick were anointed and the dying received viaticum, their last Holy Communion.

We also have tales of Native Americans having been taken to Spain, Christianized and, as was a common practice then, Europeanized in the process. One such story tells of Paquiquinejo, an Algonquin, who was transported to Spain and there took on the name Don Luis. Another, a youth who went with him, was thought to have been a young Native American, an "underling" later known as "the altar boy." Paquiquinejo, who was related to Virginia's Powhatan, later returned to La Florida, in the vicinity of the Bahia de Santa Maria (St. Mary's Bay, now the Chesapeake). Upon his return, he reverted to Algonquin dress and his native religion and led an attack in which eight Jesuits were killed. There is developing speculation that, in the raid, an altar boy was allowed to live and that he is identified as the younger Alonso de Olmos, the son of the tailor of Santa Elena and later a soldier in St. Augustine.[21]

Both the forced conversion of Native Americans (or their willing conversion that led to abandonment of their tribal cultures) and the early existence of slavery are parts of the unfortunate record of the Santa Elena settlement and, thus, of the prehistory of the Diocese of Charleston. At the same time, it has to be noted that a certain religious beauty persists in this history. One of the stunning display boards at the Santa Elena History Center in Beaufort is entitled "The Church." It shows a schematic of an early chapel and notes that there was a structure on Parris Island (then Santa Elena) not unlike the small mission churches that dot rural South Carolina to this day. The prominent painting on this display shows a priest in a white "fiddle-back" chasuble, as it is sometimes termed, elevating the host. Gold candlesticks adorn the altar, and a gold monstrance is off to the side, ready for exposition. It speaks of the chapel's adornments: a crucifix, a painted image of Christ, a leather canopy over the altar area, fine vessels and vestments.

Fort San Felipe became a wreckage after a Native American revolt in 1576. Fort San Marcos, built by the nephew of Pedro Menéndez, opened in 1577 and lasted until 1587, when Santa Elena was vacated. By that time, Sir Francis Drake was gaining control of the Carolinas and Florida. One year later, in 1588, the British would defeat the Spanish armada in a historic coup. Spain thereafter concentrated its resources on Cuba, Mexico, Central and South America.

The loveliness and lushness of the islands in and around Port Royal Sound (once the Bahia de Santa Elena) have birthed and nourished Native Americans, French and Spanish settlers, Englishmen, Gullah-Geechee people enslaved and then freed and, now, migrants from Mexico, along with retirees fleeing the cold of Canada and the northeastern and upper midwestern United States. Parris Island, the Marine Corps training base, active since 1915, can be seen as an indirect descendant of the early Spanish naval forces that settled on the sea islands.

The other descendants of Santa Elena would have to include a church, a school, a mission and an outreach center. St. Peter's parish still has its historic church in downtown Beaufort. That church was built by an Irish immigrant, Michael O'Connor, and dedicated by Bishop Ignatius Reynolds in 1846. The parish moved closer to Parris Island when it relocated to a larger property on Lady's Island and built a sizable church in 1987, a school in 1991 and a still larger church with a capacity of 1,200 people in 2006. Holy Cross Mission on St. Helena Island was established in 1963, first at a storefront church and then at a gas station, a facility called the Soul Palace and, finally, on a property where a new facility was built in 1972. Worshipers from Fripp, Harbor, Dataw, St. Helena and smaller surrounding islands occupy this mission.[22] The former Franciscan Center, now St. Francis Center, has been in existence on St. Helena Island for nearly forty years as an outreach ministry.

The parish, the school, the mission and the outreach center tend to the care of souls while also tending to many basic needs. In some sense, things have come full circle as an escalation of Spanish-speaking residents and migrants has reshaped the ministries of the Catholic facilities in the Beaufort area. Every Sunday, third-millenium Catholics receive *el Cuerpo de Cristo*, knowing that they can help educate or be educated, assist their neighbors with home repairs or basic household needs and feed or be fed at Catholic-run institutions.

Before Jamestown and before Plymouth, Santa Elena established itself, though briefly, where the Diocese of Charleston came to be. True to its name, St. Helen, a Spanish padre uncovered the Cross, confirmed the true faith and bore the Body of Christ into South Carolina.

Chapter 2

FROM SETTLEMENT TO COLONY TO STATE

F rom the end of the Santa Elena settlement to the arrival of John
England in Charleston, Catholics in the Carolinas and Georgia had
a spotty history. Dominican and Franciscan friars and Jesuit priests
traveled to the sea islands and made forays into the interior. Sebastian
Montero, "a secular priest," is said to have catechized the Wateree tribe in
what is thought to be the present Anderson County in the late 1560s and
early 1570s.[23]

The Catholic faith, though far from widespread, was established in some
quarters in Georgia and Florida by Spanish Franciscans over the next
hundred years. His Excellency Gabriel Diaz Vara Calderon, bishop of Cuba,
oversaw Florida and Georgia and considered the English colony of Port St.
George (now Charleston) as one of his borders as of 1674–75.[24] Charles II of
England renamed Port St. George after himself, dubbing it Charles Towne.
Father Scott Buchanan has noted that Charles II "was secretly Catholic" and
that "one of the ironies of history" is that the practice of Catholicism was
deemed illegal once the colony was established.[25] From that time forward,
until somewhat after the United States had a Constitution, Catholicism was
officially suppressed, and for decades many Catholics—including members
of the Yemasee tribe and German, Scottish and English colonists who had
been Catholic—joined Anglican churches.[26] By the late 1600s, the taking
of oaths that professed loyalty to the Established Church (of England) was
required for a man to vote on any matter. By 1697, the Carolina legislature
had enacted the free practice of religion for all Christians except "Papists."[27]

Among the worst days for Catholics occurred when James Moore was the royal governor of the Carolinas. Between 1702 and 1706, he pushed the occasional Spanish settlers south and sentenced captured priests and native converts to executions so bloody that many Protestants, including their clergy, were horrified.[28]

Surprisingly enough, Catholic men, despite the lack of a legal right to practice their faith, were gradually granted the right to vote on civic matters, although governance of the Carolinas was organized not on townships or counties but on the boundaries of Anglican parishes.[29] The British colonial period saw a paltry number of Catholics attempting or able to practice their faith in what would become John Carroll's diocese and finally John England's. As Buchanan has observed, "The few Catholics who remained in the Carolinas did so with great difficulty, most often relying on priests who were quietly passing through the area, usually from Canada to Louisiana, for the sacraments."[30] It was during the eighteenth century that historians record suspicion that priests were making inroads into the Carolinas in disguise.[31] An additional problem arose when, in 1755, Acadian Catholics, who were fleeing British rule in Canada, were dropped off in the Charleston area. Some few of them stayed at Sullivan's Island, while others scattered, returning to Canada or wending their way south to Louisiana,[32] where they became known as the Cajuns. French traders were known to have been traveling with priests bent on converting natives, so the Acadians fell into a situation that might be called guilt by association—association by virtue of language, national origin and religion. These Acadians were Catholics, and the combination of their tongue, their refugee status and their religion made them suspect. No one was quite sure where their core loyalties might lie.

When the American Revolution began, the handful of Catholics in the Carolinas were divided between partisans of the Revolution and British Loyalists. Loyalists in some cases retreated from the colony after the war had been won and the Union confederated.

Among the Catholic heroes of the post-Revolutionary period were Irish Catholics who had joined the Revolution, along with the Le Bon family residing in Lexington and later Brush Creek in the Upstate region. They were French Catholics whose patriarch had first come to North America with the Marquis de Lafayette. Le Bon later returned with his wife and brother. Another was the Sumter family, whose son, Colonel Thomas Sumter Jr., married a Franco-American, Nathalie De Lage, in 1802. Mrs. Sumter, as she came to be known, was the daughter-in-law of General Thomas Sumter Sr., who was considered a war hero. Thus, she was accepted into Charleston's highest social circles even while she was conducting "dry Masses" (prayer and hymns) and catechism classes each Sunday on the Sumter plantation.[33]

Among Mrs. Sumter's catechetical students were slaves who were Catholics and converts to Catholicism. Historical accounts of the Stono slave rebellion of 1739 note that Mrs. Sumter's slaves were preceded by slaves who had arrived on American shores as already baptized Catholics. Buchanan has suggested that the unsuccessful Stono slave rebellion was not only about the fact of slavery itself but also occasioned by the power struggle between Spanish and British, which affected their religious background. Buchanan noted that it was the desire of slaves, some of whom came from Angola and the Congo, "not only [to] be free persons but also [to] practice their faith without hindrance."[34]

A Heritage of Slavery

Slavery was part of South Carolinian culture from the earliest days. The settlers of Santa Elena, as noted earlier, brought slaves with them, and Spanish conquistadors conscripted native tribal peoples as slaves. The later planters used slave labor. The buying, selling and employing of slaves and their families persisted until 1865. Catholic families and Catholic clergy alike had slaves.

All this was true despite the fact that Pope Paul III in 1537, in *Sublimis Deus*, had condemned the slave trade and the treatment of African slaves and indigenous peoples as though they were livestock. We may attribute the centuries-long persistence of slaveholding among Catholics to several factors. One was the fact that papal documents were written in Latin and generally were accessible only to theologically educated clergy. Another was the slowness of transportation and communication. A telling factor, however, was the lack of "ecclesiastical censures and penalties" to be applied to those who violated the prohibitions levied by Paul III.[35] This opened the way for slavery to be tolerated from the era of Bishop (later Archbishop) John Carroll of Baltimore and the bishops of Charleston through Patrick Lynch. Bishops and clerics accommodated civil society's mores and held to a theory of gradualism in terms of improving the treatment and status of slaves.

That having been said, it remains important to consider what we know today of slavery and the slave trade. Long before the 1970s television miniseries based on Alex Haley's *Roots* and more than fifty years before the making of the film *Amistad*, Robert Hayden, an African American poet, in the 1940s published the poem "Middle Passage." It recounted the fevers that ravaged the sardine-cramped quarters, the chains, the rapes, the stench, the prayers for death and the loss of those who "leaped with crazy laughter/to the waiting sharks, [and] sand as they went under."[36]

Any history of the United States, or of any diocese within it, has to come to terms with the fact that the U.S. Constitution for some eighty years protected slavery and legitimized the slave trade in slaveholding states. These states deemed slavery essential to their economic well-being. As Hasan Kwame Jeffries has noted, "It is often said that slavery was our country's original sin, but it is much more than that. It was responsible for the growth of the American colonies, transforming them…to glimmering jewels in the crown of England. And slavery was a driving power behind the new nation's territorial expansion and industrial maturation, making the United States a powerful force in the Americas and beyond." But this, too, is the case: "Slavery was also our country's Achilles' heel, responsible for its near undoing."[37]

If discrimination against Spaniards and Catholics was an early theme, racial discrimination was and has been a nearly constant one. It has affected the whole history of South Carolina and the Church, all the way through the shootings at Mother Emanuel AME Church in 2015 up until the present day. Yet the problem is not unique to the South and its so-called peculiar institution.

Slavery actually encompassed the northern American colonies and much of Europe. Europeans and Americans were involved in the seizure and transport of African and West Indian people. The brutal conditions of the slave trade and the practices of slaveholding enriched white traders, planters, factory owners and shopkeepers. The regard of enslaved people of color as subhuman (three-fifths of a person, according to prescriptions for census-taking in the U.S. Constitution) laid the foundation for institutionalized racism and the overtones of racial discrimination that have persisted. American affluence escalated as transatlantic dependence on cotton, sugar, rice and tea grew exponentially. Trade and textile industries were part of a network of interdependence on livestock, lumber and crops tended and nurtured by enslaved persons, with the profits going to privileged white gentry. Slavery was a financial boon—but not merely to the South. Simply to cite one example, historian Christy Clark-Pujara noted how Rhode Island's ports "dominated the slave trade" and "created subsidiary industries that most Rhode Islanders depended on including farmers, tradesmen, merchants, distillers, sailors, day laborers, clerks and warehouse managers."[38]

By the time there were the beginnings of an established parish, St. Mary's in Charleston (1788), there was an array of personalities of Irish, French, Scottish and occasionally German or Portuguese origin, who were devoted Catholics who also managed to be content with slavery. Rare ones would occasionally provide for enslaved people and "mulattos" in their last wills and testaments.[39] Mixed with some of these acts of charity, there remained a backdrop of fear. Charlestonians, for example, feared something like the uprisings in Haiti and the ascent of "a black Napoleon, Toussaint l'Ouverture,"[40] which gave them all the more reason to shield and preserve the civil order that they knew.

Just as twenty-first-century people find it difficult to question the sometimes twisted history of the commodities they use and the customs of the present day, seventeenth-, eighteenth- and nineteenth-century South Carolinians relied on the system, things largely as they were, to provide both wants and needs. Even to disciples of Christ, stability and silent consent often rank high as civic virtues—and tend to make these disciples uncritical of their cultural environs. As far as sin is concerned, it seems perennially easier for people to confess things they have done rather than things they have failed to do—including challenging the status quo. It is also easier to identify personal sin than to implicate oneself in something more abstract like social sin.

The Priests

In the scattered world of South Carolina Catholics, there were priests who made an impact, some of very short duration and some much longer. In 1520, when Francisco Gordillo returned to Santo Domingo with native slaves in tow, it was considered an "embarrassment" to the region's official, Lucas Vasquez D'Ayllon.[41] Subsequently, it was a priest, Dominican Father Antonio de Montesinos, who actively protested the enslavement of these people. He is recorded in Salamanca as having died as a "martyr in Indies," with no particulars about his martyrdom noted.[42]

Father Sebastian Montero has been named as the priest first attempting to evangelize the tribes surrounding the San Felipe mission at Santa Elena in 1566. In 1569–70, Jesuit Juan Rogel tried to encourage the native peoples to plant, rather than hunt and gather, and form villages. His hope was to build communities and then embark on a campaign of Christianizing the peoples. He was convinced, however, that they were bent on demon worship and decided that the task was too daunting.[43] A Father Sedeno, a Jesuit, was martyred in the area now considered Virginia, and Franciscan friars based in St. Augustine were under attack, with at least one, Fray Miguel de Aunon, martyred in what has been known as St. Catherine's in Georgia near the end of the sixteenth century.

It is a matter of record that Bishop Juan de las Cabezas Altamirano (from either Havana or Santo Domingo) toured mission territories in 1606 and proceeded "to confirm some 2,000 natives, some of whom came from Carolina." But there was no stable mission and certainly no parish. Instead, there was "a *visita*, a center of instruction, at Santa Elena [likely ministering to a native village, as the Spanish settlement was gone] and one at Satuache [Salkahatchee?], a village of the Edisto River."[44]

As mentioned earlier, the occasional priest traveled through South Carolina and ministered to Catholic people. Many fell away and practiced one or another Protestant faith or none at all; some visitors and settlers who presented themselves in simple Quaker dress were suspected of being priests conducting clandestine sacramental rites. The survival of the faith depended on family leadership, lay catechists or, later, people like Mrs. Sumter. There may have been the occasional ordained minister, but that was a rarity. When William Hilton encountered a "fryar and two Spaniards"[45] as he scouted the Santa Elena region—and, likely, Hilton Head and surrounding islands— they were presumably what later were called circuit riders, traveling to touch base with people in an expansive and untamed mission territory.

In the eighteenth century, after the American Revolution and as the Constitution of the United States was being drafted, prominent Charlestonian Catholics reached out to the vicar of the bishop of Cuba and to Bishop John Carroll in Baltimore. Bishop England himself repeated what Charlestonians had told him: that the first Mass in Charleston was celebrated by an Italian priest en route to South America and drew about a dozen people at the home of an Irish Catholic at some point in 1786. In 1788, there was a teacher of French and Latin who was known as Mr. Paulin who ultimately began celebrating Mass. His time was short-lived, as Bishop Carroll, who seems not to have known of Father Paulin's sojourn in Charleston, appointed Father Matthew Ryan to this outpost of his widespread American diocese.[46]

By 1790, plans to do something with a former Methodist meetinghouse fell to a newly appointed priest, Father Thomas Keating of Philadelphia, while Father Ryan was sent to Emmitsburg to build St. Joseph Church. As of 1791, with more constitutional toleration, the South Carolina legislature had passed a resolution that allowed the "Roman Catholic Church of Charleston" to incorporate and thus purchase land and commence with plans to build a church for the community already known as St. Mary of the Annunciation.[47] Father Keating, unfortunately, had to make a hasty return to Philadelphia, likely due to illness, in late 1792 and died there in March 1793.

Keating's successor was Father Simon Felix Gallagher, a scholar, who was priest of Dublin. He proved to be both a resoundingly accomplished intellectual and a thorn in the sides of the bishop, and then the archbishops, of Baltimore. His vestry was accustomed to laity taking the lead and making many decisions regarding policy, while Father Gallagher was busy teaching and then becoming headmaster of the College of Charleston. As he was not particularly engaged in the project of building a church, Archbishop Carroll decided to replace him as pastor with a French priest, Angadreme Le Mercier, and a power struggle ensued. By 1812, Father Joseph Picot de Cloriviere, formerly an active opponent of Napoleon and a latecomer to Holy Orders, was appointed—but not to replace Mercier, who was sent back to Savannah, from which he had come.

Cloriviere was sent to assist the reappointed Gallagher. To his lasting credit, Cloriviere sought out the black Catholics of Charleston, catechized them and increased the number of communicants of the church he served from 8 to 130. Then he went back for a visit to France, where he was awarded for his service to the French Crown during the Napoleonic era. When he returned, he found that Father Gallagher had recruited a Father Robert Browne to assist him, and the local vestry was determined to bar Cloriviere from serving them.[48] It seems that a combination of ethnic and political issues may have been behind this, but there was also a problem, persistent for decades, of local vestries or curators, as other European immigrants termed them, presuming that they ought to enjoy a level of autonomy regarding parish funds and ministerial appointments.

The new archbishop of Baltimore, Leonard Neale, Carroll's successor, reprimanded the vestry and the priests. As of 1816–17, Cloriviere was the only lawfully appointed priest serving the Charleston community. Neale died after a very short term as archbishop, and his successor, Ambrose Marechal, sustained the appointment of Father Cloriviere and kept Gallagher, Browne and their supporters under interdict. Masses were celebrated not at St. Mary's (with its rectory on the site of the home bequeathed to Charleston's Catholics by Mary Watson) but rather at a location somewhere between Hasell and Market on King Street as a result of the controversy over parish governance.

Finally, Archbishop Marechal dispatched two Jesuits, Benedict Fenwick and James Wallace, to negotiate with the trustees (the vestry) and to outline conditions for their resuming good standing with the institutional Church. In the end, Father Cloriviere was sent to a new ministry as chaplain to Visitation sisters in the District of Columbia; Fenwick was appointed pastor; Wallace took on the leadership of the Catholics in Columbia, South Carolina; Father Browne embarked on a European trip; and Father Gallagher, who had not been given faculties and thus "had no authority in the parish, sang with the choir every Sunday."[49] This resolution of problems in Charleston was put into effect in 1819. By 1820, an appropriately exasperated archbishop had won Vatican accession to his recommendation to form a new diocese and allow for a somewhat more local exercise of church governance.

Slavery in the South was one matter. Another was a tradition of resisting centralized authority. John England was about to face both in the social character of his new bishopric.

Chapter 3

BISHOP JOHN ENGLAND
AND A NEW DIOCESE

He had a flair for the dramatic and a sense of humor too. Columbus, Georgia, was an all-Protestant town—one reputedly not a stranger to fervid anti-Catholicism.

The townspeople had heard that the new Catholic bishop, an Irishman, had booked a room at their none-too-swanky hotel. For John England, pastoral tours around his diocese meant horseback or horse-drawn cart and intermittent stops in whatever facilities were available when his landing spot was three hundred miles or more from Charleston. His diocese, the seventh established in the United States, encompassed South Carolina, North Carolina and Georgia.

Curiosity seekers had gathered in Columbus as if they were about to see a freak show. Who knew what the bishop would be like and how he might be gussied up? According to a story told by Joseph Kelly, a redfaced, perspiring traveler coated with a layer of pollen and road spew arrived while the locals were awaiting the bishop. The traveler divested himself of a jacket and hat, washed up and slugged down a glass of wine. Only then did he pull a ring from his pocket and identify himself as the much-anticipated bishop.[50]

A YOUNG BISHOP IN A NEW LAND

John England had been a priest a scant twelve years when he was designated bishop of the new Diocese of Charleston on July 11, 1820. His journey to

America was fraught with gladness, sadness and perhaps terror. His own journal tells of how pleased he was to baptize a nephew on the day he was consecrated bishop in Ireland, September 21, 1820, and shortly thereafter to celebrate Mass with the students of Carlow College. He was the school's first alumnus to be named a bishop, so there were elements of a victory tour for the college and for John England. At the same time, he hated to leave his mother, who was so overwrought that she stayed in bed the day he set out for Belfast, where he would board a ship.

It took from October 22, 1820, until December 26 for the new bishop to get from Belfast to Hunting Island, South Carolina, and then finally to Charleston on December 30. He described the trip as "a very tedious and unpleasant voyage."[51]

The young bishop was energetic and resolved to get to know and serve his large diocese pastorally. The three-year journal he kept of his first episcopal years, his "Diurnal," offers an almost breathless account of travels to Savannah, Augusta and Warrenton in Georgia and Columbia in South Carolina. All the while he was celebrating Masses, preaching, baptizing, hearing confessions, confirming, blessing marriages, inspecting parish books and premises and meeting trustees. He made it a point, when he was a mere two months into his diocesan position, to meet "black adults," as he called them; Cherokees; and, with regret, persons who had married outside the faith and those who had, for one reason or another, renounced their faith or simply given up its practice and were thus considered apostates. In June 1821, he reported sadly meeting "about ten Catholics French, Portuguese, and Irish, generally extremely negligent" in Edenton, North Carolina.[52] At the same time, he recounted that he spent time "giving instruction to some Negro children" and being offered an Episcopal church in Fayetteville as a venue in which he could preach.

When people look at the long tenure of Bishop England in the city of Charleston proper, they recall his dedication to education, philosophical societies and the arts. He reached out to the civic community and saw fit to embrace causes with people of various faiths. England is credited with establishing book clubs and promoting cultural societies, as well as founding the first Catholic newspaper in the country, the *United States Catholic Miscellany*.[53] His cathedral, St. Finbar's, was the site of regular liturgical celebrations and other parish activities.

As an immigrant to the still young United States of America, Bishop England had to acclimate himself to an emerging American culture and some already established customs. He promptly showed himself eager to serve those he termed "Africans," for the most part freed slaves, and so he regularly presided at Sunday vespers for Charleston's African community. Yet he also had to confront the reality of slavery in the South and the practice of slaveholding among much of the Catholic population.

THE BISHOP AND SLAVERY

John England found himself in a quandary in the three-state diocese, which had a collective population of Catholics comparable to the early twenty-first-century head count at a parish like St. Gregory the Great, Bluffton or St. Mary Magdalene, Simpsonville. These Catholics lived on or around working plantations, and those plantations had slaves.

There were few Catholics who knew that popes in 1435 and 1537 (Eugene IV and Paul III) had stridently condemned the slave trade and the treatment of native peoples from Africa and the newfound Americas as chattel. These papal condemnations, in an era of limited linguistic ability and literacy and slow communications, had limited currency. It fell to bishops to discern how best to communicate and apply magisterial teachings to concrete situations.

Historians note that Bishop England brought with him from Ireland a knowledge of the holding of indentured servants. These were people who were working for a family or a master for a specific period of time in which they would receive room and board and work toward financial independence. England also bore an abiding compassion for the oppressed, and he did know papal teachings. He had seen enforced poverty firsthand, and his family had suffered anti-Catholic prejudice. Among his early acts as bishop was to celebrate Mass and vespers each Sunday for Africans. In 1829, he established the Sisters of Charity of Our Lady of Mercy, who had a founding commitment to educate needy girls, including free Africans, and give religious instruction to female slaves. In 1831 and 1835, he opened schools for girls and boys of African descent. These suffered temporary closure as anti-abolitionist sentiment heated up, but he had reopened at least one of these schools by 1841.

Despite these efforts, Bishop England is sometimes faulted for compromising on slavery. On one hand, he is hailed for public actions on behalf of free Africans. On the other, he is criticized for finessing the stance of Pope Gregory XVI. In 1839, news came from abroad that this pope had reiterated the Church's condemnations of the slave trade.

Bishop England interpreted this to mean that it was immoral for Catholics to seize people from their homelands and market them as commodities. He did not, however, read the pope as opposing existing domestic slavery. England indicated that slaveholding was a part of human history and that scripture acknowledged the existence of slavery. He did not strongly emphasize the Church's regard for slaves as fully human persons and did not highlight St. Paul's admonition to Philemon to receive the slave Onesimus "no longer as a slave but more than a slave, a brother."

Historian David Heisser has written, "England abhorred slavery but stated that his church permitted retention in servitude of descendants of those originally enslaved. He hoped that American slavery would not continue, but he saw no quick end to it. He worked [instead] to improve the condition of blacks."[54]

Perhaps John England was living another of Paul's admonitions—one addressed to Corinthians: "I fed you milk, not solid food, because you were unable to take it." Without journals available that might have recorded England's reflections on the question of existent slavery, it is hard to know how he might have grappled with or reasoned through the stance he ended up taking.

The American Way

On another matter, we have a very clear public record. That is the insistence that Catholicism could coexist compatibly with the Constitution of the United States. The question has been a recurring one. In the twentieth century, when Alfred E. Smith, a Catholic, ran for president, anti-Catholic sentiment reared up, insisting that Catholics owed a loyalty to the papacy that made it impossible for them to be patriotic Americans. The candidacy of John Fitzgerald Kennedy occasioned the same charges. Hate mail appeared in voters' mailboxes, and Kennedy had to appear before a convention of Protestant ministers to argue that his faith would not ask him to be unfaithful to the Constitution of the United States. From 1822 on, Bishop John England faced repeated claims that he, particularly because of his promise of obedience to the pope, owed his first allegiance to a foreign power, namely, the pope and the papal states.

Such varied journals as Washington's *City Gazette*, Boston's *Gospel Advocate*, Georgia's *Missionary* and a host of others have been described as "pumping forth anti-Catholic bilge water."[55] Bishop England took every opportunity to refute their accusations and explain both the meaning and the limits of papal power. It should be noted that papal infallibility, which applies to formal and strictly official (*ex cathedra*) declarations on matters of faith and morals, was not defined until 1870. Bishop England nuanced his comments on papal authority, saying that even if papal infallibility were defined, it would be limited to doctrinal matters. He also vigorously defended the need to have some authority beyond the words of scripture itself and human reason to be able to ensure authentic interpretation of the Word of God.

Underlying so much of the vitriol against the Church was a mix of doctrinal dissent among Christians and a political fear of the temporal power of the papacy. In 1826, England addressed Congress and offered reassurance that the pope had no ability to supersede the freedom of the ballot box for Catholics, nor did being Catholic require a monarchical view of government. Brian Cudahy, a scholar who has studied the origins of Bishop England's progressive view of religious freedom, attributed much of it to the influence of an Irish Capuchin, Arthur O'Leary, a cleric from County Cork. O'Leary was an essayist who advocated for religious toleration and spoke of the importance of "liberty of conscience."[56] Long before the Church at large did, John England stood for a firm distinction between Church authority and state governance and publicly praised what Jefferson invoked as the appropriate "wall of separation" between civil government and religious authority.[57] England had trust in both faith and reason and recognized that people of conscience would come to different conclusions. One of the main points in his extraordinary address to the U.S. Congress was that civil rulers had no competence in defining doctrine and that ecclesiastical authorities, such as the bishop of Rome, had no right to direct citizens to overthrow their governments. He did, however, concede that bishops in a particular country did have a role in making moral judgments affecting politics and civic leadership. Cudahy interpreted this as an early affirmation of "episcopal collegiality."[58]

Aside from prizing the mutual engagement of the bishops of a particular nation, England also believed in consultation as part of decision-making. He encouraged input and participation from lay Catholic leaders, even though he had initially had to deal with the stresses of trusteeism in Charleston's history. In his own practice as bishop, England devised a diocesan constitution and promoted the regular involvement of lay consultors. Historian and theologian Patrick Carey has noted that Bishop England promoted "an American Catholic consciousness" that prized the Constitutional guarantee of freedom of religion; separation of Church and state; "voluntaryism," especially as it was expressed in Catholics' development of their own schools, hospitals, orphanages and so on; a political philosophy of "republicanism"; and a sense of the importance of Church councils—"local diocesan, as well as…national and universal."[59] England's role as an articulate interpreter and defender of the faith may well have laid foundations for much later developments, including the thinking of

John Tracy Ellis, SJ, and his contributions to the Second Vatican Council's "Declaration on Religious Freedom" (*Dignitatis Humanae*).

Of this aspect of Bishop England's role, Patrick Carey has written, "From John England's arrival in 1820 until his death in 1842, American Catholicism was gradually but steadily transformed from a low profile, numerically insignificant, and nationally unorganized minority into an increasingly numerous, aggressively self-defensive, and well-organized national community. Bishop John England and Immigrant Irish Catholicism played a major role in the dramatic change."[60]

THE LEGACY

Indefatigable is an adjective easily applied to John England. He spent himself for ecclesiastical, educational, cultural and societal causes. He traveled extensively, wrote prolifically, preached dynamically and made both friends and enemies around the diocese and around the country. From May until December 1841, he made one of his occasional trips to Europe, in this case in the hopes of raising funds.[61] When he returned to Charleston, it was obvious that his physical health had deteriorated. Carey noted that he had been in contact with victims of dysentery while abroad and had ministered to them. From Lent of 1842 on, he was unable to leave his bedroom. Monsignor Madden, historian of the diocese from its beginnings until its 144th year, noted that "[t]hroughout the diocese prayers were offered that his life would be spared. To this appeal of his faithful were added the prayers of the congregations of Episcopal Churches of Charleston and the Jewish Synagogue."[62]

When Bishop England died, flags were lowered to half-staff, bells tolled, gun salutes sounded and judicial and military affairs suspended their sessions. The Irishman nicknamed "the Steam Bishop" because of his fervor and energy[63] left behind a growing spiritual enterprise. He was an advocate for the American way and for ecumenical and interreligious cooperation. His legacy is felt to this day and makes it no surprise that Catholic schools have sought out those on the margins, that a parish in Kingstree to this day worships in what was a Jewish synagogue and that twentieth-century Baptists who borrowed Camp St. Mary's when they were building a church returned the favor in the twenty-first century by lending their church-school to John Paul II Catholic School when its opening was threatened by construction delays. These were gestures of respect that gentlemanly John England would have understood and approved. He had, to be sure, the grace of a cosmopolitan and collaborative spirit.

Chapter 4

RELIGIOUS SISTERS AND BROTHERS TOO

A children's book, *Fire and Forgiveness*, tells, in brief, the story of the legendary Mother Baptista Aloysius, an Ursuline sister, and her dealings with General Sherman. It seems that Mother Baptista, the sister of Bishop Patrick Lynch and a native South Carolinian, had joined the Order of St. Ursula based in Cincinnati and was instrumental in returning sisters from her order to the state after a brief hiatus. In many ways, she seems to have been the typical sister-principal. She expected her female students to have good study habits and good manners and to be faithful to sacraments and prayers. She also expected that gentlemen would keep their word, especially gentlemen who would seem to have a debt of honor owed to her.

She had taught General William Tecumseh Sherman's daughter in Ohio and seems to have been on friendly terms with his wife.[64] On that basis, she felt comfortable remaining in Columbia when much of the city evacuated as General Sherman's army approached during the Civil War. He had pledged that the students and sisters would have a safe haven in the Ursuline convent school. What Sherman did not anticipate was that some of the Union soldiers would go on a drinking spree and begin looting the largely abandoned city before tossing firebrands and setting much of Columbia ablaze as high winds on a chill winter night caused fires to leap from one property to another.

As the threat drew closer, Mother Baptista took the girls in hand—some two hundred of them, from kindergarten through high school age—and guided them to St. Peter's Church (established by Bishop England in 1821 and in the twenty-first century a minor basilica). Despite rumors that the church might be bombed, which caused the sisters and students again to evacuate temporarily, officers promised solemnly to protect it. This time, the promise held good.[65]

An embarrassed General Sherman later apologized and offered the sisters "any house" in town. The forthright Mother Baptista replied that people's houses were not his to give away, but she did demand that he and his soldiers help the Ursuline convent and school to move when they themselves found a suitable location. After a woman who has been identified as a Union widow fed the sisters and girls, they found temporary lodging at the Methodist Female College and finally found a home at the Preston House, which belonged to a grandfather of Confederate general Wade Hampton. Mother Baptista had prevailed on Sherman to save it, which he did. After the Civil War ended and Reconstruction began, Mother Baptista, always a righteous-minded soul, returned the residence to the family. The house at Blanding and Pickens Streets is now one of Columbia's historic sites and is open to tourists.[66]

Not surprisingly, the record of Mother Baptista Lynch is not reserved to children's reading and edification, with its lessons of survival, restitution and eventual peacemaking between her and Sherman. When the University of Georgia Press released its three-volume series, *South Carolina Women: Their Lives and Times*, one of the first women to show up was Mother Mary Baptista Aloysius. The essay on her life records that Mother Baptista, Ellen Lynch, was a self-assured leader, a highly competent educator with a strong belief in training girls in the liberal and practical arts and a determined refounder who managed to rebuild her convent school, in improved form, by 1869.

Her biographer in the Georgia series, Nancy Stockton, described her as a determined, even formidable, personage when it came to her mission and ministry but solicitous and self-sacrificing when it came to her person.[67] Stockton noted that it took a strong woman to become a religious sister, much less an Ursuline superior, in tumultuous times. Anti-Catholic slanders and anti-Irish prejudices were so rife that the patriotism of all Catholics was held in question, and the abuses rumored to occur in convents had caused an Ursuline convent in Boston to be burned by a mob in 1834[68]—when Ellen Lynch was a young girl and a mere thirty-one years before the convent school she ran was engulfed.

A product of her times, Mother Baptista also assumed that slavery was an established way of life, a necessity for the South and an institution attested to in sacred scripture. Her intellectual prowess did not extend to questioning things as she found them in the cities and state that she called home. That is not to make light of a whole culture's entrenchment in slavery, but describes what is regrettably common in human history: a ready acceptance of the structures and mores of the society in which people find themselves.

Ursuline Academy, where she was superior, was a progenitor of today's six-hundred-student Cardinal Newman School (grades seven through twelve), a coeducational, multiracial and multiethnic secondary school that in January 2016 moved to an expansive new campus in Columbia. The school has received recognition for its students' philanthropic projects, for athletics and for many academic achievements.

The Ursulines, who established Catholic higher education in Columbia, were not, however, the sisters who first exerted influence in the diocese. Stockton repeated a story about Mother Baptista's having at one point traveled alone on the Mississippi River out of her religious habit and in women's mid-nineteenth-century dress for safety's sake. After what she termed "a disagreeable time," she decided that she would be safer if she traveled in the future wearing what she called "the costume of the Sisters of Mercy of Charleston, which is so universally known and respected throughout the U. States."[69] This is the community founded by John England in 1829.

THE SISTERS OF CHARITY OF OUR LADY OF MERCY—AND OTHERS

As noted in chapter 3, Bishop John England quickly resolved that there should be a community of women ministering in his diocese and, in 1829, founded the group then called the Sisters of Our Lady of Mercy. Four young women (Mary Joseph; Honora O'Gorman; Teresa Barry, later the first Mother General elected by the sisters; and Mary Elizabeth Burke) responded to Bishop England's desire to have sisters in his diocese. Drawn by their own sense of a vocation to touch the lives of "the poor, sick, orphaned, and uneducated,"[70] the four came with him from Baltimore to establish the foundation, which grew as young women were recruited from within the diocese and abroad. Within ten years of their founding, the sisters had a modest tuition-based school for girls, a temporary hospital, a free school for girls and a school for free children of color. They provided catechetical instruction for white and black children, slave and free children. By the fortieth year of their existence, they also had a branch in Savannah and an academy in Sumter. During the Civil War, they ministered to injured Confederate and Union soldiers with compassion and care. Catechetical programs, Catholic elementary schools, academies, Bishop England High School, a junior college, an orphanage, infirmaries and hospitals, a nursing school and outreach centers serving the poor of any race, creed or color have been among their ministries in the 190 years of their existence (as of December 8, 2019). South Carolina, Georgia and New Jersey in particular have seen the sisters' ministries, conducted in a spirit of charity and mercy.[71]

It perhaps comes as no surprise that in the most recent years, one of their own, Sister Mary Joseph Ritter, a graduate of Bishop England High School and a general superior of their community, has been singled out by W. Thomas McQueeney as one of the "Visionaries, Luminaries and Emissaries of the Holy City."[72] While she has served in many roles in her historic religious community, the one that McQueeney celebrates is her leadership of Our Lady of Mercy Community Outreach on Johns Island, outside Charleston—a facility and ministry established by Sister Bridget Sullivan, OLM, shortly before Hurricane Hugo roared into the Charleston area with the fury of a Category 4 hurricane.

History records that the Outreach opened a matter of days before Hurricane Hugo battered the South Carolina coast and even the Midlands in 1989. As Hugo struck, some 25 percent of the people on Johns Island and parts of the surrounding James and Wadmalaw Islands were living at or below poverty level.[73] These folks were in need of basic provisions—food, clothing, household materials and so on. In the aftermath of the devastation of Hugo, there were still more needs: clean water, infant and child care items, medical and dental attention, shelter, roof and siding repairs or replacement. In response to these needs, the Outreach escalated its programs by seeking volunteers, donors and materials and partnering with organizations including Habitat for Humanity, grant providers and numerous other charitable groups. Another Sister of Our Lady of Mercy, Sister Carol Wentworth, spearheaded the Outreach response to some of the shelter needs by heading what was cleverly called the Nun Better Roofing Company. A subsequent work generated by the center was Neighborly Assistance in Living Safely, known by the acronym NAILS.[74]

The islands served by the Outreach have built and built up again, but the poverty of many whose families have lived there for decades remains, though sometimes quite hidden—away from gated communities and golf courses and roads to the beaches. The work of the Outreach has continued, meeting not only the physical and medical needs of an impoverished population but also offering English as a Second Language classes, GED training and coaching for job interviews.

Sister Mary Joseph Ritter has received a number of honors for her selfless efforts. These include a civic award from the Coastal Community Foundation, the Seton Medal for educational and charitable works and the highest papal award given to the laity, the Pro Ecclesia et Pontifice medal. Without taking away from her merit, it has to be said that the recognition given to Sister Mary Joseph is in many ways an honor to all of the sisters who have lived and worked as Sisters of Charity of Our Lady of Mercy since their long-ago founding. Her community today has used its resources of persons, experience, facilities and finances to support numerous social services and educational projects—through hands-on ministry, networking and grants.

Religious communities have a history of service in outreach missions across the state, whose works are described in chapter 12. The first of these was the OLM-founded Neighborhood House, established in Charleston in 1916. Others include the Felician Center in Kingstree; the Franciscan Center, now known as the St. Francis Center, on St. Helena Island; the Mercy Mission in Hardeeville; Our Lady of Mercy Mission in Gloverville; and St. Cyprian in Georgetown operated by the Daughters of Charity until recently being taken over by Catholic Charities. There are countless other parish and regional outreach programs, religious and secular, in which sisters lend a hand to assist or refer those facing personal and familial setbacks. Prison ministry, hospital and hospice visits and so many other works of service rely on the sisters of the diocese.

Religious Orders and Congregations

Since the early centuries of Christianity, desert fathers and mothers, *abbas* and *ammas*—celibate contemplative men and women—have gone apart from mainstream society to pray without ceasing, to live simply and to offer service, as they are able, to those who come their way. Shortly after the fall of the Roman empire in the West, communities of religious men and women, beginning with the Benedictines, have organized themselves for the purposes of prayer and work, *ora et labora*, with lifetime vows committing them to the structured communities (initially monasteries) in which they have been initiated and formed. These organized groups, subject to approval by diocesan bishops or the Roman Pontiff, have been powerhouses of prayer for the universal Church, for the United States and for South Carolina.

We must recall that religious men were here even before the sisters were. The record of Santa Elena and of the century and a half between its existence and the establishment of the Diocese of Charleston recount visits from and ministry provided by Dominicans, Franciscans and Jesuits. The scattered Catholics of the Carolinas and Georgia, like so many in the American South, sometimes kept the faith simply by teaching and praying with their families and occasionally by gathering with neighbors for non-liturgical worship. When an itinerant priest happened by, people gathered to have marriages blessed, children baptized, confessions heard, the Holy Eucharist administered and the sick anointed. When Bishop England arrived, he included among his priests Jesuits and found evidence of the visits of itinerant missionaries belonging to several religious orders. There were no sisters, however, until John England took it on himself to found a group of sisters and also to recruit the Order of St. Ursula from Ireland to serve in the Diocese.

From the founding of the OLM sisters and the arrival of the Ursulines onward, women religious from a diversity of orders and congregations have bolstered Catholic parishes and created institutions that provide education, healthcare and social service, while also ministering to the spiritual needs of numerous individuals and living lives of fervent prayer.

Two women religious who are numbered among the saints have touched the Diocese of Charleston. Mother Katharine Drexel, Philadelphia heiress and founder of the Sisters of the Blessed Sacrament, came to the diocese during the bishopric of Henry Northrup. She was instrumental in establishing Catholic schools and parishes ministering to African Americans, while also using her influence to encourage outreach to Native Americans. Mother Teresa of Kolkata (Calcutta) visited in the early 1980s, during the years of Bishop Ernest Unterkoefler's term of service, and brought her message of the Christian call to revere and serve the poorest of the poor. The sisters, brothers and priests of the diocese have attempted, through two centuries, to bring their gifts to meet and serve Christ in his people, including the least and most marginalized of the brothers and sisters.

In the Diocese of Charleston, the Sisters of Charity of St. Augustine have provided numerous grant-funded opportunities for sisters to offer direct service to the poor, literacy training, development of parenting skills, retreat programs and service to those with developmental challenges.

Many have done so through the Collaboration for Ministry Initiative, which has funded an annual gathering of sisters to share faith, vision and mutual concerns for ministry, under the umbrella of the Sisters of Charity Foundation of South Carolina.

The Sisters of Charity of St. Augustine have their own unique story in connection with the diocese. In 1851, the CSA sisters arrived in Cleveland as a break-off from their French community. The intent was to establish themselves as "hospital sisters." This they did in Ohio. In the summer of 1938, newlyweds from Columbia, South Carolina, James and Flora Younginer, traveled to California. Mrs. Younginer became critically ill and was taken to a Catholic hospital for care. After an extended illness, from which Flora Younginer recovered, the couple returned to Columbia offering high praise for the quality of care extended both to Flora and to her new husband, James. They were so taken by their experience that they, who were not then of the Catholic faith, approached an Irish pastor and begged him to search out the prospects for bringing a group of sisters to the capital city to build a hospital. He promptly reported their interest to Bishop Emmet Walsh, who then heard of the work of the sisters in Ohio while he was at a bishops' conference.

From there, he extended an invitation, and the sisters discerned that they were being called to mission territory. The whole country, however, was barely beginning to regain some stability from the throes of the Great Depression. Bishop Walsh noted his delight in welcoming the sisters but notified them that there must be a postponement of their arrival because the diocese had no funds to contribute to the project. The Younginer family, meanwhile, went about raising a downpayment on property and the project. The hospital was built without delay. It came to light only much later that the sisters had mortgaged their motherhouse in order to build what became Providence Hospital in Columbia. While it was under construction, they shared a convent with the Ursuline sisters.

Just as the OLM sisters ultimately determined that they would have to sell their hospitals in the latter twentieth century, the Sisters of Charity of St. Augustine had to do likewise in Columbia in the twenty-first. Both groups have used the proceeds of sales to support a variety of initiatives among the most needy in the state and in support of religious and lay leaders who have undertaken efforts to meet unmet needs.[75]

This sort of boon to the diocese is part of what seems to be a larger movement to increasing engagement in joint efforts among the many groups of women religious. As was noted in her book, *Sisters in Arms*, Jo Ann Kay

McNamara observed a third-millennium trend toward what she called "a larger global sisterhood."[76] Sharing ministerial projects, community housing and fostering the education of sisters from impoverished parts of the world are now a matter of course among congregations, which at one time relied solely on their own sisters for staffing and leadership.

Men's congregations have banded together with diocesan (secular) priests and both national and international conferences to address demands of underserved populations and also to confront matters of internal organization and discipline.

As of 2019–20, the Diocese of Charleston counts twenty-two congregations of women religious and sixteen of men (religious brothers and priests) serving in the diocese. Over the years, women's groups have ranged from American foundations like Maryknoll to international groups, which include sisters, brothers and priests from Europe, Africa, India, Central and South America, the Philippines and Vietnam. Each group of religious women and men has its own unique charism, spirituality and mission. Distinct among these are the two contemplative orders that make their home in South Carolina.

The Trappists and the Poor Clares

In many ways, these are the titans of the Church of Charleston. While laity and religious alike pray, often and fervently, none of them design their every day around a horarium of prayer and meditation as do members of contemplative orders. Thomas Merton, the great Cistercian spiritual writer, once speculated that the world might by now have blown itself up if it were not for the prayers of these men and women living a largely silent and obscure life. The monastic day of the Trappists begins with their rising at 3:00 a.m. and retiring after Compline, the final prayer of the daily Liturgy of the Hours, at 8:00 p.m. Simplicity of life and dress, unadorned liturgical space, a vegetarian diet and quiet work (selling eggs for years from the monastery hen houses, more recently raising mushrooms and stocking the monastery giftshop) provide for the monks' needs. In addition, the monks offer spiritual direction, provide housing for retreatants, host concerts and conferences and welcome visitors to their gardens.

The Trappists, members of the Order of Cistercians of the Strict Observance, are a group dating back to 1664 in France, as a reform of the Cistercian order that had evolved from the Order of St. Benedict. Thus, Trappist roots actually go back more than 1,500 years.[77] The Trappists who came to South Carolina were invited to form a new monastery, an offshoot of Gethsemani Abbey in Kentucky (made famous by Merton and his 1947 memoir, *The Seven Storey Mountain*), at the urging of Bishop Emmet Walsh in 1949. Clare Boothe Luce, author, ambassador and convert whose life was greatly influenced by the celebrated Bishop Fulton J. Sheen, and her husband, Henry Luce, publisher of such successful magazines as *TIME, LIFE, Sports Illustrated* and others, donated the property outside Moncks Corners (actually, Cordesville). The Henry Luce Foundation has continued to fund such projects as installing the chapel organ and building the monastery library, which is open to the public.

Silence, simplicity, hiddenness and hospitality are some of the marks of the contemplative, monastic life. So, too, is community—life shared with others who have responded to a similar call to give all and to throw in their lot with others who might or might not have been their friends and companions in another way of life. The Trappists of Mepkin are ordinary men who have chosen to seek God and to reverence persons in a unique but centuries-old way. A mere six years after their arrival in South Carolina, a similar community of women arrived.

The Order of St. Clare, with its roots in the thirteenth-century Franciscan movement initiated by both Saint Francis of Assisi and Saint Clare, came to Greenville in 1955, during the diocesan leadership of Bishop John Russell. The dozen sisters who established their monastery in the Diocese of Charleston came from Jamaica Plain in Massachusetts. Initially located in Greenville proper, the sisters opened a new monastery in 2008 that includes a separate retreat house, La Foresta, on their property, which abuts Bunched Arrowhead Heritage Preserve in the ascent to the Blue Ridge Mountains. In many ways, the lives of the sisters at Travelers Rest are comparable to those of the Trappists. Their days are devoted to prayer, contemplation, crafts, hospitality and spiritual direction in the solitude of an enclosure, or cloister. They self-describe their roots in St. Clare's vision for the community, "the privilege of highest poverty," which they term "evangelical poverty," in the Franciscan spirit. St. Francis, who was named patron of ecology by St. John Paul II, also inspires in them a reverence for creation all around them and a commitment to living lightly on the land. They advertise their ecumenical retreat house as a place where their visitors can engage in solitary prayer and reflection, join the sisters for Eucharist and the Divine Office and "enjoy the healing power of nature."[78] In very recent years, the Poor Clares have participated both behind the scenes and in person with the Collaboration for Ministry Initiative and have enlisted their volunteers to provide useful take-home souvenirs and table favors for the annual gathering of the sisters of the diocese.

Both of these groups, the Trappists and the Poor Clares, lead lives of seeking and interceding. They plumb silence and the heart of God and bring to God the needs of individuals and the whole world. While their lives can be idealized, they share the ups and downs of any fervent life of prayer and the need to continue to find means of support for both older and younger members and their facilities. Both groups today are facing the challenge widespread among religious communities of men and women in the United States: an aging membership. Despite the occasional dark night, the monks and nuns meet and greet others with smiles, offer both homespun and erudite counsel and strive to uncomplicate their lives as much as possible. Thus, their gift is often that of the "joy of the Gospel" of which Pope Francis has so often spoken. They offer a spirit of serenity while they engage in practical work to support themselves in their monasteries. They welcome guests into their quiet, sacred spaces and provide, in a tradition as old as that of St. Benedict and St. Scholastica, gentle hospitality.

Chapter 5

PINCKNEY COLONY
AND THE PINCKNEY LEGACY

E very spring, signs go up along U.S. 278 in Bluffton, inviting the
general public to turn onto Pinckney Colony Road and pick daffodils.
There are fields of them—sunny yellow and standing strong—along
a road that traces its way alongside homes, most of them set back, plus a new
Latino evangelical church, a stable and grazing space for horses, marshes
that ebb and flow with the tides and expanses of land that have been planted
for centuries. One mile in is St. Andrew Chapel, Bluffton's original parish
church that celebrated its seventy-fifth anniversary in 2007 but dates much
farther back. The story of how the first Catholics of the Walterboro/
Bluffton/Hilton Head/Hardeeville/Ridgeland area unknowingly birthed
one of the two largest parishes in the diocese (locally sometimes referred to
as a megachurch) begins with the Pinckney family.

Family biographer Mary Pinckney Powell recorded how the first Carolina
Pinckneys trace their roots to a family known as Picquigny, who arrived in
England with the eleventh-century Norman invasion. They migrated to
the area known as Bishop Auckland and Durham and, originally Catholic,
were said to have founded a convent in Yorkshire in the thirteenth century.
From the time of Henry VIII on, they were Anglicans and registered
parishioners in a church named St. Andrew's.[79] In the late seventeenth
century, Thomas Pinckney set out for the colonies in America, settled in
Charles Towne (Charleston) in 1692 and, a childless young widower,
returned briefly to England, where he was charmed by a young woman
named Mary Cotesworth, married her in Durham Cathedral and brought

her back to properties he owned in Charleston and Ashepoo. He was a successful exporter and importer, and it is from his family line that American revolutionaries and political leaders arose.[80]

Charles Cotesworth Pinckney (1746–1825) was the American-born grandson of the settler Thomas Pinckney. Charles Coteswoth Pinckney was British educated, widely traveled on the European continent, a trained lawyer, an aide de camp to General George Washington, later a military commander and prisoner of war and an active participant in the framing of the United States Constitution. Then he was a serious contender for a seat on the first Supreme Court, appointed to be minister to France under the presidency of John Adams and a Federalist candidate for vice president and president in 1800, 1804 and 1808. Both state historian Walter Edgar and Powell credit him with participating in an intervention that inserted into the U.S. Constitution the prohibition of an establishment of religion and of any "religious test" associated with holding "office or public trust."[81]

The military and political background of the Pinckney family was also one deeply embedded in the Protestant Church of England and in America. Thus, it is not surprising to find that one of Charles Cotesworth's familial line served as rector of St. Jude's Church in Walterboro while also celebrating services for Presbyterians and Baptists as well, along with his own Episcopalians.

The Catholic Pinckneys come from the family line of Charles Cotesworth's uncle, William, and his son, William Cotesworth Pinckney, owner of Dawn of Hope Plantation in Ashepoo. A son of this Pinckney, William Cotesworth, became the medical doctor known as Cotesworth Pinckney, who married a Catholic, Elizabeth Perry Bellinger. Elizabeth came from the Bellinger family, who attributed several converts to the influence of and admiration they had for Bishop John England. Elizabeth herself is said to have conducted her own search, visiting several Protestant denominations, a Unitarian church and a Jewish synagogue before she determined to convert to Catholicism. She became a fervent one, sending her sons to St. John's College in New York, the school that would become Fordham University. One of these sons, Eustace Bellinger Pinckney, did not finish college, although his brother did. Mary Powell has speculated that he took upon himself care for his mother and came home to manage the Colleton County properties and become a successful rice planter as the South edged toward the Civil War. Eustace Bellinger Pinckney shortly met and married Julia Lynch of Cheraw,[82] the sister of the Most Reverend Patrick N. Lynch. Biographer Mary Pinckney Powell remarked of the mother who ingrained Catholicism in Eustace Pinckney and his descendants, "What more could she ask of her son, since he showed no inclination toward the priesthood, than that he become engaged to the sister of the…Bishop of the Diocese of Charleston?"[83]

Tragically, but commonly enough in days without preventive medical care, anitbiotics or surgical anesthesia, Julia Lynch Pinckney died at age twenty-two in 1861, leaving her husband, Eustace, with two young children. The *Charleston Catholic Miscellany*, in its obituary, referred to her thus: "A dutiful daughter, an affectionate wife, and a tender mother, and from childhood a fervent and pious Catholic, she was tried in the sufferings of a long illness, borne with cheerful resignation and she died strengthened by the sacraments of the Church."[84]

Shortly after Julia's death, Eustace became a Confederate soldier and fell in love with and married "a charming young lady of Huguenot ancestry from the Sea Coast of South Carolina, Mary Martha (Daisy) Porcher." Her family owned the Calhoun Plantation in Bluffton, on what is now called Pinckney Colony Road, and it there that she and Eustace took up residence after the end of the Civil War, when tremendous debt and high taxes beset landowners. Eustace determined to sell his Colleton County property and purchase Calhoun to save it. At one point, the Porcher property, purchased by Daisy's father, approached one thousand acres.[85]

Daisy Porcher Pinckney was an athletic young woman, trained "in all the social graces of a Southern lady," and definitely sturdy stock. She lived to raise sixteen children, two of whom were Julia Lynch's son and daughter, and fourteen her own. Her family property was considered fertile "tidewater land," with "the finest soil for the cultivation of indigo, sea island cotton, cattle raising, rice, corn and timber."[86] Daisy inherited the property from her father, James Porcher, when he died in 1891, as an act of gratitude for her decades of supporting and caring him through the Reconstruction era. This bequeathal meant, of course, that Calhoun Plantation could stay in the Pinckney family for years to come.

So, too, would the chapel that Eustace and Daisy built. Fifteen years before her death in 1924, Daisy had become Catholic, probably through the ministry of one of the circulating priests who had become regular visitors to their home, Father Daniel Berberich. Eustace Bellinger Pinckney had kept the faith with predictable difficulty, and Daisy supported him in that, even before her own conversion. One of their granddaughters, Marion Pinckney Crosby, has told of Masses celebrated at Eustace's dining room table when various traveling priests arrived. Her grandfather, who knew the Latin responses, was the altar server. When Daisy and Bishop Henry Pinckney Northrup (likely a distant relative) pressed the family to build a chapel, Marion Crosby's and Mary Powell's grandfather and uncles felled trees, hauled and dried logs and built one.[87] The chapel, first opened in 1915, was initially called St. Mary in the Woods. In 1932, a new chapel was built, and Bishop Emmet Walsh renamed it St. Andrew's.

The naming of the chapel suggests more than one connection. It may be mere coincidence, but the Anglican church of the Pinckney family in the Bishop Auckland–Durham region was St. Andrew's. There also is a suggestion that St. Andrew was the name requested by a significant donor. While the land and the original chapel were all constructed with Pinckney family efforts, the new St. Andrew's, built after the 1929 stock market crash and on the verge of the Great Depression, relied on a grant from the Catholic Extension Society. A Wilhemina Wegman of Rochester, New York, donated much of the needed funding in honor of her deceased husband, Andrew, who had been a successful printer and publisher.[88]

Another name, St. Mary's, was long retained in the region because of the presence of Camp St. Mary's. This summer camp was championed by one of the many priests who traveled in and out of the Lowcountry region, a young Irishman named Father Linehan. He conceived of it as "a religious vacation school," and it began in 1928. With the help of Eustace and Daisy's children and their children after them, Camp St. Mary's began on their property. Planning and conducting the camp involved Catholics from Ridgeland, Hardeeville, Switzerland (South Carolina) and Bluffton, along with priests, seminarians, Sisters of Charity of Our Lady of Mercy and African American neighbors who served as chefs and cooking staff. After a number of successful years drawing young people from around the state (and especially Charleston), another property was purchased in 1935, with the blessing of Bishop Emmet Walsh, just across the Okatie River from the Pinckney family compound.[89] The property, now under other ownership, is located near the current John Paul II School.

St. Andrew Chapel long served roughly 150 or fewer parishioners from the Hilton Head/Bluffton/Hardeeville/Ridgeland area. In 1950, Bishop John Russell officially designated the mission church as a parish and appointed its first full-time pastor. A new church, St. Gregory the Great, was built and dedicated in 2000, as an influx of families from the Northeast and Upper Midwest moved into new retirement communities and family neighborhoods. The population in the area began to explode. From a little over 1,200 parishioners when the new parish church was built and renamed,[90] the parish reached a population approaching 11,000 by the eve of the diocesan bicentennial. As is true in so many other areas of the diocese, a growing Hispanic community has added to its numbers and activities.

St. Andrew Chapel continues to serve as a site for daily morning Masses, occasional weddings and funerals, retreats and days of recollection. Holy Resurrection Greek Orthodox church uses the chapel for Sunday and Easter Triduum celebrations, an ecumenical outreach begun when Monsignor Martin Laughlin was pastor and also administrator of the diocese.

The Pinckney presence and heritage continues to live on, and among the descendants of Eustace Bellinger and both Julia Lynch and Mary Martha Porcher Pinckney can be found teachers, lawyers, doctors, nurses, landscape architects, authors, musicians, highway patrolmen, county councilors, athletes, coaches and people who still love the land, its oysters and shrimp and abundant produce, its trees and its flowers.

LIKE MANY OTHER MISSIONS

Stories like that of the Pinckney family and their heirs were replicated in many quarters of what was a tri-state diocese. The slow growth prompted by a few devout families in South Carolina contrasts sharply with the relations between families and parishes in the American urban centers, mining towns and industrial hubs from which a significant number of "snowbirds" and new residents of the state have originated. In those areas from which many of the new settlers have come, groups of immigrants arrived and bonded with relatives and friends who had arrived slightly before they did or shortly thereafter. These were people who spoke their languages and shared their cultural and religious roots. Churches rapidly sprang up as priests who were themselves immigrants arrived, and masses of devout parishioners scrimped and saved to build churches beautifully appointed with statuary and stained-glass windows where they could pray and hear preaching in Italian, German, Slovak, Polish, Hungarian, Lithuanian and other European languages.

In the South, however, with the possible exception of French New Orleans, Catholics found themselves an anomaly. They were what scripture calls "strangers in a strange land" (1 Peter 2:11), surrounded by Protestant Christians who often misunderstood the people they sometimes termed "papists." Itinerant Catholic priests provided ministry in family homes as they were able. If there was a small cluster of Catholics, the priests inevitably used the house-church model that developed, out of necessity, in the apostolic era.

This is exactly what happened in places all over South Carolina. St. Joseph in Anderson began with a French-speaking family who on occasion welcomed a priest traveling from Montreal. What was Sacred Heart in Camden began in the latter nineteenth and early twentieth centuries because a few Catholic families felt the need for a place to worship. Eventually, in Camden, Charlotte Thompson, who was a convert with a devotion to Our Lady of Perpetual Help, donated funds to build (and rename) a new church in 1914. St. James in Conway was built with the assistance of a traveler named named Prashack who happened to stop by in the 1950s. Before Conway ever became a mission, Masses had been celebrated in Catholic families' homes and local social and fraternal organizations. St. Joseph Mission in Darlington and St. Anthony in Florence can claim the same: beginnings in family headquarters. Sacred Heart in Blackville was built with the muscle and money of families named Maher, Quinn, Farrell, Molony and Kelly. More than a decade before the Civil War, Dr. Burt of Edgefield had a family chapel that preceded St. Mary of the Immaculate Conception, and Arthur Morgan's home in Georgetown was a worship site from a similar period. The Herlihy home on Edisto Island saved Catholics a seventy-mile round trip to Yonges Island before St. Frederick–St. Stephen Mission grew. The Caggiano family of Gaffney outfitted a chapel in their basement in 1950 before Sacred Heart was dreamed of. St. Michael Mission in Great Falls credits the Azouri, Francis and Mitchell families with their founding. Parishioners in Greenwood cite the Turners, those in the Hampton mission remember the Mulligans and parishioners in Summerton express gratitude to the Joseph, Nimmer and Shaleuly families. Mr. Waddy Francis's home in Lancaster preceded St. Catherine's as a place to gather Catholics, as did the home of Charlie Purcell and others in the Newberry area. Pageland Catholics used the homes of Kay Owens and the Sikes family for worship, and as their community grew, they turned to a turkey hatchery and a lodge with a restaurant to borrow space for worship.[91]

Perhaps the earliest of these family sites for Catholic devotions and catechism instruction was the expansive property of Thomas Sumter Jr. and his wife, Nathalie DeLage Sumter. Sumter's father was a militia leader of the American Revolution akin to Francis Marion, a planter and later member of the first Congress and advocate of the Santee Canal project; his family was not Catholic.[92] His French daughter-in-law was, however, and the family eventually built a chapel on their property and later built the first Catholic church, St. Lawrence, in what is now Sumter County—this despite the fact that the elder Sumter had endured the burning of his own house in a British raid in the early days of the Revolution and, like so many others, faced an uphill climb to reclaim property and fortune. The story of Mrs. Sumter has been detailed in a biography written by Sister M. Ignatia Gavaghan, OLM, for the Sumter County Historical Commission.[93]

As mentioned earlier, there were times, as in the case of Pageland before St. Ernest Mission, when all sorts of places were used as worship sites until momentum rose to support the construction of a parish church. Some of the chapels and mission churches were constructed using designs typical of other Christian denominational churches, while others renovated existing spaces sold to them, like the former Knights of Columbus clubhouse (or "hut") that became the first Sacred Heart Church in Charleston.[94] Some mission churches, like Our Lady of La Vang in Greer, have expanded into parishes even in the past decade, and some new mission churches, like San Sebastian in Greenville, have been established in the same period. Others maintain a relatively small population and continue to be pastored by priests operating in the circuit rider mode of old. Newberry, with its missions in Joanna and Laurens, or Orangeburg, with missions in Allendale, Springfield and Barnwell, are just two examples.

It is well to mention that while South Carolina and so many other areas of the United States have a history of anti-Catholic sentiment, there is also an ample historical record of generous worship-sharing on the part of other denominations. As far back as the time of Bishop John England, Episcopalians, Lutherans and Methodists allowed the traveling bishop to use their churches at various locations across his tri-state diocese. In the present Diocese of Charleston, parish records recount similar inter-church hospitality. St. Thomas Episcopal Church in Abbeville donated the bell for Sacred Heart. Lutheran churches in Mauldin, Mount Pleasant, Goose Creek and Spartanburg all shared or opened their doors to Catholics before St. Elizabeth Ann Seton, St. Benedict, Immaculate Conception and Jesus, Our Risen Savior were built. Lee Road United Methodist Church let Catholics from Greer and Taylors worship in their building, and St. Mary Magdalene in Simpsonville, another sprawling parish, used Ebenezer United Methodist for a time. A nondenominational community church, River Hills, let Catholics who formed All Saints, Lake Wylie, use its premises. In very recent times, Okatee Baptist Church in Ridgeland offered the first-year students at John Paul II School the use of its Sunday school rooms as the Catholic school's building was being completed. Before the end of the school year, as John Paul II occupied its finished space, local Knights of Columbus went in and repainted Okatee Baptist classrooms. Shortly thereafter, John Paul II School made a substantial donation to help Okatee Baptist repair its roof after a severe windstorm. Ecumenism, it seems, has been in effect in the diocese before, during and after the Second Vatican Council. It has proved to be a saving grace.

Chapter 6

THE SOUTH'S PECULIAR INSTITUTION AND
OUR LADY OF THE CONFEDERACY

Visitors to Charleston who tour the Cathedral of St. John the Baptist will see smaller altars to the left and right of the main altar. The one to the right, dedicated to the Blessed Virgin, for nearly a century and a half bore a finely sculpted statue that was known colloquially as Our Lady of the South or Our Lady of the Confederacy. She came to Charleston in late 1865 with the only bishop, namely Bishop Patrick Neeson Lynch, known to have required a presidential pardon to return to the United States. In more recent years, she shifted residence to a shrine in Kingstree, dedicated to Our Lady of South Carolina, Our Lady of Joyful Hope.

How is it that a boy brought to this country as a one-year-old—the son of a prosperous family, graduate of one of Rome's best theologates, hand-picked for episcopal succession by John England—ended up being a legate to the Vatican on behalf of the Confederate States of America? And how is it that a man who was "haunted" by the specter of slavery and appalled by the fact that Irishmen were assigned tasks considered too dangerous for slaves became himself, by 1860, the owner of ten slaves and later, by virtue of a legacy to the diocese, eighty-five more?[95]

To this day, there are longtime southerners who claim, as did their parents, grandparents, great-grandparents and farther back, that slavery offered Africans a better life. That is the case despite the annals of Frederick Douglass and the historical and literary accounts of the horrors of seizure, the Middle Passage, the conditions of slave markets and the record of floggings and lynchings.

THE LYNCH FAMILY AND THEIR SON

The family of Conlaw Peter Lynch, Bishop Lynch's father, was considered "lace curtain Irish" as opposed to "shanty Irish." The motives for their arrival on the shores of the Carolinas seem to have been mixed. The birth of Conlaw and Eleanor McMahon Neeson Lynch's firstborn, Anna, took place very shortly after their marriage.[96] Ten months later, their second child, Patrick, was born, on March 10, 1817. Eleanor's father had disinherited her. Along with that social disgrace, there were threats of famine and typhus. These circumstances seem to have combined to cause Conlaw and Eleanor to seek a new start in a new home.

Both Conlaw and Eleanor came from families accustomed to advantages. Both had French and Irish ancestry, and there was even a Lynch castle in Galway. The McMahon family included political activists and statesmen.[97] When they boarded a ship to America, they knew that they were leaving behind a rich family history, but they seem to have been determined to make a new one. They landed first in Newfoundland in Canada, then in Philadelphia and then in Georgetown, South Carolina. Conlaw was savvy and extroverted enough to make connections with John L. Wilson, who in 1822 was elected governor of South Carolina. It was he who pointed the family in the direction of the Great Pee Dee River and the trade center developing in Cheraw. It wasn't long before Conlaw had established himself as a designer and builder, a millwright and owner of a sawmill and a brickyard. He ended up building homes, the Cheraw Merchant's Bank, a central market and St. Peter's Church in Cheraw.[98] Three of the Lynch's twelve children died as young adults. The other nine went on to become distinguished professionals and church leaders.

Patrick Neeson Lynch, that second child, studied at Cheraw Academy and by age twelve was mastering Greek and Latin classics. Identified early as a promising future cleric, Patrick entered Bishop England's Seminary of St. John the Baptist in 1829. Patrick and a fellow student, James Corcoran (by that time an orphan), attracted the attention of Bishop England, who by December 1833 had arranged for them to undertake studies at the Jesuit-run Urban College in Rome. Commonly known as the Urbanum after its founder, Pope Urban VIII, it was the seat of Propaganda Fide, the curial office for the Propagation of the Faith. The young men, Corcoran and Lynch, arrived in Rome in May 1834. During their time there, Vincent Pallotti (founder of the Pallottine Fathers and later canonized a saint) was the spiritual director.[99]

On Passion Sunday 1840 (then celebrated a week before Palm Sunday), Lynch was ordained in Rome. In September of that year, he received his doctorate in sacred theology magna cum laude, as well as a notable number of honors in ecclesiastical history, canon law, morality, dogmatics, Greek and philosophy.[100]

Father Lynch, the accomplished scholar, returned to Charleston and was immediately appointed to the faculty of the diocesan seminary. On April 11, 1842, Bishop England died from the long illness that had beset him after a trip to Europe. Records of the Fifth Provincial Council of Baltimore, 1843, indicate that Lynch had been one of the contenders to succeed Bishop England but was deemed too young and not quite the picture of health himself.[101]

Once the new bishop, Ignatius Aloysius Reynolds of Kentucky, had been appointed, Lynch became embroiled in controversy stirred by a growing anti-Catholic movement. Ironically, it was spurred on in the Carolinas by a fellow Cheraw Academy graduate, Reverend Dr. James Thornwell. By the mid-1850s, the anti-Catholic American Party, also called the Know-Nothings, had gained political leverage in both of the Carolinas and won two Congressional seats.[102] Lynch began to use both the written word and speaking opportunities to respond to an array of defamatory claims laid against the Catholic faith and Catholics themselves.

The other controversial topic, always the elephant in the room, was the maintenance of slavery and the move to expand slavery westward in the midst of a burgeoning abolitionist movement. The abolitionist cause was largely led by Quakers, Unitarians and members of a number of evangelical Protestant groups, most of whom resided in the New England and mid-Atlantic states.

THE BISHOP AND SLAVERY

Ignatius Reynolds, the second bishop of Charleston, appears to have had a more retiring personality, perhaps even a lackluster one. He was an adept administrator and fundraiser, but he also suffered some setbacks and found covering a tri-state diocese daunting. During his tenure, the Diocese of Savannah was established in 1850, which left both Carolinas to the bishop of Charleston. Bishop Reynolds took on the first of the two heated controversies, the anti-Catholic movement, particularly through the vehicle of the diocesan newspaper.[103] Meanwhile, antislavery sentiment was heating up in other parts of the country, and the disposition of possible new states in the Union was prompting feverish debate. The successor of Ignatius Reynolds, who died in March 1855, was Patrick Neeson Lynch, installed as the third bishop of Charleston in March 1858, and his side on both controversies was quite clear.

Despite his cosmopolitan experience and vast learning, Lynch was a product of his time and the culture in which he had been nurtured from early childhood. His mentor, Bishop England, who had sought to educate free Africans and catechize slaves, continued to interpret papal directives in such a way that he tolerated domestic slavery. Lynch was of a similar mind. He did advocate for keeping married slaves and their families together, and he also insisted on the obligation of slaveholders to feed, clothe and shelter slaves and care for elderly ones who were no longer fit for labor. He was said to have engineered, behind the scenes, temporary loans of healthy male slaves to substitute when one young man or another was ill so as not to reflect poorly on an unhealthy slave. Lynch's brother, Dr. John Lynch, was known in Columbia as a man who provided medical care for slaves. Slaves tended to rely on ineffective home remedies until their situations had become desperate, likely because they feared their owners' detection of any apparent weakness or defect. Among the slaves bought by Bishop Lynch was a woman named Flora, who in 1863 "was not certified as being of sound health."[104] It seems that Bishop Lynch and his brother, John, were of a mind to provide medical care for slaves and to protect slaves whose health had suffered serious setbacks.

Bishop Lynch also appears to have been following not only the thinking of Bishop England but also that of Francis Patrick Kenrick, the bishop who consecrated him. Bishop Kenrick had published a treatise on moral theology shortly before he became bishop of Philadelphia and subsequently archbishop of Baltimore. In that treatise, he argued that in a received social system it was permissible to cooperate as long as one maintained humane provisions and practices and did not directly defy the moral law.[105] With such reasoning afoot in his time, Lynch was known to have accepted slaves from the estate of a McKenna family and sent one to serve as maintenance man for his sister, Mother Baptista Lynch, when she was the Ursuline superior in Columbia.[106] However the implications of slaveholding may have been judged from a later historical perspective, it seems that the children of Conlaw and Eleanor Lynch were attempting to live within the southern system while also attending to the well-being of slaves and making strenuous efforts to keep slave families together—a policy not required by South Carolina law.

The Bishop and the Confederacy

Whenever the War Between the States is discussed, slavery is, of course, treated as the issue at the forefront. But along with it is the contentious issue of states' rights versus what to some seemed to be an increasing federalization of power. It seems that the principle of subsidiarity was ingrained in Lynch long before it was articulated in Church teaching: the idea that power and decision-making should reside at the most local level possible. This concern for more regional control over governance may well have influenced him to stand with the Confederacy and go to the Vatican to intercede on its behalf. Lynch also seems to have been persuaded that there was a fundamental inequality of races, and this later led him to defend the existence of separate institutions for the races as the South settled into the troubled period of Reconstruction.

In February 1864, Lynch had headed to the Vatican at the behest of Jefferson Davis, in the hopes of obtaining recognition of the legitimacy of the Confederate government. He did not manage to convince the pope or papal advisors to take such a stance. The conditions of warfare blocked Lynch from returning, so he occupied himself with a variety of church activities and arranged for the purchase of the statue of the Virgin mentioned at the beginning of this chapter. Once the Confederacy surrendered in April 1865, it took a pardon from President Andrew Johnson to allow him back into an American port.

After the Civil War

While Bishop Lynch's extended stay in Europe strained relations with other prelates, he did ultimately return to full engagement with the bishops of the United States and rather quickly resumed his attendance at numerous ecclesial events, including the elevation of bishops and a cardinal. He also attended sessions of the First Vatican Council. He distinguished himself as an orator in both the South and the North and spent considerable time raising funds to rebuild churches, orphanages and schools destroyed during the Civil War.

Lynch expended himself in many ways. While he was busy erecting parishes in Greenville and Charleston, including two African American parishes, he was also attempting to pay off massive debt, incurred not only from the damages of war but also as a result of a raging fire in Charleston in 1861 that had leveled the cathedral. Meanwhile, he was busy solidifying plans for additional liturgical sites, expanding diocesan services and reviving the diocesan newspaper. Amid the sometimes frantic activity of the postbellum era, Bishop Lynch saw one of the projects for which he had pressed finally fulfilled. In March 1868, news came that a new Apostolic Vicariate of North Carolina, predecessor to the Dioceses of Raleigh and Charlotte, was being formed. This effectively separated North Carolina from South Carolina as his episcopal territory.[107]

Historians Heisser and White noted the persistence of rumors that Lynch would be named an archbishop or perhaps coadjutor bishop to New York's John Cardinal McCloskey.[108] There is a certain irony to this, since McCloskey's predecessor, John Hughes, an Irishman like Lynch, was very clear about their opposing sides when it came to the Civil War. Perhaps the weight of history made it impossible for Lynch to advance in ecclesiastical circles, but he retained a significant influence.

By 1880, Bishop Lynch had managed to complete many of the projects he had initiated or at least to get them on solid footing. He reduced the diocesan debt from $400,000 (massive in those times) to approximately $10,000. This seems attributable to his wide circle of friends, his oratorical skill and his exhausting work ethic. One item of unfinished business was restoration of the cathedral. This project was left to Bishop Henry Pinckney Northrop, former apostolic vicar of North Carolina. A pro-cathedral had to remain in use for well into the 1890s and early 1900s. The Cathedral of St. John the Baptist was not completed until 1907. Some would say that it was not truly complete until the erection of the steeple in 2010.

When Lynch died on February 26, 1882, the secular press noted his intellectual prowess and diverse interests. People spoke of his passion for astronomy and geology, as well as his proficiency in whatever skills might be needed to conceptualize ways to engineer jetties and dredge Charleston Harbor so that more ships might dock there. Along with participating in many civic endeavors, Bishop Lynch was instrumental in the creation of artesian wells in Charleston and the promotion of a variety of institutions devoted to health and welfare. He was known among Catholics as a friend of priests and prelates and a friendly acquaintance of Pope Pius IX. He was a loyal brother to the Lynches, but he was also hailed as a friend to clergy of many other faiths and of their congregations. He advocated racial segregation but also averred that he did indeed believe that all were beloved by God and that salvation was available to all.

Bishop Patrick Lynch lives on in the annals of the Diocese of Charleston and the early historical records of what are now the dioceses of Raleigh and Charlotte. Aside from that, his name has been given to one of the divisions of the Ancient Order of Hibernians active in the South Carolina Lowcountry. Perhaps that is due to the fact that Bishop Lynch had actively encouraged an Irish migration to South Carolina. In 1867, Bishop Lynch wrote to a member of the Irish Parliament, John Maguire, urging him to encourage his countrymen to come to the Palmetto State, which the bishop identified as "probably, the most Irish of any of the States of the Union" and certainly a place where his countrymen would find "earnest sympathy for the struggles of Irishmen at home." He went on to claim that "nowhere will the Irish immigrant be received with a greater welcome, or be more generously supported in all his rights."[109] The group that has adopted Bishop Lynch as patron is dedicated to what might be considered Lynch's first loves, aside from assiduous theological scholarship and devotion to the Church: Friendship, Unity and Christian Charity.[110]

Chapter 7

RECONSTRUCTION AND A
GEOGRAPHY OF GRACE

At the end of the Civil War, much of Columbia was ash and debris, Bishop Lynch was stranded with his Confederate credentials in Europe and many plantations had been ravaged. Grandparents, parents, aunts and uncles, siblings, cousins and small children were mourning their dead. Lincoln had been assassinated. Slaves, who revered him as their advocate, were dismayed even as they rejoiced in newly realized freedom. It was a freedom without much direction as to where and how they might shape new lives. Much the same could be said of every white citizen. Souls were in tatters.

It was incumbent on all in the Diocese of Charleston, with the rest of the South, to construct a new social and economic order. Clergy and religious knew what missionaries to the unchurched in foreign lands have discovered: tending to people's bodily needs—for food, clothing, shelter, medical care and meaningful work—must lay the foundation for spiritual healing and the stabilizing of a religious culture.

Historians tend to define the Reconstruction era as beginning in 1865, when General Robert E. Lee surrendered his army to General Ulysses S. Grant at Appomattox, Virginia, and ending when Union troops were officially withdrawn from the South in 1877, after a court-dealt compromise awarded a contested presidential election to Rutherford B. Hayes. In reality, however, Reconstruction (and indeed basic construction) extended out many years—with economic crises, political upheavals, family problems and reversals of gains made by the freed slaves marking many decades. Memories festered, and there were those who held on to hope that the old order might somehow be restored.

In 1881, the *Charleston Post and Courier* carried news from Daniel Heyward of Beaufort, who had visited General Lee. Lee was in Savannah and en route to Florida in a state of broken health. Heyward reported that the ailing Lee had denounced Sherman's bloody and fire-fueled March to the Sea as "the act of a savage, and not justified by the usages of war."[111] The sting of Sherman's memory has lasted more than 150 years, as could still be seen in 2019 on a billboard along South Carolina route 462 near Coosawatchie denouncing Sherman and his troops as terrorists, arsonists and thieves. Although the Confederate flag has been removed from the state capitol grounds, there are various locations where relics of the Confederacy are displayed or sold. The response of the Diocese of Charleston emphasized rebuilding and healing, but for many years, it also populated its churches and schools along color lines.

Economy

Until the later nineteenth and early twentieth centuries, South Carolina resisted industrialization. Paper mills came to the coast and textile mills to the north of the state in those periods. Meatpacking arrived in some rural areas, but it was much, much later that transportation corporate powerhouses like BMW and Michelin came to the Upstate and Boeing established itself in Charleston, adjacent to the airport. During Reconstruction, the state relied on what it always had: the fruits of the plantations, banking, medical and legal professions and education.

In addition to cotton production, which occupied acres and acres of land, rice fields yielded the famous Carolina rice. Indigo, sugar cane and tea all had their day. So, too, did tobacco and a variety of fruits and vegetables that found a favorable growing climate: peaches, watermelon, peanuts, pecans, tomatoes, corn, cucumbers, sweet potatoes, squash and numerous greens—especially collards. All of these, naturally, required skilled planters, pickers, harvesters, winnowers, packers and haulers. Other cottage industries developed too, like the Charleston-area sweetgrass basketmaking that is still one of the sought-after crafts of the region. Along the coast, oyster and shrimp boats provided support and income, and in the more wooded interior areas, deer hunting yielded venison. People learned to cook and eat what they could; the Civil War era had honed survival skills.

It was during Reconstruction that the losses of the war, human and material, came home. Manpower and skill sets were lacking. An economy that had survived and thrived on slavery had to reinvent itself or, in some cases, starve, even though the soldier-stomped land was resilient and eventually would recover.

REBUILDING AND BUILDING ANEW

As mentioned in previous chapters, it fell to Bishop Patrick Lynch to rebuild the fire-ravaged Charleston, including schools, churches and the bishop's residence—lost in what appears to have been an accident, not an act of war. Mother Baptista's academy in Columbia was among the ruins of that city, which was indeed the consequence of the war. Father Leon Fillion, Bishop Lynch's vicar general, contracted typhoid fever and died while Lynch was in Europe.[112] There were debts to pay, and once he was able to return to the diocese, Bishop Lynch had to spend a great deal of time fundraising to restore both the works of the diocese and their sites.

Similarly, the brief history of Eustace Bellinger Pinckney and Mary Martha Porcher Pinckney notes that planters and landowners in general were often faced with having to sell whole plantations or parts of properties in order to save others and secure provisions for their families. Formal education at boarding schools for children who were previously considered southern gentry was virtually inaccessible, and providing free schools for anyone—the child of a former Confederate or of a former slave—seemed impossible when the tax base had been shot apart.

Surprisingly enough, the impetus to add missions, parishes and schools somehow continued—though at a necessarily slowed pace. Under Bishop Lynch's guidance, St. Peter Church for freed slaves opened in Charleston, and St. Anthony Church was established in Florence. There was an effort by a Mr. Devereaux to remodel a former Jewish synagogue so that it could serve temporarily as a "pro-cathedral." And so, by the end of September 1866, Bishop Lynch had a useful structure.[113] Plans began for a parish church in Aiken, and collections were taken up with an eye to replacing a storm-ruined church on Sullivan's Island and for a prospective new one in Blackville. Then a faltering attempt was made in Anderson, and attention shifted to the prospect of founding a parish in Greenville.[114] Amid the ongoing hope for new Catholic parishes, the future of schools and orphanages remained a concern.

The Sisters of Our Lady of Mercy managed to open St. Joseph's Academy in Sumter in 1866.[115] St. Peter Catholic School in Columbia began admitting students in 1872, and four schools started up in Charleston between 1874 and 1878: Cathedral School for Boys, Parochial School for Girls, Central Catholic (a boys' school) and St. Peter's. The Ursulines, whose Columbia convent and school had been ruined, lived for a time on a farm called Valle Crucis, which served a very small number of students. The Sisters of Our Lady of Mercy bought Alston Mansion on Meeting Street to serve as Our Lady of Mercy Academy and so were able to move orphaned girls to their motherhouse on Queen Street. The community received a grant of $12,000 from the U.S. Congress in 1871, an expression of gratitude for the sisters' compassionate care of soldiers from both sides of the conflict during the Civil War.[116] Orphaned boys moved to a newly purchased property in 1878.[117]

As can be seen, there was progress, but there was also regress. In one location after another, weakened buildings began to fail, as did the health of overtaxed priests. Bishop Lynch asked the Vatican to take North Carolina on as an Apostolic Vicariate so that he could focus on restoring South Carolina. The request was granted, so he mounted ever more vigorous plans to support the diocese where Church losses were still said to have exceeded $300,000.[118] That would be the rough equivalent of $4.5 to $4.6 million today (according to two online inflation calculations). In addition, there was another $60,000 in losses incurred by the St. John's Saving Association, which the bishop had set up as a source of financial security for immigrants.[119] Bishop Lynch was on the road more than not, and his sister, Mother Baptista, finally wrote to him to ask, "Ah, my, when can you cease to be a carpet-bagger bishop?"[120]

Elsewhere, much of South Carolina was staggering under the enormity of the projects and perplexities residents faced. Historian Walter Edgar has recounted the way in which labor and industry suffered in the aftermath of the war. Much to the surprise of Carolina planters, once slaves realized that they had truly been freed, many left the state and, in some cases, the country, heading to Liberia. Others stayed on as wage-earning laborers. The southern economy was not prepared for that, and in the meantime, whites had incurred significant debt and had mortgaged property. Interest rates escalated. Rice fields had to be worked, but in many cases there were no hands to work them. Women accustomed to servants suddenly found themselves having to do housework. Men unused to plantation chores and heavy lifting found themselves without farmhands. Homes and barns had to be rebuilt and fields re-tilled and planted, and the workforce was stripped. Not only had many freed slaves left, but nearly one-third of the men who had voluntarily joined or been drafted into the Confederate army had also been killed in battle. Others had returned with limbs missing. The Blue Ridge

Railroad project, expected to be a boon to the Upstate and an opportunity for immigrant workers, failed, in part, due to inability to construct a tunnel but also as a result of a bond scheme.[121]

White southerners sometimes staged "bread riots" in places like Richmond and Savannah. The city of Charleston barely avoided them, mainly because of its active public assistance program. Those who returned from armed conflict were war-weary long before Lee's surrender, as were their families. Poor and middle-class white Carolinians increasingly resented the way in which they seemed to bear the brunt of war. Rumors fueled resentments as the perceived "elite" seemed far less affected by the deprivations of war. Promises from leaders that secession would have no bloody consequences had been irretrievably broken.[122]

The stage was set for already existing racism to become more virulent.

RACE

Historian Henry Louis Gates Jr. has observed that in the Reconstruction era, when all African American males were free, 80 percent of them registered to vote, and in many cases they won the majority of seats in southern state legislatures.[123] That is exactly what happened in South Carolina. African Americans joined the Republican Party, the party of Lincoln, which had been the object of scorn by political leaders in the immediate antebellum period. Francis Cardozo, a Presbyterian minister educated in England and Scotland, was the first person of color elected to state office in South Carolina—that of secretary of state.[124] African Americans briefly occupied the majority of seats in the statehouse in Columbia, chaired committees and were elected to the U.S. Congress. Meanwhile, they were often vilified in the press as illiterate and child-minded.[125] When the first African Americans enrolled at South Carolina College (now the University of South Carolina), and Richard D. Greener, a black Harvard graduate (later U.S. consul to Vladivostok), was awarded a position on the faculty, most of the existing faculty and student body resigned.[126] The normal school, the public school teacher training program common at the time, operated on the USC campus, at Rutledge College. Its enrollment is described as made up "almost entirely of black females"[127] in the heyday of Reconstruction. Thus, political and educational progress for African Americans also gave impetus to white flight.

Decades of coexisting during slavery had done nothing to undo southern taboos. Racial intermarriage was unthinkable despite the presence of numerous biracial children fathered by "masters." Sharing schools, athletic events and social circles was considered an open invitation to the "miscegenation" of intermarriage. In the immediate aftermath of the Civil War, white legislators had attempted to impose "Black Codes," which would have treated free slaves (or anyone designated "colored") as subjects of white legal guardians while also imposing exorbitant fees for trade and travel. These codes did not pass muster with the federal government, which retained an occupying force in South Carolina until the official end of Reconstruction.[128] A new state constitution had been passed in 1868, which accorded many rights to citizens of color, but it was resisted or ignored as much as possible by many white South Carolinians.

Walter Edgar noted that self-segregation was the route taken by many former slaves who remained in South Carolina. They found security in their own neighborhoods, schools and churches and, by and large, did not trust the white world.[129] In short order, an active Ku Klux Klan had risen across the South, and murders, whippings and church burnings ensued, with the result that African Americans formed their own militias. Social turmoil and a reign of terror afflicted both races.[130]

Whatever gains had been made by African Americans in South Carolina were rapidly rolled back once Rutherford B. Hayes, the new president, withdrew federal troops and agents in 1877. While some arenas of integration persisted, many rapidly disappeared, and black voters were disenfranchised by voter registration regulations and required oaths (supporting segregation of the races) until 1948.[131]

The legal imposition of segregation in public places and institutions was a fact of life that people of every faith, including Catholicism, acceded to and lived with. Monsignor Madden's history speaks of ministry to "colored Catholics" for decades and decades after the Civil War, and the first ordination of a black priest recorded in his diocesan history occurred at the cathedral in Charleston in February 1958. The man receiving Holy Orders, with Bishop John J. Russell officiating, was Kenneth Henry, a member of the Conventual Franciscans and son of Mrs. Estelle Henry of Charleston.[132]

The Spirit

War can bring out the best of human valor and sacrificial love. It can also leave minds shattered and spirits saturated with a desire for revenge. Dealing with both outcomes falls to those who minister and practice the healing arts.

One of the comforts and one of the unique possessions of South Carolina's African Americans was the slavery-born tradition of spirituals. Students of the genre often remark on how the musical style reflects African, especially West African, roots and mingles soulful sadness with hope. Using the songs sung in All Saints Parish in Waccamaw, Charles Joyner remarked on how themes of the Old and New Testaments provided texts that expressed "the total involvement of religion in everyday life."[133] He noted that not only did stories of Moses and the Exodus, David's victory over Goliath or Daniel in the lion's den offer hope in God's saving power, but they also suggested that God's justice would come, one way or another, to those who were the perpetrators of oppression. The spirituals did more than that, however. They also "voiced [slaves'] deepest values and proclaimed—and partly shaped—their sense of community."[134]

Community was, above all, what a newly freed people most sought and depended on. Inevitably, in a locale where not everyone wanted to share community with them, they turned to those who had most intimately shared their journeys and borne their crosses.

Healing, therefore, requires structure and institutions where people can find comfort. The history of the Diocese of Charleston shows that Bishop Lynch continued to set up parishes and schools for African Americans. In many ways, he was doing what was common across the state. Slaves and freed Africans had for decades joined the Catholic, Baptist, Presbyterian, Methodist and other churches. Denmark Vesey, executed after an attempted slave revolt, had been a Bible study leader and parishioner at Second Presbyterian in Charleston.[135] The Episcopal Church, which had many African American adherents, failed to seat African Americans at their general convention, with the result that many found the Reformed Episcopal Church a spiritual home that was more welcoming. But in the post–Civil War era, relations with predominantly white congregations were fraught with tension. Perhaps the undercurrent of resentments and distrust helps to account for the rapid growth of traditionally black denominations, such as the African Methodist Episcopal Church and AME Zion Church, in South Carolina.[136]

To this day, it is commonly remarked that modern-day Africa is rife with Catholics, and African priests and sisters have joined the ranks of those ministering in the Diocese of Charleston and surrounding states. African Catholicism boomed after the slave trade and much of the colonial era had faded. But African Americans continue to make up only a small fraction of the registered Catholics in the diocese. Much of that has historical roots. There are, however, noteworthy strongholds of African American Catholic faith and action visible and growing in the diocese.

Chapter 8

CATHOLIC HILL, ST. GERARD AND MORE

In diocesan lore, allusions to Catholic Hill sound like the lead-in to a detective story. St. James, the mission in what has long been known as Catholic Hill, seems to have disappeared from consciousness and public record for more than forty years. Part of the history of this traditional African American church is connected to the Bellingers, who intermarried with the Pinckneys.

Located outside Walterboro, St. James is said to have its beginnings with an appeal made to Bishop John England by a group of vestrymen who wanted to form a parish community in an area called Thompson's Crossroads (or, in later records, Ritter). In the late 1830s, a chapel was built there, and it appears to have included some of the Catholics of the Bellinger family, along with servants and slaves. According to parish records, the church burned irreparably in 1856, and in the midst of the Civil War and Reconstruction, no one in the Walterboro area or the diocese seems to have been aware of it.[137]

It seems that after a long lapse, the Jesuit Father Louis Folchi, who was brought to Charleston to organize St. Peter's Church (a parish founded in 1868 for African Americans), assisted in reclaiming the forgotten community of Thompson's Crossroads.[138] In 1872, Bishop Lynch began corresponding with a religious community of men, the St. Joseph's Missionary Society, also known as the Mill Hill Fathers, who expressed interest in serving the black community. Upon their arrival in 1875, Folchi began a mission tour around the state. He was particularly interested in black Catholics, but he was also attentive to any small faith community he discovered. He went to the Beaufort/Port Royal area and wrote that he believed that it would be important for "missionaries for the colored people" to visit the Walterboro area. He noted, "I found there are a good many of them who still retain enough of the faith and are anxious for a priest."[139] It would seem to be a good wager to think that the "good many" were concentrated around Thompson's Crossroads—the faith community of Catholic Hill.

Some twenty-two years later, Father Daniel Berberich, the one who had served and been so influential with the family at Pinckney Colony, found himself in Catholic Hill, where he undertook building a church and a school. Father Berberich served St. James until 1909. After that, it became a mission stop for priests from various sites in the Lowcountry. Now St. James is a mission of St. Anthony in Walterboro with a roll of fifteen registered households and up to forty regular attendees at Sunday Masses. While some might consider this a "remnant people" in the mold of the Israelites of the time of the Blessed Virgin and St. Joseph, the important point seems to be that the faith has held on—and did indeed persist despite decades of interruption, families' movement away from the area and the ups and downs of civic society and the economy. The parishioners of St. James credit the Holy Spirit, of course, but also one man, Vincent of Paul Davis, for maintaining Catholic teaching and devotion throughout those mysteriously forgotten years.[140] That devotion has paid off over the years. Parishioners from Catholic Hill have remained active in the Diocesan Council of Catholic Women and have contributed their presence and voices at African Catholic heritage days and a bicentennial dialogue with black Catholic theologians held on October 11, 2019. St. James is one of those mission churches that testify to and personify a classic hymn: "Faith of Our Fathers." It is living still.

A Number of African American Parishes

Some of the traditionally African American churches in the diocese, like St. Peter's in Charleston, no longer exist independently but have merged with others. In the case of St. Peter's, the merger made them a part of St. Patrick's. There remain a number of active parishes and missions in South Carolina that were largely or fully African American in their attendance and early history. Those identified as such include St. Jude in Sumter, which has now merged with St. Anne to form a combined parish. St. Jude High School (Sumter Catholic) operated from 1959 to 1970, and it included a St. Jude Boarding School for girls from 1963 to 1970. The combined St. Anne–St. Jude parish maintains a significantly higher population of registered African American parishioners than any other in the Columbia deanery, with the exception of St. Martin de Porres. St. Anne–St. Jude School continues and for a time was able to incorporate a diverse group of high school students from what was once St. Francis Xavier High School, a private Catholic secondary school in Sumter. St. Martin de Porres in Columbia continues to serve a relatively large African American population and offers an occasional Mass in Igbo, the language of a major tribal group in Nigeria. The parish maintains a small school that is dedicated to serving African American students from the Waverly neighborhood in Columbia. St. Martin's Church welcomes registered parishioners and daily Mass attendees who serve on the faculty of USC or on the staff of local hospitals, and the mixing of races and national origins is visible to all who join in parish liturgies and celebrations.

At least two parishes evolved into predominantly African American church families: the aforementioned St. Patrick and also Our Lady of Mercy in Charleston. Over the years, Our Lady of Mercy provided hospitality and outreach by assisting the operation of Neighborhood House and Echo House.[141] Other parishes that began as exclusively or almost exclusively African American now serve a mixed population. Among these are St. Anthony of Padua in Greenville, which has an active and diversely populated school and a parish community that includes African American, Anglo and Hispanic/Latino members. St. Anthony's mission statement is firm in its commitment to its roots. It proclaims that the parish is dedicated to "welcoming all people to worship God in the genius of African American Catholic Spirituality."[142]

Other traditionally African American parishes and missions include St. Anne, Florence; St. Ann, Kingstree; St. Mary of the Angels, Anderson; St. Cyprian, Georgetown, named for an African saint and now combined with St. Mary, Georgetown; and Christ the King, Orangeburg, which merged in 1963 (parish and school) with Holy Trinity, Orangeburg, the latter being another racially and ethnically diverse parish, served at this writing by an African priest. It should be noted that Christ the King, founded in 1939, burned in what has been deemed an arson fire and was rebuilt in 1942. Like a number of other churches, it was merged with another local church by Bishop Ernest Unterkoefler in an effort to advance full integration throughout the diocese. The year was the same one known for the "I Have a Dream" speech of Reverend Dr. Martin Luther King Jr. and the March on Washington in August 1963. Some have later questioned the wisdom of the bishop in forcing some of the mergers. There has been some sentiment that the distinctiveness of the African American churches was sacrificed, but the bishop's declared intentions were the service of justice and equality.

Two other historically African American parishes should be noted. One, St. Mary in Rock Hill, had a school that helped form the first fully integrated Catholic school in the diocese, St. Anne in Rock Hill. In 1954, the year of the U.S. Supreme Court decision in *Brown v. the Board of Education*, which insisted on equal access to public education for students of all races, St. Anne became the first nonpublic school to achieve this goal. While other communities around the state were scrambling to found new private schools and academies to bypass integration, St. Anne welcomed five African American students from St. Mary's.

St. Gerard Church in Aiken noted that in its early days local African American Catholics met in one another's homes without the presence of a priest. With the assistance of Redemptorist priests, the African American faith community became a mission of Orangeburg, meeting, as they grew, in a local theater. The faith community existed long before its church did, however.

At a Black Heritage Day of Recollection in the spring of 2017, there was an animated discussion about the numbers of youths from Aiken and the surrounding area who were enrolled in boarding schools out of state: St. Emma Military Academy for Boys and St. Francis de Sales School for Girls in Northern Virginia. These were created by St. Katharine Drexel, whose religious community, the Sisters of the Blessed Sacrament, was founded with a distinct mission to Native American and African American communities. Among the missions she founded were these two schools, which enrolled young people from the 1890s through their closing in 1972. The conversation raised the issue of the dual purpose served by these schools, as well as the reason so many parents welcomed the opportunity for their children. On one hand, it was clear that St. Emma's, with its curriculum of academics, religion, arts and trade skills, and St. Francis de Sales, with its emphasis on classical education and practical arts, offered a rigorous course of studies and a sound preparation for future careers. On the other hand, the schools also offered a secure environment. The older men and women at the spring 2017 gathering, many of them from St. Gerard's, observed that going off to boarding schools may also have saved lives. There were too many arbitrary arrests, too many stories of brutal killings like that of Emmett Till in

Mississippi or Willie Earle in South Carolina and too many assaults. Mother Katharine's initiative certainly seems to have been a rescue mission as well as a spiritual and professional uplift.

The Oblate Sisters of Providence

While St. Katharine Drexel is revered for the use of her personal gifts and Philadelphia family fortune, another group of sisters gave special service to the African American community. Based in Baltimore, Maryland, the Oblate Sisters of Providence operated schools across the diocese, including St. Gerard in Aiken, Christ the King in Orangeburg and St. Peter and Immaculate Conception in Charleston. The Oblates continued in the Diocese of Charleston through the 1980s. The history of these sisters noted that they are "the first successful Roman Catholic sisterhood in the world established by women of African descent."[143] They were founded in 1829, the same year that the Sisters of Our Lady of Mercy in Charleston were founded. A Sulpician priest, Father James Hector Joubert, and four sisters of African Caribbean origin, led by the young woman who would become Mother Mary Lange, traveled to Baltimore to establish a religious community devoted to teaching and caring for African American children. By the 1950s, the sisters recorded that they had founded schools in eighteen states, including, of course, South Carolina. For a brief period of time, they also were involved in educational ministry in Cuba. Along with maintaining ministries in several states in the Union today, the sisters also serve at locations in Costa Rica.[144]

A distinguished parishioner of St. Patrick Church, Judge Arthur McFarland credited the Oblate Sisters with his youthful conversion to Catholicism. Now retired as Municipal Court judge in Charleston after more than thirty years on the judicial bench, McFarland was a graduate of Immaculate Conception School in Charleston, staffed by the Oblates; Bishop England High School, where he was one of the first African Americans to integrate the school; and Notre Dame University. Prior to his return to Charleston, he worked for a time with the National Association for the Advancement of Colored People (NAACP). In speaking of the impact of the Oblate Sisters of Providence, Judge McFarland expressed the gratitude of many African American Catholics who have been products of their schools.

An interesting side note is that one of the Oblates' founding sisters, Mother Theresa Maxis Duchemin, left the order when it was experiencing severe diminishment and had an uncertain future. She went on to cofound the Sisters, Servants of the Immaculate Heart of Mary (IHM's) in Detroit, in collaboration with Redemptorist Father Louis Florent Gillet in 1845. The IHM Sisters eventually became three groups, centered in Detroit, Michigan, and Philadelphia and Scranton, Pennsylvania. The Scranton IHM sisters aided in the founding and formation of the Sisters of St. Casimir (1907) and the Sisters of SS. Cyril and Methodius (1909). Two of these communities, the Philadelphia IHM sisters and the Sisters of SS. Cyril and Methodius, along with the early Oblate Sisters of Providence, have collectively given long service in the Diocese of Charleston—and the three together make up part of the same religious family tree.

African American Catholics Today

There are and have been African American bishops and archbishops. One of them, Wilton Gregory, now archbishop of Washington, D.C., was a protégé of South Carolina's Cardinal Bernardin. There is an African American priest now en route to sainthood, Venerable Augustus Tolton, a former slave, educated and ordained in Rome, who served in Chicago and other Illinois locations. In November 2017, *The Atlantic* published an article pointing out that the 3 million African American Catholics exceed the total number of members of the African Methodist Episcopal Church.[145]

That number, while impressive, remains only slightly more than 4 percent of the total number of Catholics registered in U.S. parishes. In South Carolina, registered African Americans comprise only 1.8 percent of the combined parish counts. There are likely numerous reasons for the paucity of numbers, such as the discrimination that caused an African American like Father Augustus Tolton to have to go directly to Rome to study (because he was refused seminary admission on the basis of race in the States)—or that it was easier to form a Knights of St. Peter Claver than to join some Knights of Columbus groups if one happened to be a man of color.[146] Catholics, as any honest study of the diocese shows, more than tolerated slavery and sustained segregation well into the 1960s. That history has to be grappled with when it comes to examining how welcome African American and other people of color may feel when they walk into our churches and seek entry into its ministries and social activities. It should be noted that Ms. Kathleen Merritt, an African American, has served as the director of the Office of Ethnic Ministries in the diocese since her appointment by Bishop Robert Baker in 2002. Bishop Robert E. Guglielmone appointed Mrs. Sandra Leatherwood—a former principal, assistant superintendent and director of elementary education—as superintendent of Catholic schools, the first African American in the history of the diocese to hold this position. Mrs. Leatherwood is a lifelong Catholic, raised in Alabama during the civil rights struggles of the 1950s and 1960s. During her tenure at the helm of the Cathoic Schools Office, she has advanced many causes for the diocese, including diocesan-wide accreditation and the development of a strategic plan to strengthen schools, and also served on the Executive Board and the Commission on Standards for the National Catholic Association.

As is noted in chapter 17, the number of African-born Catholics in the diocese has swelled as professionals and priests and religious have come to the state. Whatever may be said of the state's history of hard-core segregation, it is clear that in 2020, Catholic parishioners are appreciative of the chaplains, administrators and pastors from Africa who have come to lead them. They begin to realize, with the whole Church, that Africa, a continent that has produced a current count of twenty-six members of the College of Cardinals, is a vibrant locus of Catholicism. At one time mission territory, Africa is now providing the diocese with missionaries to America.

Chapter 9

WARS, MOVEMENTS, UPHEAVALS

INTO THE TWENTIETH CENTURY

Following the tumultuous and trying times of Civil War and Reconstruction, the twenty-four-year term of Bishop Patrick Lynch's episcopal service was followed by the record-breaking thirty-three years of Bishop Henry Pinckney Northrop. It was a different South Carolina and yet an old one that he faced.

According to state historian Walter Edgar, the immediate post-Reconstruction period found political parties calling themselves Conservatives, Bourbons and Redeemers organized to reverse much of what Reconstruction had wrought.[147] Opposed to Lincoln's Republican Party and all that it stood for, they systematically took legislative and judicial steps to ensure that "black Carolinians did not threaten the white minority's control of state government."[148] This was after the barely dozen-year spell in which African American men had been voting in large numbers and holding public office. De facto segregation ensued in many areas, and then Jim Crow laws mandated it. Political machinations after the departure of federal agents ensured that it would be difficult, if not impossible, for African Americans to vote, and the Confederacy was honored in ceremonies and statuary. Clearly, despite the end of slavery, South Carolina saw in all sorts of places signs and evidence "of the resurrected old order."[149] As the brief spell of African American engagement in public life was broken, enforced segregation affected churches, schools, the workplace and every arena of life.

The Early Economy

Before the Civil War and into the Reconstruction era, South Carolina's economy might best have been described as agricultural and mercantile. After that, and largely coinciding with Bishop Northrop's episcopacy, it clearly retained these endeavors but took on new ones, too, particularly in industry and transportation. Rice culture decreased, and tobacco, with the growing popularity of smoking and snuff, rose. Cotton remained a big product, but cotton gins altered labor and textile mills employed new workers who lacked the skills of planters and pickers.[150] Railroad travel increased, trolley tracks were laid and by the early twentieth-century motor cars had begun to appear on the scene, which meant that the new roadways and tracks had to be maintained and periodically improved. Electrical power required plants, and sanitation meant that reliance on old wells would have to be supplanted by water and sewer lines—things that often were incredibly slow to come to poorer rural areas and towns where low-paid laborers lived.[151]

Insufficient wages, poor health and child labor were issues only gradually being addressed, and according to Edgar, women often were the driving force organizing initiatives to address literacy and public health needs.[152] Among these women were Catholic sisters, who had long taken a lead in these fields. It is interesting to note that despite the beginnings of a tourist trade in South Carolina, prohibition had no small support—probably due to the strong Baptist presence. Women were welcomed when they took on public initiatives and formed a statewide Woman's Christian Temperance Union, but that was not enough to get the South Carolina legislature to endorse the Nineteenth Amendment, which gave women the right to vote.[153] Overall, the last decades of the nineteenth century and the early decades of the twentieth saw the rich becoming richer and the poor growing poorer, with affluence remaining the province of white men and their families and poverty falling to both African Americans and working-class white people.

During all of this, the Church flourished, and Bishop Northrop is credited with completing the seventeen-year project of building St. John the Baptist Cathedral, dedicated in 1907; founding numerous parishes and missions; supporting the inclusion of a School of Nursing in the OLM-run St. Francis Xavier Hospital; encouraging the opening of new Catholic elementary schools and girls' academies in Aiken, Charleston and Columbia; and founding Bishop England High School in 1915.[154] During Bishop Northrop's term of office, Mother Katharine Drexel was instrumental in reestablishing a church, St. James, for the long-lost Catholic Hill community (see chapter 8) and setting up two schools for African American children in Charleston. Then, within months of Bishop William Russell's taking the helm of the diocese, the United States became engaged in World War I.

WAR, DEPRESSION AND WAR AGAIN

In the late 1890s, the United States had been engaged in the Spanish-American War and war in the Philippines, both of which required armed forces. Comparatively few South Carolinian young men were involved in these conflicts, and Edgar noted that the poor health of many of those who volunteered caused them to be rejected—as many as one-third of those who presented themselves.[155] This seems to have been an obvious outcome of poor sanitation, the living conditions of mill towns and other areas where poorer laborers lived and the nonexistence of antibiotics and other twentieth-century medical advances.

In South Carolina, there had been notable sentiment against war in general, and there had been some public protests prior to U.S. entry into World War I, but once war was declared, more than 300,000 of South Carolina's men volunteered. Only one-sixth of them actually saw military service.[156] British poets Rupert Brooke (died in 1915), Wilfred Owen (died in 1918) and Siegfried Sassoon (who died of old age), along with Alan Seeger, American author of the well-known "I Have a Rendezvous with Death" (died in 1916), put into verse the horrors of a war in which poison gas and new munitions wrought havoc and resulted in tremendous bloodshed. Black and white young men came from a state that prided itself on military installations. They served in various branches of the armed forces, and a number of them were awarded Medals of Honor. Sadly, those who returned found that race relations were as they had been and that postwar benefits were accorded only to white men.[157] As the nation hurtled into the Roaring Twenties and the Jazz Age, South Carolina did not seem to fare so well as some other parts of the country, and the stock market crash of 1929 and the Great Depression meant that the South was again afflicted.

Even before the October 1929 crash on Wall Street, there were signs of economic stress in the state. A number of mills and plants were sold off, and banks had begun to fail before the national economic earthquake hit.[158] Less cotton was being successfully marketed, and surprisingly enough, less tobacco was selling too. As observers of the period noted, tobacco planters rode a kind of giddy elevator to overproduction and were then stunned when demand did not coincide with their supply.[159] In addition to overestimating markets, many farm areas were suffering the effects of overplanting and failure to rotate crops. Not surprisingly, in most areas, people were publicly committed to banning alcohol but privately resisting Prohibition, so selling moonshine or otherwise illegally acquired whiskey became a lucrative business.[160] Walter Edgar described what the 1930s brought to the state: "In 1935 the state's population was three times what it had been in 1850, but the amount of food produced was about the same. Consequently, poorer Carolinians subsisting on a diet of pork, cornbread, and molasses were more susceptible to disease."[161] This reality assuredly affected the citizenry at large and, as a consequence, affected parishes, schools and other Catholic institutions throughout the state.

The New Deal measures initiated by FDR provided food, conservation work and public projects like bridge construction and road building. The massive Santee Cooper damming and electrical power production[162] fed, clothed and sheltered citizens who previously would have resented the federal government's incursion into their lives. Cultural projects, federally funded, produced histories and literary works. While DeBose Heyward apparently did not need funding, his novel *Porgy*, which, in collaboration with Gershwin became the opera *Porgy and Bess*, is often cited as a product of a Charleston renaissance that managed to coincide with the downturn of the 1920s and 1930s.

Some of the works of the New Deal also buttressed what was a weaker South Carolina industry, tourism, and made it stronger. There was a time when men's beachwear included buttoned T-shirts and close-fitting pants as long as knickers and women's covered a similar amount of skin and included skirting. Tourism, especially to beach areas, became an attraction of South Carolina as city-weary families seeking cool breezes headed for shore points. The public initiatives generated by Roosevelt provided better roads, with the result that tourism became more inviting. More and more hotels grew up in the Myrtle Beach area, and places like Folly Beach outside Charleston, though generally housing people in cottages, gained a certain cultural prestige by association with Heyward and his work on *Porgy*. Lake Marion, created by the Santee Cooper project, provided more than electrical power, as its scenic expanse provided and ideal site for fishing and boating.

While the New Deal helped with survival, if not economic recovery, the entry of the United States into World War II provided full or nearly full employment statewide and also occasioned an influx of workers from other areas of the country to supplement the workforce depleted by the absence of more than 184,000 enlisted men and women who claimed South Carolina as home.[163] Army and navy bases boomed, and some that had been shuttered reopened. Walter Edgar also cited the little-known existence of twenty-eight prisoner of war camps located in South Carolina. These housed captured military personnel, most of them from Italy or Germany.[164] All of these installations required workers. The economic upheavals that had gradually plagued the state in the earlier part of the century seemed definitively ended, and a new prosperity did persist in some quarters. After the conclusion of the war and in the decades ahead, South Carolina attracted new inhabitants and new industry.

What did not abate was racial tension. In his book *Civil Rights in South Carolina*, James Felder recounted, in chapter after chapter, the twentieth-century revival of Ku Klux Klan activity and the frantic efforts made by politicians to stem the tide of integration. African American teachers and business people in the war years and the postwar era began joining the NAACP, and lawsuits were increasingly being filed to press for equal pay for teachers, equal school facilities and school buses for children of color and desegregation of public parks and other facilities. In both World War I and World War II, black and white military personnel had served with equal distinction, but when they returned home, they found that they could not attempt to get equal pay or equal treatment without losing friends, business and partnerships. Strom Thurmond, who initially seemed progressive in his attempt to handle the lynching of Willie Earle in the courts (the subject of Dr. Will Willimon's lecture at Mount Hermon Lutheran Church in Columbia on October 15, 2019), became, as a U.S. senator, a rabid segregationist and Dixiecrat. As is commonly known, the initial affection for FDR and gratitude for the saving efforts of the New Deal fell away as he, Truman and the Democratic Party increasingly advocated for equal rights.

Edgar and Felder recounted how, even after the 1954 Supreme Court decision banning segregation in public schools, South Carolina conspired in many ways to dodge it, including attempts to privatize schools. Along with St. Anne Catholic School in Rock Hill (noted in chapter 11), the Lutheran Theological Seminary of the South in Columbia is cited as one that rapidly integrated—in 1954.[165] Bishop Ernest Unterkoefler, who assumed the see of Charleston in 1964, was from the outset a proponent of racial justice and was insistent on inclusion of all races in the Catholic schools. His predecessor, Bishop Francis Reh, was also known to support integration, and the Diocese of Charleston Archives includes a letter to him from U.S. Attorney General Robert Kennedy that includes twenty-six pages of Kennedy's testimony to the House Judiciary Committee in support of civil rights legislation. The letter was dated October 22, 1963, exactly one month before the assassination of President John F. Kennedy. Alhough the intent of the letter is not recorded, its implicit purpose was to encourage Reh in his efforts.

Catholic schools responded quickly to the call to integrate schools, although some continued to have an almost all-white student population. As school and facility integration inched along in other public quarters, numerous issues continued to arise. Unterkoefler was the only white person speaking at a January 1976 Columbia rally in support of making Martin Luther King Jr. Day a legal holiday.[166] The most recent widely known display of the persistence of white supremacist thinking in the region was Dylann Roof's assault on Emanuel AME Church in 2015 in Charleston. The Emanuel shootings finally led to Governor Nikki Haley's leadership in persuading the state legislature to remove the Confederate flag from the capitol grounds—something for which Charleston's mayor Joe Riley, a lifelong parishioner at the cathedral, had marched one hundred miles in the year 2000.

Chapter 10

CHANGE AND MORE CHANGE

The twentieth century was a time of eleven popes, from Leo XIII through John Paul II; eighteen American presidents, from William McKinley to William Jefferson Clinton; and nine bishops of Charleston, from Henry Northrop to Robert Baker. Of the popes, one, John Paul I, had the startlingly short papacy of a little over a month, while Popes Pius XII and St. John Paul II endured for more than twenty years, with St. John Paul II having achieved nearly twenty-seven by the time of his death in 2005. Two American presidents were assassinated in this period, McKinley and Kennedy; Franklin Delano Roosevelt died shortly into a never-to-be-repeated fourth term of office; and at least two faced well-advertised public scandals, Richard Nixon, who resigned, and Bill Clinton, whose impeachment seems to have been a near miss. Bishop Francis Reh held the see of Charleston for only two years before he was assigned to the North American College in Rome, while Northrop, spanning two centuries, had thirty-three years. Bishop Ernest Unterkoefler remained for twenty-six years, with his term beginning as the Second Vatican Council was approaching conclusion.

On the world scene, global concerns moved from the German threat of World War I and World War II through the war in the Pacific with Japan to decades of tension between the West and both Soviet and Chinese Communism. The famed gassings of World War I paled in comparison with Hitler's concentration camps and "final solution" regarding Jewish people and those of other faiths who resisted Nazi madness and then, even more terrifying, the constant threat of nuclear war after the United States unleashed atomic bombs on Hiroshima and Nagasaki. Then guerrilla warfare, made famous in Cuba and Southeast Asia, and escalating terrorist acts added to all of these to change the face of human armed conflict. Meanwhile, peaceful uses of atomic energy, in terms of nuclear power plants (which proved capable of critical accidents) and nuclear medicine, added both dangers and opportunities to everyday life.

Protests and marches had certainly been held before, and the Boston Tea Party, which helped instigate the American Revolution, might well be counted among them. Marches for workers' rights, women's rights and equitable treatment for African Americans became more commonplace in twentieth-century America. The sit-ins and demonstrations that marked the cry for racial justice in the United States were succeeded by protests against the war in Vietnam and the draft. Marches and other public displays also were held in support of, and in opposition to, legal abortion and gay/lesbian rights as the decades rolled on toward the millennium. Elsewhere on the world stage, a so-called velvet revolution toppled the Soviet Communist empire and the Berlin Wall, and Chinese students attempted a revolt in the ill-fated Tiananmen Square protests against Chinese Communism. Arab-Israeli conflicts flared and slightly abated and flared again.

Communications in the later nineteenth century had been enhanced by telegraph and Alexander Graham Bell's telephone. Radio broadcasts went from trials to household commonplace as the twentieth century ensued. Televisions with rabbit ears on sets and antennae on rooftops went from rare to everywhere as broadcasts went from black-and-white to color and from shut-down hours to 24/7 operation. Cable systems vastly expanded the networks available to customers, and the digital age was in the works. In the 1960s, students were still using slide rules to do calculations in physics classes; by the 1970s, calculators had become common. Computers in the Bell Telephone Laboratories were the size of gymnasia locker rooms in the mid-1960s. By the end of the century, personal computers were everywhere, and they kept shrinking in size. In the early 1990s, television commercials started referring to "the information superhighway," and the Internet was born. Telephones went mobile and cell and then added Internet and photographic capacities. The accoutrements of the American home transformed in undreamed-of ways. Gas stoves coexisted with microwave ovens, and gadgets galore—from electric drills and power saws through automatic washers and driers to kitchen blenders—became standard. Farm equipment and irrigation systems became more and more technologized.

In the arena of transportation, horse-drawn carriages, coaches and trolleys gave way to automobiles and public buses. Riding lawn mowers supplanted push mowers. Trains continued to operate, but passenger trains became rarer as more and more people owned cars and used them for drivable distances. The first air flights by the Wright brothers at Kitty Hawk, North Carolina, in 1903 led, in short order, to military airplanes and commercial ones—and then to the space race, culminating in 1969 with the first landing of a man on the Moon and then continuing to all manner of adventures and explorations, space shuttle flights and the establishment of space laboratories and stations and, finally, an international space station in 1998.

Politics and business catapulted into a new world of simulcasts and on-the-spot communications and coverage. It was hard not to know of things unless one chose to go "off the grid." Information overload and information exhaustion, with sometimes dubious means of discernment of the factual from the fictitious, became an increasing challenge as the world edged into the twenty-first century and propagated fears of a Y2K (Year 2000) meltdown of all computerized systems and the possible consequence of worldwide social chaos.

For all of this, the so-called First World is the point of reference—and primarily the United States. While affluence and magnificence seemed almost an affliction in some quarters, poorer people and poorer nations missed out on the many advantages and gains of the twentieth century. There were still deaths from starvation, and there were credible warnings about environmental degradation, global warming and water crises. And no matter how civilized peoples and cultures fancied themselves, there remained tribal and ethnic conflicts that spilled blood and bred lasting resentments, and human trafficking set new forms of slavery on the world scene. American politicians squabbled about the pros and cons of foreign aid, while religious leaders appealed for sanity and generosity. Meanwhile, moral conflicts about human rights, warmaking versus pacificism, sexual mores and the simultaneous existence of outlandish prosperity and dire poverty chafed the consciences of adherents of many faiths.

What often seemed resolved was that people would increasingly live in irresolution. Beneficent souls and saints arose, as they always have, but new issues continued to wrack consciences and press for focus on self-interest and self-satisfaction. In 1974, the United States Supreme Court deemed procured abortion a woman's right, tempered only by some considerations of the trimester of fetal development. This outraged Catholics, evangelicals and others who found—and find—it basic to faith that human life begins with conception and is meant to end with a natural death. Euthanasia, in the form of assisted suicide, became legal in some nations and states, and the Church's pro-life ethic, based on God's sovereignty over life, faced another secular challenge. Guns abounded, and mass shootings, even in schools, became more and more frequent news. Multinational corporations and all manner of global monetary organizations did little to abate stresses and suffering. In the midst of head-spinning changes in people and society, the Church itself underwent change as it tried to read "the signs of the times," a slogan of the Second Vatican Council, and respond without diluting any of its core doctrines and practices.

A Changing Church

"Jesus Christ is the same yesterday, today, and forever," proclaims the timeless Letter to the Hebrews (13:8). Some have described Christ's Church, however, as both changing and changeless. The phrase *semper reformanda* ("always reforming") signals the fact that the Church continues to be called to proclaim God's Word in ways understandable to people and to invoke scriptural and traditional resources to address new moral and cultural issues, while also updating and at times correcting its discipline and practice.

The First Vatican Council, 1869–70, attended by Bishop Lynch, was cut short by strife in Italy. Its intent to address certain cultural currents never got fleshed out, and it is primarily known for proclaiming papal infallibility on solemnly declared teachings on faith and morals. The Second Vatican Council, convoked by St. John XXIII and held from 1962 to 1965, drafted dogmatic constitutions, but its intent was primarily pastoral; the changes that ensued from the council reflected that intent. Its purpose was, as the sainted pope declared, *aggiornamiento*—updating, in response to the dizzying rate of social change and the competing philosophies and governing systems affecting people's lives.[167] Bishop Unterkoefler attended all of the sessions of the council, as did Bishop (then Archbishop) Hallinan.

Perhaps one of the things that led Ernest Unterkoefler to be so much at the forefront of the civil rights movement was the council's emphasis on moral engagement with the world and the call to transform society in such a way that it better conforms with the vision of the Kingdom of God. That, too, would seem to be the basis for Cardinal Bernardin's leadership of the Catholic bishops of the United States in their quest to address the arms race, the vexing problem of anti-population weapons and the principles of the Catholic just war tradition. One of the major documents of Vatican II was *Gaudium et Spes*, the Pastoral Constitution on the Church in the Modern World, and among the issues it addressed were family life, the economy and poverty, the obligations of civil society, life issues and war. Before Vatican II, Catholics in America tended to be more reticent when it came to politics. Perhaps that was partly because their patriotism was often suspected by their detractors, who would question—as they did when Al Smith and again when John Kennedy ran for president—whether their true loyalty was to the Vatican state. In any case, as Catholic social teaching gained articulation and momentum from the time of *Rerum Novarum*, released by Leo XIII in 1891, Catholics increasingly found themselves defending workers' rights, resisting totalitarian regimes and engaging civic struggles on the basis of social-moral principles.

The council did not change only Catholics' sense of responsibility as members of civic society, however. Its dogmatic constitutions, *Sacrosanctum Concilium*, *Dei Verbum* and *Lumen Gentium*—on liturgy, sacred scripture and the nature of the Church, respectively—reclaimed a number of traditions and also led to a number of new ventures in Church life. The first area of reform was the celebration of the Eucharistic liturgy and sacramental rites. A liturgical reform movement had been underway for several decades, and it culminated with a commitment to permit Mass to be celebrated in the vernacular, the language spoken by the people of any region, and for laity to interact, respond and participate more fully than they had. Interestingly enough, the idea of having the Gospels and the Eucharistic liturgy in the language of the people had precedent in the ninth century, when Saints Cyril and Methodius received papal blessing for their liturgical books in Old Slavonic. Their idea, like that of the Council Fathers, was to emphasize comprehensibility of the liturgy to the faithful. The council continued to revere the classic Latin, Greek and Hebrew of the liturgy and the traditional Gregorian chants—all of which it sought to preserve—but its pastoral concern was for the active involvement of the faithful. Similarly, updating of the rites of initiation, vocation and healing were pressed on with a concern for employing traditional elements but vivifying the celebration. People saw baptismal rituals, confirmation, ordinations, weddings, anointings of the sick and the sacrament of penance celebrated in new words and new ways as they were renewed and endorsed.

After centuries of hesitancy in terms of biblical study by the laity (occasioned by a fear of private interpretation leading to doctrinal breakaway), Catholics were vigorously encouraged to immerse themselves in the Word and engage in Bible study groups. The Lectionary was revised to provide a fuller cycle of scripture readings for daily and Sunday Masses, the Divine Office was updated and clergy were instructed to offer scripture-based and scripture-inspired homilies more diligently. New translations of the Old and New Testaments were commissioned, and what had been the family Bible on a coffee table became more likely a personal copy of the Bible to be used for religion classes, parish Bible studies and personal meditation.

The Dogmatic Constitution on the Church clearly articulated its hierarchical nature but also made clear the call of all the baptized to be active disciples, engaged in the mission of the Church. It spoke of the universal call to holiness. Much of this teaching opened the way to the explosion of lay ministry that the Church saw in the decades after Vatican II. It also opened the way to the restoration of the permanent diaconate. Some sources, including diocesan ones, credit Bishop Unterkoefler with having been the first bishop in the United States to ordain permanent deacons, but other sources suggest that he ought to be called *one* of the first. There are indications that Bishop Fulton J. Sheen ordained a former Episcopal priest as a Catholic deacon in 1969 but that, regrettably, the man returned at some point to the Episcopal priesthood. Deacon Paul McCardle was ordained by the Bishop of Kansas City in 1970, a year before Bishop Unterkoefler imparted Holy Orders on three permanent deacons, the first of whom was Joseph C. Kemper Jr. In any case, Bishop Unterkoefler saw the importance and urgency of restoring the permanent diaconate and took steps to develop a solid deacon formation and discernment program available to qualified married and single men.[168]

Among the many developments prompted by Vatican II was energy for ecumenical engagement. Rather than regarding Orthodox and Protestant Christians as schismatics and heretics, the Council Fathers emphasized that the historical reasons for division among Christians were centuries old and that unity in common Christian faith and baptism ought to be celebrated. Both commonalities and differences ought to be topics for dialogue, while joint efforts on behalf of social well-being were also not only appropriate but also encouraged. In the Diocese of Charleston, ecumenism gained a new impetus, but it was not an altogether new idea. John England's *Diurnal* records how Lutheran, Presbyterian, Episcopalian and Methodist pastors allowed him to use their churches or halls as he traveled around his vast diocesan territory. Philosophical discussions with people of various faiths were something England participated in and sometimes initiated. Bishops after him followed suit. England and his successors often found themselves in a position to join with ministers in common efforts to assist people, whether in time of war or plague or aftermath of earthquake or hurricane. Ministry to the poor made no religious distinctions, and John England was adamant in his support of religious freedom and the Constitution's non-establishment clause.[169] Ecumenism in the diocese today is expressed in the participation of Catholics in numerous outreach efforts and in the diocese's membership and support of the Fellowship of South Carolina Bishops (successor to LARCUM, the Lutheran–Anglican–Roman Catholic–United Methodist dialogue), the South Carolina Christian Action Council and the Interfaith Partners of South Carolina. The vision continues to be that articulated by the Second Vatican Council in its decree *Unitatis Redintegratio* (on ecumenism) and its declaration *Nostra Aetate* (on interfaith understanding).

The efforts of the council showed up in quite a number of external changes visible to the people of the Diocese of Charleston, but they continue to be called to remember that the basic principles of the faith, the dogmas of the Church, the love of God, the presence of the Risen Lord and the action of the Holy Spirit remain even as planet Earth and its peoples whirl about the sun and traverse the universe.

Chapter 11

A Steady Boom in Catholic Schools

Madame Nathlie DeLage Sumter, the French wife of Thomas Sumter Jr., catechized in her own home in the nineteenth century. Edward Bohun Bellinger (died in 1924) was the full-time teacher of the children of Pinckney Colony. Just as mothers and fathers continue to homeschool today, we can be sure that South Carolinians were teaching trades, housekeeping skills, literary and other arts, mathematics, history, geography, music and religion to their offspring. At the same time, citizens and non-citizens alike recognized the value of structured schools with established curricula and well-tutored teachers. Bishop John England built on millennia-old principles when he began creating schools for boys and girls, white or free black, and offering catechetical instruction to slaves. Like many others institutions, Catholic schools in the Diocese of Charleston arose and fell or have arisen and persisted. (Appendix C gives their chronology.) A look back gives the rationale and backdrop for their existence.

Why Catholic Education

Catholic education stands in a long, honored tradition. From the Chosen People of Israel, Catholics have inherited the inclination—and, indeed, the obligation—to pursue wisdom. Often quoted, and sometimes used as a school or seminary motto, is the familiar injunction from the book of Proverbs: "The fear of the Lord is the beginning of wisdom" (Proverbs 9:10). Solomon's famed desire for wisdom was the sum of reverence for God, a breadth of knowledge, common sense and an "understanding heart" (1 Kings 3:9). The Jewish people have been known for ages for their love of scholarship. It is not surprising, then, that the oft-used title for Jesus sprang from this reverence for learning. Jesus was known to his followers as rabbi, or teacher. To be a disciple is to be a knowledge-hungry student. The Great Commission given by Jesus to his apostles before the Ascension was the command to teach all nations and baptize them (Matthew 28:19).

From the early centuries of Christianity, the Church relied on scholar saints. The Fathers of the Church—Irenaeus, Basil, John Chrysostom, Augustine—were immensely learned. When Saints Benedict and Scholastica founded their monasteries in the sixth century AD, their devotion to prayer and work, *ora et labora*, implied not only devotions and physical labor but also studying and preserving tomes of learning. Benedictine Jean LeClerq delivered an explanation for the steady dedication of Christians to study. The title of his classic work is revelatory: *The Love of Learning and the Desire for God*. It often goes unrecognized, but it was Catholics who formed the great university system of Europe. The University of Padua is where St. Thomas Aquinas studied, and he taught at the University of Paris in the thirteenth century. From the ages of monks, nuns and friars, a classic liberal education was linked with catechetical purposes.

For that reason, Catholics in the earliest days of the colonies and the United States concluded that catechesis via Sunday school or some other vehicle—for example, released time from public and other schools for religious instruction—served a noble purpose. But they sensed that it was also vitally important to establish schools that provided an integrated curriculum of religion, science, mathematics, language, history and the arts. When Charleston was still part of the Archdiocese of Baltimore, St. Elizabeth Ann Seton was organizing Catholic schools that were free and open to the poor. Mother Seton died just days into John England's first acts as bishop of Charleston, but he had her spirit, as is shown in the rapidity with which he opened a seminary and schools, including ones that were free to children of African descent.

England brought with him, too, the Irish heritage of dedication to broad-based learning. Years later, Cardinal John Henry Newman, canonized on October 13, 2019, voiced the commitment to a well-rounded education that typified his nineteenth-century leadership at the Irish College (Catholic University of Ireland, now called the University of Dublin) in his book on education, *The Idea of a University*.

Catholic Schools in the Diocese

In every one of the decades of its existence, the Diocese of Charleston has opened a school or multiple schools. According to the 2018–19 report of the National Catholic Education Association (NCEA), there are at present 1.8 million students in Catholic schools, approximately 7,000 of them in the Catholic schools of South Carolina. Nationwide, they are made up of 21 percent overall racial minorities and are approximately 18 percent Hispanic/Latino. The Catholic Schools Office of the diocese is committed to welcoming a diverse population of students and providing a holistic education. The school population in the autumn of the 2019–20 school year was slightly more than 13 percent Hispanic/Latino and overall 30 percent minority—Hispanic/Latino, Asian or Pacific Islander, African American or African, Native American or mixed race.[170]

Of the slightly under 6,300 Catholic schools reported by NCEA, 33 are in the Diocese of Charleston (0.5 percent, recalling the minority position of Catholics in the region). Accredited since 2012 and renewed in 2017 by the Southern Association of Colleges and Schools (SACS/AdvancED now Cognia), the diocese, as of this writing, covers a system of 4 diocesan secondary schools, 2 combined pre-K through grade 12 parish schools and 1 moving toward becoming a classical secondary school, currently accepting students in pre-kindergarten through ninth grade (tenth in 2020). The remaining 26 are parish or regional elementary schools enrolling three- (in some cases) and four-year-olds through middle school, ending with grades six or eight. The one and only private secondary school collaborates with the diocese on many of its initiatives. The State Department of Education certifies elementary teachers, and the superintendent of Catholic schools has agency to approve continuing education programs and workshops for certification. Secondary school faculty must have either a major or a minor in subjects they teach and are AP certified if teaching Advanced Placement courses.

In the twenty-first century, schools have become increasingly technologized and are required to continue improving and updating their technology plans. They have also become increasingly diversified, not only racially and ethnically but also in their offerings of a rich academic curriculum and provision for students with diagnosed learning differences and other physical challenges. This has been made possible through Exceptional SC, which provides tuition grants for such students and tax credits to those who support this program. Through concerted efforts and education of principals and pastors through Notre Dame University resources, an increasing number of

Hispanic/Latino students have been invited to enroll. In addition, principals have been intentional about encouraging African American and Asian students' enrollment. Because of the quality of Catholic education, parents of children and youth who are not Catholic make up 23.4 percent of the students enrolled in Catholic schools in the diocese in 2019–20.

In 2015, Bishop Guglielmone endorsed a Strategic Plan for Strengthening Catholic Schools, which has focused on mission and Catholic identity, academic excellence, operational vitality and governance and leadership. Numerous stakeholders were involved in the process that led to the plan, and currently several initiatives are underway to buttress financial support of the schools. In-service days on diocesan and regional levels and retreats for faculty, staff and principals have provided for curriculum and methodological training and updating as well as spiritual enrichment. Like diocesan accreditation and the formation of a Diocesan Catholic Schools Advisory Council, the Strategic Plan was developed under the leadership of Superintendent Sandra Leatherwood.

CATECHETICAL PROGRAMS

From the outset, Catholics in the colonies and the states have imparted religious belief and practice to their children. Parents, often assisted by grandparents, always have been charged by the Church to fill the role of primary educators of their offspring. In the early days of the diocese, literacy training and catechism lessons often went hand in hand, led or assisted by local clergy, religious or trusted laity. The Baltimore Catechism, published in 1885, was the long-standing handbook to ensure fluency in Catholic doctrine. After the Second Vatican Council in the 1960s, new textbooks, audio-visual materials and varied methodologies were developed for catechetical instruction. Most recently, the emphasis on missionary discipleship has birthed methods that are doctrinal and experiential, often led by youth ministers.

While Bishop England and every bishop since continued expanding formal educational institutions, they also took on the responsibility of providing catechisms and setting up opportunities for adults to gain additional formation in their faith. Religious sisters in particular were sought to teach in Catholic schools while also providing religion classes for young people and training for catechists. Groups like the Sisters of Our Lady of Christian Doctrine were brought in to set up "a vocational and a crafts school" in

Horse Valley outside Aiken in the 1940s.[171] Maryknoll Missionary sisters and the Missionary Servants of the Blessed Trinity came to Colleton County in the mid-1950s, and the Sisters of St. Mary of Namur took up ministry in Williamsburg County[172] around the same time. With others, they made inroads into small mission areas as social work was mixed with religious instruction for Catholics of all ages.

The diocesan synod convened by Bishop Thompson from 1992 to 1995 concluded with many action items to sustain and expand Catholic schools and Catholic religious education programs. These included the development of a consistent diocesan-wide religion curriculum and theological and practical preparation of catechists. During Bishop Baker's years, a biennial Fire at the Beach catechetical conference began, along with numerous regular catechetical days. Fire at the Beach evolved into On Fire with Faith and then joined with Hispanic ministry for larger-scale faith formation days for adults.

With the United States Conference of Catholic Bishops' release of a renewed Christo-centric high school curriculum and an adaptation for youth ministry, high school religion teachers and youth ministers across the state became aware of these materials and adopted or adapted them as appropriate. By the onset of the 2010–11 school year, basic catechetical certification was required of all Catholic school teachers within five years of their hire. The idea was that the teacher must be able to render accurately the basics of what Catholics believe, whether or not he or she formally teaches religion classes. That same year, a diocesan religion curriculum for pre-kindergarten through grade eight was adopted for schools and parishes, and it has recently been updated and supplemented with topics on Catholic social teaching that can be implemented across the curriculum. Workshops, webinars and various audio-visual resources now enable catechists, directors of religious education, teachers and principals to gain basic, intermediate and advanced catechetical certification in the diocese. The development of these programs was spearheaded by heads of the diocese's Office of Catechesis and Christian Initiation between 2008 and 2020. The Spanish School of Faith (Escuela de la Fe) similarly provides foundational and more advanced training in theology and pastoral ministry. The program is intensive, requiring three years of study amounting to 120 hours of classes, 24 hours of which are acquired in three annual conferences, and a final synthesis paper in Spanish. The School of Faith was developed by Dr. Gustavo Valdez, secretary for Hispanic ministry.

In 2015, with the blessing and encouragement of Bishop Guglielmone, a Formation for Ministry program debuted for all diocesan and parish staff.

Each year, new topics in theology, practical ministry or spiritual development are introduced by Franciscan Sister Kathy Adamski, leader of the program, with an eye to facilitating employees' understanding of Catholicism and also being effective and pastoral in their dealings with parishioners and the general public. The Office of Spirituality and Formation for Ministry has taken on oversight of many adult faith formation activities and provision for spiritual direction for adults. All of these offerings spur participants on the theological enterprise described by St. Anselm as "faith seeking understanding."

HIGHER EDUCATION

It confounds people accustomed to an abundance of Catholic colleges and universities when they discover that, in the three states of Bishop John England's original diocese, there is only one Catholic college. Belmont Abbey, outside Charlotte, North Carolina, was founded by Benedictine monks in 1876 and chartered as a college originally known as St. Mary's College in 1886. The name of the abbey was adopted as the college name in 1913. Belmont is a small college, with an enrollment of roughly 1,500 students, traditional and nontraditional. It offers an array of majors in humanities, social sciences and professional studies—including theology and pastoral ministry, criminal justice, computer information systems, finance and marketing, as well as concentrations in sports and motor sports.[173]

As a way of providing for additional opportunities in Catholic higher education, a cohort of graduate students in theology and pastoral studies was temporarily formed with Ave Maria University during Bishop Robert Baker's tenure in the diocese. Under Bishop Guglielmone, the Office of the Permanent Diaconate, led by Deacon André Guillet, made an agreement with St. Leo University, based in St. Leo, Florida, in the Diocese of St. Petersburg. It is another school with Benedictine roots—and one noted for being far ahead of other schools in racial integration (dating from the late 1890s) and distance learning.[174] The terms of the agreement allow eligible men in diaconate formation, their wives and other ministerial personnel to complete requirements for a Master of Arts degree in theology. Those not seeking the master's degree are awarded a Certificate of Completion for the Undergraduate Certificate in Theology, which can be applied to credits needed for a bachelor's degree. Professors from St. Leo and those contracted as adjunct faculty teach courses on site in the diocese, typically at

Our Lady of the Hills in Columbia or, on occasion, at the Pastoral Center in Charleston.

In addition to this program, the Catholic Schools Office, acting on recommendations of accreditors and the strategic plan, has aggressively developed an internal program of orientation for new principals and an Aspiring Leadership Program, which is open to teachers and assistant principals who have been identified as having potential for school leadership. The program, led by Sheila Durante, a former principal in the diocese and former superintendent of Catholic schools in the Diocese of Providence in Rhode Island, allows participants to attain certification in Catholic school leadership and also, for those meeting graduate requirements successfully, master's degrees in education from Loyola Marymount in California, Creighton University in Nebraska, Loyola University Chicago and Marymount in Virginia.

To attend to the needs of undergraduates around the state, Catholic campus ministry plays an active role. It retains presence on a full-time basis at larger colleges and universities that grant undergraduate and graduate degrees and full-time regional ministry or part-time ministry—sometimes by salaried campus ministers, sometimes by volunteers—for students at many smaller colleges. Priestly leadership and sacramental ministry on campuses has received new impetus from Vicar General Monsignor D. Anthony Droze, and FOCUS (The Fellowship of Catholic University Students) and Evangelical Catholic have embarked on a peer-level ministry on larger campuses— namely, the University of South Carolina, Coastal Carolina University and Clemson respectively. For several years, too, the Catholic Extension Society has provided grants to create a statewide data base of graduating high school seniors, whether in Catholic or public schools, to help them connect with Catholic campus ministry at the colleges in which they are matriculating.

In many ways, lifelong learning is a standard part of Catholic culture. The Diocese of Charleston—from the time Father Simon Gallagher taught at and then presided over the College of Charleston and Bishop England began opening schools, until the present day—Catholic leaders have followed the maxim of a Protestant woman of color born in 1875 in South Carolina, the famed educator Mary McLeod Bethune: "Faith is the first factor in a life devoted to service. Without it, nothing is possible. With it, nothing is impossible."[175]

Chapter 12

OFF THE BEATEN PATH

MISSION CHURCHES AND CENTERS ACROSS THE STATE

Society Hill, South Carolina, was founded in 1736, as signage at the entryway to the town proudly proclaims. Today, it has attractive cottages, a few larger homes with pleasant gardens and some small business. Anyone traveling south on U.S. 15 from Rockbridge, North Carolina, say, will notice that the western edge of town intersects Route 52 to Cheraw and both 52 and 401 to Darlington. If one happens to be a Catholic, both of those communities might have weekend Masses attended by thirty-five to seventy-five persons. The closest stop on 15, though, would be Bennettsville, where the St. Denis Mission would welcome thirtysome people. This area lies north and a bit west of Myrtle Beach, the seat of its deanery. There are some significant businesses, truck depots and warehouses nearby and Hartsville boasts the Governor's School for Science and Mathematics, but the area gives a good pictographic image of why the Catholic Extension Society has long rated the Diocese of Charleston as mission territory.

Something of the same is true on the northern and western edges of the state. The Greenville deanery and the parish churches of Sacred Heart in Gaffney and St. Andrew in Clemson serve Union and Walhalla, the sites of St. Augustine Church and St. Francis of Assisi Mission, respectively. Getting to the church in Union requires a jog off U.S. 176 into the downtown Union area, one with appeal similar to that of Newberry and other well-established towns that deserve adjectives like *charming* and *quaint*. St. Augustine, a stately spare white church, stands at the entryway to Union's modest business district and announces, on its public signage, that there is a Mass at 8:00 a.m.

on Sundays. Walhalla's church lies some miles above Lake Hartwell and, approaching the Chattooga River, lies near the northeast corner of Georgia; on Route 28, it is south of Highlands and Franklin, North Carolina. In some sense, Walhalla, like the Poor Clares' Travelers Rest, comes close to intersecting the original tri-state makeup of the Diocese of Charleston. While Union typically hosts a congregation similar in size to that of Bennettsville, Walhalla can count on upward of 130. Over the years, each of the missions mentioned has invited converts and people coming into full communion with the church to Rites of Election and Calls to Continuing Conversion celebrated in their deaneries and to initiation at the Easter Vigils held in their communities or at their central parishes.

With relatively spare head counts, one of the questions that presses on every bishop, every diocesan curial member and each diocesan department is how to serve and touch the lives of people of faith whose residences might tend to be written off as boondocks.

Outreach

Panhandlers and street people can be found almost anywhere. Strolling a block or two from the Pauline Book Store on King Street in Charleston will likely result in a meeting with someone pleading for help. A turn around the corner from the Baha'i Center in Columbia or just off the ramp exiting Neglia Hall at St. Peter's on Assembly Street will more than likely result in an encounter with a homeless person. A visitor to Myrtle Beach may well discover that the scruffy-looking person crossing Ocean Boulevard is not a biker but a person who snuggles at night amid dune grass or under some flimsy cover. In areas not so populous, a simple drive into the parking lot of a Kroger's or Publix might put the driver face to face with a man or woman with a cardboard sign asking for help. South Carolina has its homeless and its hidden poor. Some of these are in highly populated areas, while others are practically off the grid. With its Gospel demand to attend to the needs of the least of the brothers and sisters, a variety of pious associations, religious led and lay fraternal organizations follow the demand of both Old and New Testament to care for those most in need.

The diocese has a long history of tapping laity for the service of charity. Monsignor Madden's history, which concludes with the beginning of Bishop Unterkoefler's term, recounts how Knights of Columbus, the Hibernian

Society (as it was earlier called), the Council of Catholic Women, the Council of Catholic Men, the Catholic Benevolent League, the Cathedral Benevolent Society and the St. Vincent de Paul Society have been among those offering financial and interpersonal help. Storms, fires, yellow fever, an earthquake and the early twentieth-century flu epidemic left people in need. The plight of accident victims, the sick, victims of war, impoverished immigrants, widows and orphans and the unemployed or underemployed have all been addressed by groups such as these. Individual parishes and their parishioners have taken up causes as needs became evident. Up to and through the writing of this history, such groups support children and adults with special needs, women with problem pregnancies, the homebound, victims of domestic violence, migrant workers, new immigrants, the elderly and the poor. Initiatives like pro-life pregnancy centers, the St. Clare Home slated for Greenville and Rachel's Vineyard all assist pregnant women and offer healing for those suffering post-abortion trauma. Local food banks, organizations providing free medical and dental care, after-school programs and tutoring, hospitals and elder care facilities all rely on volunteers, many of whom are Catholics living in the diocese. In addition, the Diocese of Charleston sponsors and staffs and provides chaplains for ministry to prisoners and seafarers arriving in the Port of Charleston.

Over the years, the Catholic Extension Society (earlier known simply as the Extension Society) has been very responsive and financially supportive of projects to assist ministries and parishes reaching the more marginalized citizens of the diocese. Founded in 1905, the society in its very early years began helping construct or expand churches in Union, Kingstree, North Charleston, Mine Creek (near Aiken) and Batesburg—along with Charleston's Neighborhood House, which was pioneered and has continued under the leadership of the Sisters of Charity of Our Lady of Mercy.[176] In very recent years, the society has provided support to sisters coming from Mexico to provide ministry to Spanish-speaking parishioners in the Lowcountry and those seeking training in youth and young adult ministry, among other things.

Another group known for their outreach are the Sisters of St. Felix. In 2012, twenty years after their arrival in Kingstree, they won the Catholic Extension Society's Lumen Christi Award for their long service on what was considered "the wrong side of the tracks" in Kingstree and for the way in which it has expanded to embrace many in Williamsburg County.[177] Their services include a food pantry, cooking classes, computer classes, a clothes closet, home visits, catechetical classes at nearby St. Ann Church, assistance with home repairs and legal advocacy. Like all of the sister-run programs, the Felician Center relies on grants, donations, volunteers and broad ecumenical support and cooperation.

The Felician sisters joined an effort that women religious have undertaken in the diocese since its earliest days. The Sisters of Charity of Our Lady of Mercy, founded in Charleston in 1829, were the first to establish schools and to serve slaves and free Africans by offering catechetical instruction and schooling. They established orphanages, infirmaries and hospitals and were distinguished in providing nursing care to both Confederate and Union soldiers during the Civil War. For this, they received many letters of support and appeals to the U.S. Congress from the South Carolina legislature and from former Union soldiers who were pressing for federal assistance to repair the sisters' war-damaged orphanage.[178] The OLM sisters opened Neighborhood House in Charleston as a center for, as they term it, "home nursing care and social service" in 1915. This rapidly grew to become a center for training in life skills and homemaking, prenatal and child care, visits to prisoners and those in elder care facilities, catechetical classes, provision of food, measures to prevent juvenile delinquency, parenting programs and other outreach to the poor.[179] Now past one hundred years of existence, Neighborhood House has added special services such as a soup kitchen, "resiliency" services and programs for those facing or recovering from drug addiction.[180] It continues to rely on the support of the OLM sisters and an array of other donor sources and volunteers for its expansive outreach.

Our Lady of Mercy Outreach Center on Johns Island opened just two weeks before Hurricane Hugo hit Charleston in 1989. The Category 4 hurricane blew apart homes and businesses, took steeples off churches, caved in roofs, uprooted trees and flooded streets and homes. It reached into the Midlands after making landfall on the coast. While all of the sister-run and Catholic Charities centers provide similar services in the realm of food, clothing, housewares, home repairs, utility assistance, educational and supportive services and referrals to other appropriate providers, the Johns Island ministry puts a special emphasis on "self-sufficiency" and "self-worth." The staff and volunteers prepare people for job interviews and help them find training programs and educational opportunities, with the aim to raise families from poverty.[181] Several unique features of that center include an arrangement with Roper St. Francis for dental and obstetric-gynecological services and a collaboration with Medical University of South Carolina and Trident Technical College allowing students to get credit for service they provide to uninsured or otherwise non-paying clients. The facility also hosts area ministers several times a year, a quilting group and other community ventures.

Another of the sister-run outreach centers is the St. Francis Center (formerly the Franciscan Center) on St. Helena Island, initially run by Sisters of St. Francis from Wisconsin; by the Sisters of St. Francis of Philadelphia from 1987 to 2012; and, beginning in 2013, by the Sisters of Saints Cyril and Methodius. This center distributes food four days a week; operates a thrift shop that offers extremely low-cost clothing, housewares and furnishings; offers emergency assistance in a variety of forms; has a special outreach to migrant workers; has helped to repaint, refurnish and supply a local family-operated home housing formerly homeless men; offers educational assistance to adults needing to develop English language skills; provides tutoring for children on an as-needed basis; and refers homeless people to local agencies and facilities for short-term stays. In addition, the St. Francis Center hosts individuals making private retreats and also welcomes groups for days of recollection.[182]

In addition to these centers, Echo House in North Charleston, founded by the OLM sisters, was long supported by the service of Franciscan and Dominican sisters. The Daughters of Charity were responsible for the work of outreach centers in Georgetown and Gloverville. These have now been assumed by Catholic Charities. Sisters from the Georgetown mission relocated in 2018 to serve the Mercy Mission of Hardeeville, originally founded by the Religious Sisters of Mercy of Chicago. This mission, too, is now operated by Catholic Charities, an agency whose statewide outreach is an important service to those who live on the margins.

CATHOLIC CHARITIES OF SOUTH CAROLINA

While Christians have been engaged in works of charity since the first decades of the Church's post-Pentecost existence in the first century AD, the organization officially known as Catholic Charities USA dates back in the United States 110 years. Founded in 1910, it claims its origin and inspiration with the Ursuline Sisters in New Orleans.[183] By the late 1940s, when Bishop Emmet Walsh was attending its board meetings, Catholic Charities had been established in the diocese for several years. In 1957, a dozen years after the organization's 1945 arrival, Reverend Joseph Bernardin, the future cardinal who is the subject of chapter 14, was Catholic Charities' diocesan director. During Bernardin's tenure in that office, the diocese hosted the meeting of the Southeastern Region of the National Conference of Catholic Charities.[184] Around the state, Catholic Charities of South Carolina, even more widespread in its outreach than in Bernardin's day, describes itself as dedicated to "direct services, consultation, education and advocacy."[185]

Catholic Charities has centers across the state, with regional offices and special services in North Charleston, Mount Pleasant, Charleston, Beaufort and Jasper Counties, Columbia, Conway and Greenville. There are also branches across the state offering specific assistance to those in need of immigration legal services, prison outreach, restorative justice (for former prisoners returning to the civic community and work world), those victimized by human trafficking, disaster relief, pregnancy and family services. A recent initiative is the creation of the Clean of Heart Facilities, currently located in Columbia and Myrtle Beach and slated for development in additional areas. These offer homeless people a place where they are provided with toiletries and can shower and launder clothing. In the first seven years of its existence, Clean of Heart served more than one thousand individual homeless people. Some of the beneficiaries of this service have returned to thank the staff and volunteers for the simple help they received en route to job interviews or reconnection with family members.[186]

Catholic Charities also operates the Carter-May Home in Charleston, an assisted living facility serving laity and clergy that is staffed by local medical and administrative personnel and several religious sisters originally from India. Elsewhere, Catholic Charities reaches out to the elderly poor via food pantries and emergency assistance. Another initiative promoted by Catholic Charities in the diocese is promotion of the annual Lenten Rice Bowl collection, led by Catholic Relief Services in cooperation with Catholic Charities USA. The cash donations collected in parishes and schools and outreach centers across the state are used for national and international aid to the needy, but 25 percent of the collection remains in participating dioceses. Another new program, tested in autumn 2019, was called "Matthew 25; Call to Christian Service Workshop." Its pilot sessions were offered in Aiken and anticipated for a variety of locations. The workshop emphasizes the outreach component of missionary discipleship and the understanding that service to Christ is offered by way of our direct service to the poor.[187]

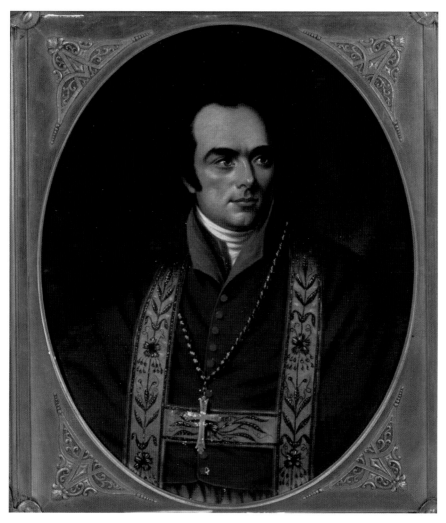

John England, the first bishop of Charleston, was appointed to lead the new diocese in 1820. A man of boundless energy and deep faith, he served the tri-state diocese until his death in 1842.

Bishop Ignatius A. Reynolds served as the second bishop of Charleston from 1844 to 1855. During his tenure, he established a number of new parishes and oversaw the construction of the Cathedral of Saint John and Saint Finbar, dedicated in 1854.

The Lynch family arrived in South Carolina from Ireland when Patrick N. Lynch (bishop from 1858 to 1882) was an infant. Educated in the state and in Rome, Bishop Lynch served as the third bishop of the diocese in the years leading up to and through the Civil War and then the era of Reconstruction. It fell to him to help rebuild the diocese both materially and spiritually.

Henry Pinckney Northrop was the fourth bishop of Charleston from 1883 to 1916. A native South Carolinian and a convert, he marshalled resources to complete the new Cathedral of St. John the Baptist and to expand Catholic presence in parish life, healthcare and education, including the establishment of Bishop England High School.

From 1916 to 1927, William T. Russell of Baltimore served as fifth bishop of Charleston. His leadership covered the span of the entrance of the United States into World War I and its aftermath. One of four episcopal leaders of the National Catholic War Council (later the National Catholic Welfare Council), he was instrumental in nurturing lay Catholic movements and organizations.

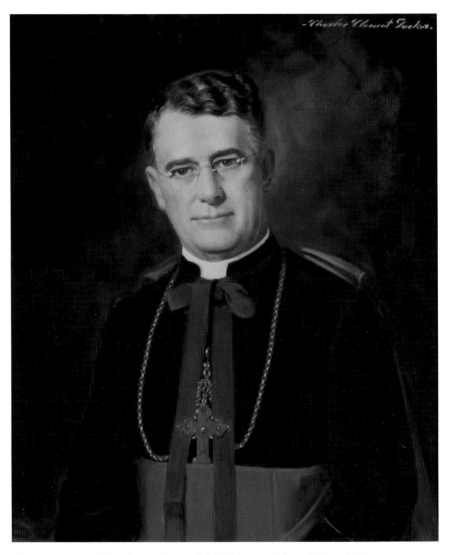

The sixth bishop of Charleston, Emmet M. Walsh, served from 1927 to 1949, carrying the diocese through the Great Depression and World War II and the initial years of the Cold War with Soviet Communism. Born in Beaufort, he devoted himself to youth by spurring the development of new Catholic schools and Camp St. Mary. He also invited new communities of women religious and the Trappist monks to establish themselves in the diocese.

The seventh bishop of Charleston, John J. Russell, from 1950 to 1958 served as the pressure to respond to the postwar baby boom affected Catholic life. Bishop Russell appointed Father Joseph Bernardin diocesan youth director and also named him secretary to the bishop. Toward the end of his term, before his departure for Richmond, Bishop Russell convened the relatively brief Eighteenth Synod of Charleston.

The eighth bishop of Charleston, Paul J. Hallinan, served the diocese from 1958 to 1962 before becoming the first archbishop of Atlanta. During his years, he supported the construction of new parochial schools and initiated plans for the construction of Cardinal Newman High School in Columbia. He also responded to anti-Catholic sentiment that had heightened expression during the presidential candidacy of John F. Kennedy.

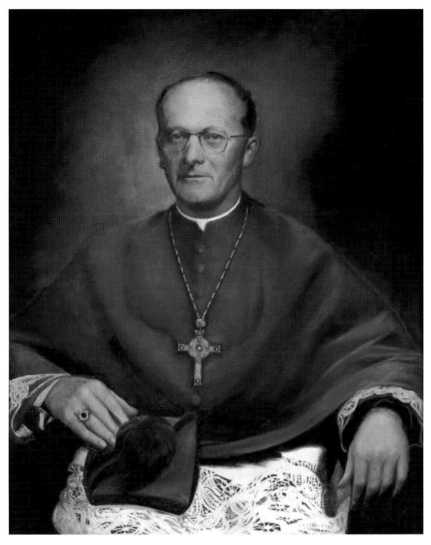

The ninth bishop of Charleston, Francis T. Reh, served a mere two years, from 1962 to 1964. He served during the years when the civil rights movement was escalating and was faced with the challenges of a growing diocese. In 1964, he was appointed rector of the North American College in Rome.

The long-serving tenth bishop of Charleston, Ernest L. Unterkoefler, spanned the years from 1964 to 1990, years of vast changes in civil society and Catholic culture and practice. Along with his commitments to post–Vatican II renewal and racial justice, he was actively involved in ecumenical ventures.

The eleventh bishop of Charleston, David B. Thompson, served from 1990 to 1997 and convoked a diocesan synod while advancing numerous pastoral initiatives. He encouraged lay leadership and continued the process of formation for the permanent diaconate, as well as for other ecclesial ministries.

Hailing from Ohio and Florida, Robert J. Baker was the twelfth bishop of Charleston. During his years as shepherd, 1999–2007, South Carolina was experiencing population growth as industries, retirees and new immigrants moved to the state. Bishop Baker focused on ministering to the ethnically and racially diverse communities in the diocese before his move to Birmingham, Alabama.

A New York native, Robert E. Guglielmone came to the diocese in 2009 as its thirteenth bishop amid a time of many transitions. The call to a new evangelization had been emphasized by Popes John Paul II and Benedict XVI and was taken up anew by Pope Francis. Construction projects to house new secondary schools and establish a diocesan pastoral center have taken time and energy. The bishop's pastoral leadership has been felt by Catholics, the ecumenical community and civic leaders around the state as the diocese prepared for its bicentennial.

Above: Before there was a diocese, the Carolinas and Georgia were part of the Diocese and then Archdiocese of Baltimore. St. Mary Church in Charleston was established in 1789.

Left: This drawing depicts Bishop John England testifying before the U.S. Congress in 1826 in defense of religious freedom and the compatibility between democratic government and the Catholic faith.

The family of Conlaw Peter Lynch, father of future bishop Patrick Lynch, worked with fellow parishioners to construct the church for the small Catholic community in Cheraw in 1842.

ROMAN CATHOLIC CATHEDRAL OF ST. JOHN AND ST. FINBAR.

Left: The successor to the wooden cathedral of St. Finbar, this second cathedral of the diocese was named Saint John and Saint Finbar and dedicated in 1854. This brownstone structure burned in 1861, not the result of the Civil War but rather the outcome of a factory fire that spread across much of the city of Charleston.

Below: In late 1861, a devastating fire broke out in a factory in Charleston and spread throughout much of the city. During the Civil War and the era of Reconstruction, temporary facilities served as the bishop's home church. The new cathedral of St. John the Baptist was finally completed and dedicated in 1907.

The Sisters of Charity of Our Lady of Mercy, founded in 1829, tended the wounded and sick of both Confederate and Union forces during the Civil War in both South Carolina and Virginia.

St. Francis Xavier Infirmary, Calhoun Street.

The predecessor of today's Roper St. Francis and Bon Secours St. Francis Hospitals in Charleston was the St. Francis Xavier Infirmary, founded and staffed by the Sisters of Charity of Our Lady of Mercy in 1882.

ANDREW JOHNSON,

PRESIDENT OF THE UNITED STATES OF AMERICA,

TO ALL TO WHOM THESE PRESENTS SHALL COME, GREETING:

Whereas, *P. N. Lynch, D. D.,* of *Charleston, South Carolina,* by taking part in the late rebellion against the Government of the United States, has made himself liable to heavy pains and penalties;

And whereas, the circumstances of his case render him a proper object of Executive clemency;

Now, therefore, be it known, that I, ANDREW JOHNSON, President of the United States of America, in consideration of the premises, divers other good and sufficient reasons me thereunto moving, do hereby grant to the said *P. N. Lynch,* a full pardon and amnesty for all offences by him committed, arising from participation, direct or implied, in the said rebellion, conditioned as follows, viz: this pardon to begin and take effect from the day on which the said *P. N. Lynch* shall take the oath prescribed in the Proclamation of the President dated May 29th, 1865, and to be void and of no effect if the said *P. N. Lynch* shall hereafter, at any time, acquire any property whatever in slaves, or make use of slave labor; and

Bishop Patrick Lynch was sent on a mission to the Vatican during the Civil War, carrying papers from Jefferson Davis, president of the Confederate States of America. With his return to the States delayed until the end of the war, Bishop Lynch required a pardon from President Andrew Johnson to return to the country.

On August 31, 1886, an earthquake shook the city of Charleston and destroyed or severely damaged many residences, churches, schools and places of business. This photo shows the bishop's house at 114 Broad Street with damage to its exterior. *USGS photo.*

St. James the Greater Church is located outside Walterboro. Several African America families were converted to Catholicism in the 1820s and 1830s. Their home community seemed to have faded from memory during the Civil War and was rediscovered in the late 1890s. Lay leaders had passed the faith on from one generation to the next. The neighborhood is still known as Catholic Hill.

The family of Eustace Bellinger Pinckney—the family credited with bringing a chapel, then a parish church and then Camp St. Mary to the Bluffton area—is shown here on a summer day.

Youths shown at an outdoor Mass at Camp St. Mary in 1933. The summer camp began first on the property of the Pinckney family in Bluffton in 1929 and became a diocesan operation from 1931 to 1967, with numerous structures and programs developed over the years.

Bishop England High School in Charleston was founded in 1915. Monsignor Joseph L. O'Brien established the school with the assistance of Reverend James May, served as its rector for more than thirty years and recruited religious sisters from various states to support the booming Catholic schools.

Founded by the Sisters of Charity of Our Lady of Mercy in 1916, Neighborhood House in Charleston has served as a social service center for more than a century. Today, groups of sisters from several communities and Catholic Charities of South Carolina have established outreach centers across the diocese.

The Oblate Sisters of Providence, a community founded by African American Catholic women, served in many traditionally black parishes and schools. Some of the first sisters to serve in the diocese are shown here in a photo dating from the early years of the twentieth century.

Typical of many of the smaller missions and churches around the state, St. Andrew in Bluffton evolved from the Pinckney family's chapel to a parish church serving the Lowcountry. Today, the parish community, now St. Gregory the Great, includes nearly eleven thousand people. The chapel continues to be used for early morning Masses, weddings, funerals and retreats.

One of two contemplative communities in the diocese is the Order of Cistercians of the Strict Observance, also known as the Trappists. They were invited to the diocese by Bishop Walsh in 1949 when Clare Boothe Luce and Henry Luce made a gift of a property of more than three thousand acres. In the early days at their monastery outside Moncks Corner, the monks are shown here in their prayer stalls.

Twelve members of the Order of St. Clare arrived in Greenville in 1995 and moved to a new monastery at Travelers Rest in 2008. The sisters devote themselves to hours of prayer and simple labor in a contemplative setting. One of their pioneer sisters is shown here.

This page: St. Anne Catholic School, Rock Hill, became the first integrated Catholic school in the state in 1954, in the immediate aftermath of the Supreme Court decision that mandated desegregation of public education and facilities. The school welcomed students from St. Mary School, Rock Hill, which had previously served African American children.

Top: Cardinal Joseph Bernardin, influential figure in latter twentieth-century Catholicism in the United States, was a native son of South Carolina. He served the diocese in many capacities before moving into episcopal ministry in Atlanta, Cincinnati and Chicago.

Bottom: Bishop Ernest Unterkoefler attended every session of the Second Vatican Council and was noted for implementing its adaptations and renewal initiatives promptly after the council concluded in 1965. He was also known as a civil rights advocate.

The Irish Travelers, tinkers and tradespeople with their own customs and clan arrangements, are one of the unique ethnic groups in the diocese. Their settlement in Murphy Village, outside North Augusta, South Carolina, is served by St. Edward Church. The statue depicts a traveler praying his rosary.

Another canonized saint, Teresa of Kolkata (Calcutta), visited the diocese in 1982. She greeted, met and addressed crowds of admirers at The Citadel in Charleston after being welcomed by Bishop Unterkoefler.

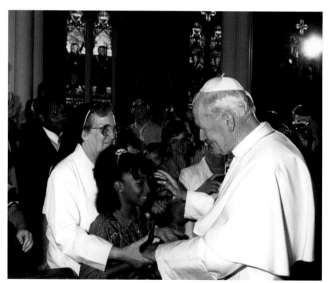

Pope from 1978 to 2005, John Paul II is now revered as a saint of the Catholic Church. His visit to South Carolina in 1987 included events at St. Peter Church, Columbia, and at the stadium at the University of South Carolina. He is shown here blessing Columbia parishioners.

Above: Years after the end of segregation, a number of historically black schools persisted in the state and across the diocese. St. Anthony School, Greenville, continues to honor its heritage in a parish that celebrates the universality of the Church and welcomes all while nurturing African American Catholic spirituality.

Right: An example of the far-flung mission churches of the diocese is St. Francis of Assisi in Walhalla, part of the Greenville deanery in the far northwest corner of the state.

Right: The Vietnamese Catholic community has participated in numerous Marian celebrations in the state, bearing the image of Our Lady of La Vang. A new parish church bearing her name was dedicated in Greer, South Carolina, in 2016.

Below: The Hispanic-Latino presence in the diocese is evident throughout the year, but especially so in December, when the Feast of Our Lady of Guadalupe prompts richly costumed celebrations.

From 1990 to 1995, the Diocese of Charleston held a synod that generated a far-reaching pastoral plan for study, action and implementation focused on ministerial and spiritual renewal. Bishop David B. Thompson is shown here signing the synod document, with Sister Bridget Sullivan, OLM, on his right.

Mayor Joe Riley, longtime mayor of Charleston and parishioner of the Cathedral, is shown leading a time of prayer in the aftermath of the events of September 11, 2001. Mayor Riley was an acclaimed civic leader and active promoter of civil rights, human rights and interreligious understanding.

St. Mary in Summerton is another example of a church with a small congregation and a traveling pastor amid a history of devout practice of the faith.

A Church on Wheels and a Prospective Saint

In 2012, Patrick and Joy Campbell, husband and wife, became Oblates of St. Benedict, lay persons committed to the way of life—work and prayer—prescribed by the sixth-century saint and followed by the Benedictine monks and nuns who follow his rule. Oblates, because they are laity with family obligations and professional lives outside a monastic setting, adapt Benedict's rule to their own circumstances. In the case of the Campbells and their nine children, that meant a commitment to evangelize and fashion what they dubbed a "spiritual SWAT Team" to equip other Catholics to fend off the wiles and snares of the devil and to be about the business of transforming the planet in accord with God's will for his Kingdom. They developed teams of persons praying for families and used social media to communicate the Gospel. The Campbells took the family on a missionary tour around North America. Their clergy connections include Father Scott Binet, currently serving in the diocese, who enlisted the family into service as "icons of joy-filled hope and ministers of mercy to the 'neediest of the needy.'"[188]

The family also gained inspiration from stories of "the heroic virtue of Fr. Patrick Quinlan," whose ministry in the 1940s corresponds so closely with their own desire to be "a Domestic Church-on-wheels." They learned of Father Quinlan in 2015, the same year that the *Catholic Miscellany* broke a story about the discovery, on a less traveled road between Lake City and Kingstree, of the long lost church on wheels that coincided with Father Quinlan's rural ministry.

Father Patrick Quinlan (1894–1971) was a spiritual pilgrim who was ordained for the Archdiocese of Hartford at Louvain, Belgium, in 1922. After serving four Connecticut parishes, St. Thomas Seminary and then the Rural Life Department for the archdiocese, he pursued the possibility of becoming a Glenmary Missioner by working with them in Ohio from 1945 to 1947. He was incardinated in the Diocese of Charleston and served St. Ann Church in Kingstree from 1947 to 1953.[189] The small community of Kingstree had previously been mission territory linked with Georgetown.

When Father Quinlan arrived in Kingstree, he found an estimated forty Catholics among Williamsburg County's forty thousand people, and he credited them for keeping the faith during the years they had been without their own church.[190] With a zeal for souls, he gradually began to establish small chapels (like those which African Americans called praise houses) around the county, the first of which was blessed by Father O.T. Carl, OP, in 1952. It was called Blessed Martin, in an area called Shaw's Place (possibly, though not certainly, associated with Shaw Plantation on the Black River). The setting up of these places of prayer was part of "the project…called the Catechumenate of Our Lady of Fatima."[191]

Father Quinlan's Catechumenate of Our Lady of Fatima was his priestly assignment from 1953 to 1971. It entailed the composition of catechetical texts, recruitment of volunteer catechists from across Williamsburg County and an attempt at forming a new congregation of brothers, along with an invitation of sisters to serve in Kingstree. The catechetical project also followed the route of a large truck, an eighteen-wheeler, which had been converted into a mobile church.

From 1949 through 1967, the "mobile church" went on a mission of evangelization across Williamsburg County and to other parts of the state. One black-and-white photo that has been preserved shows it parked and open, attracting African American visitors on one of their days at the then-segregated state fair.[192] The church on wheels was the inspiration of Father Patrick Walsh, OP, then the pastor of St. Martin de Porres in Columbia. Father Stan Smolenski, SPMA, a consecrated hermit who founded the Shrine of Our Lady of Joyful Hope in Kingstree, has related how he spent some time as a Dominican brother traveling the state like a "carnival barker for the Lord" with the mobile church. Father Quinlan connected with Father Walsh when he moved in with Dominican friars located just outside the town center of Kingstree, and he promptly made sure that his catechetical team was on the mobile church's trail so that they "could then follow up by offering classes to people in far-flung areas."[193]

The beat-up truck, missing tires and its distinctive windows, was spotted one day in 2015 by the son of Chet and Andrea Foyle of Lake City as they chose a back road surrounded by trees near an abandoned house. Father Smolenski described the surprising find as something "like discovering the *Hunley*," referring to the ill-fated submarine used during the Civil War. The church on wheels attracted curiosity-seekers as well as the devout, who came to it to pray. It exhibited ten Gothic windows (four on each side and two in the back) and had an interior with pews and an altar. Coming upon this relic of an apostolic venture has sparked new interest in what the Campbell family, cited earlier, found: a saintly exemplar—even a prospective patron saint—in the person of Father Patrick Quinlan.

Father Quinlan used "abandoned stores, garages, and even a rented former dance hall" for instruction and prayer.[194] He also inspired and enlisted people of faith in efforts to reach the unchurched and to acquaint people with some level of faith with the riches of Catholicism. Sister

Roberta Fulton, SSMN, a convert who grew up in Kingstree, remembered Father Quinlan and one of his most prominent catechists, known to her and to other young people in the area as "Miss Florence." She was lay missionary Florence Kaster. Father Quinlan had something of the spirit of St. Paul and was intent on reaching people in the most neglected areas of his neighborhood. He understood that many of the rural poor lacked decent transportation, and so it was important for the Church to come to them. He also understood that the missionary effort required many co-laborers for the Lord's expansive vineyard.

Like many a saint, Father Quinlan was willing to try one thing and then another to win souls to Christ and to build God's Kingdom. In 1954, Quinlan gained permission from Bishop John Russell to form a community of brothers whose mission would be to fan out into the rural areas of the diocese. His initial invitation enticed four men, then discerning a possible vocation with the Servants of the Paraclete, to come with the intention of being the founding members of this new initiative. They would be called the Brother Catechists of Our Lady of Lourdes or the Brothers of Our Lady of Lourdes. The candidates arrived, Bishop Russell blessed what was then called the Pius X Catechumenate Chapel and their formation began. Unfortunately, two of the candidates decided to leave, and Bishop Russell denied Father Quinlan permission to accept new candidates, so the remaining two also departed. The prospective brotherhood disbanded.[195]

The undeterred Father Quinlan then sought the assistance of the Sisters of St. Mary of Namur of Buffalo, and in 1956, they came to Kingstree.[196] Sisters from that community, which celebrated its 200th anniversary in 2019, have been engaged in catechesis, teaching and principalship at several locations around the state. To this day, they engage in diocesan, parish and outreach ministry from a base on Charleston, with one of their members, Sister Sandra Makowski, serving as chancellor of the diocese and another, Sister Roberta Fulton, mentioned earlier, assistant director for African American evangelization.

The indefatigable Father Quinlan persisted for twenty-four years in the mission with which Bishop Emmet Walsh had charged him in 1947: the "spiritual care of Williamsburg County and its people." That meant, as Jim McLaughlin has noted, "reaching out to the uninformed and misinformed, not just his 40 parishioners." At times, he also had to withstand threats from the Ku Klux Klan, which bedeviled his efforts for years.[197] The Klan, with its well-known contempt for Catholics and African Americans, sometimes brought firepower and always brought threats to life and buildings, but Father

Quinlan, his catechists and at times as many as four hundred inquirers into the faith brought the power of the Spirit.

Now the priest, whose memory is revered, is counted as a likely candidate for official veneration, beatification and canonization. Bishop Robert Baker proposed as much when he was bishop of Charleston, and the investigation into the cause continues. If Patrick T. Quinlan should ever be counted among the officially recognized saints, he would in many ways be a representative figure: one whose name stands among the many unnamed in the communion of saints, holy people who have served with grace in obscure places, off the beaten path and among the most unnoticed people.

Chapter 13

JOSEPH CARDINAL BERNARDIN, NATIVE SON

God really does help us live fully, even in the worst of times.
—*Bernardin,* The Gift of Peace

Anyone who gets his or her likeness on the cover of a national news magazine is likely to be revered by some and vilified by others. That was precisely the fate of Joseph Cardinal Bernardin, archbishop of Chicago and native South Carolinian. The cover story appeared in November 1982, when Bernardin was president of what was then called the National Conference of Catholic Bishops. *TIME* magazine featured "The Bishops and the Bomb," an article on the upcoming release of the Conference's Pastoral Letter on War and Peace, "The Challenge of Peace." This pastoral letter outlined Catholicism's commitment to peacemaking, detailed the traditional criteria for determining what constitutes a just war and questioned whether building stockpiles of anti-population nuclear weapons could ever be justified. They challenged the political theory of deterrence (which suggested that stockpiling weapons of mass destruction would keep others from using them) and provided a foundation for Christian pacifism without recommending it as a universal stance. Just as the Second Vatican Council had, they deemed the arms race—and particularly the race to produce such powerful anti-population weapons—a scourge on humanity. The letter, as long as some papal encyclicals, was instructive in terms of doctrine and discernment. It was also politically explosive, coming as it did in the Reagan era when talk of "Star Wars" defense systems and even first-strike capabilities was in the air. Joseph Bernardin, it was assumed, was not only the elected head of the NCCB but also a major contributor. He was, after all, a moral theologian who was committed to the principle that political questions are often, if not always, moral questions.

Bernardin's rapid hierarchical ascent was widely noted. Less so were his humble beginnings. He was born in Columbia, South Carolina, to Italian parents who had emigrated from Italy barely a year before his birth (April 2, 1928). His stonecutter father, also Joseph, died of cancer when his son was only six years old. His mother, Maria Simion Bernardin, became the breadwinner of the family of three—including Joseph and his sister—and made her living as a seamstress. A product of Catholic and public schools, young Joseph decided to abandon premedical studies at the University of South Carolina to enter the seminary. Always a bright and extraordinarily talented student, he completed seminary studies, earned a master's degree in education and was ordained at the age of twenty-four. After ordination, he served as a high school teacher, an instructor in moral theology for sisters of the diocese, director of vocations, director of Catholic Charities, secretary to the 1958 diocesan synod, director of cemeteries, chancellor, vicar general and administrator of the diocese in the interim between the episcopates of Bishop Francis Reh and Bishop Ernest Unterkoefler, 1964. By the time he was thirty-eight years old, he was ordained a bishop, serving initially as an auxiliary in the Archdiocese of Atlanta under one of his mentors and likely promoters, Archbishop Paul T. Hallinan, former bishop of Charleston. He was the youngest bishop in the United States. The year was 1966.

By 1972, he had been appointed by Pope Paul VI to be archbishop of Cincinnati. He had already served as general secretary to the NCCB. Aside from his interpersonal and academic skills, Bernardin had earned a reputation for being a force behind the desegregation of South Carolina's Catholic schools—in advance of the passage of the Civil Rights Act of 1964. He also gained a reputation for his pro-life efforts and teaching. By the time he was named archbishop of Chicago in 1982, he was already developing what became known as a "consistent ethic of life," a "seamless garment" approach that linked opposition to abortion with opposition to euthanasia, assisted suicide, capital punishment, war-making and indifference to the lot of the poor and suffering.

The post–Vatican II era was, as noted in chapter 10, marked by decades of rancor over changes in liturgical rubrics, eligibility for ordination, pastoral practices, official declarations regarding political stances and policies, war and peacemaking, sexual ethics, racial justice and attitudes toward people of other faiths. Catholics in the United States took to the press to publicize their opinions about what the Church ought and ought not to be doing. Often the public expressions were marked by anger and threatened to foster widespread mistrust. Bernardin acknowledged as one of his mistakes the poor planning—or poor conduct of business—at what he and other ecclesiastics thought would be a fruitful lay initiative, the Call to Action conference first held in 1976 in Detroit. What was supposed to be an open discussion of issues facing the Church produced position papers that further alienated and polarized Catholic interest groups. Thus, when "The Challenge of Peace" was issued, Bernardin was no stranger to controversy. But he was also no stranger to reevaluating and reframing. His concern was always for the good of souls, the good of the Church and the evangelization of peoples—including politicians.

The former metropolitan of the Atlanta province, Archbishop Wilton D. Gregory, a protégé of Bernardin's, has testified to the cardinal's fidelity to the deposit of faith and the mission of the Church: "I consider myself a fortunate man to have witnessed his faith and pastoral style firsthand and to have learned from his example. He never lost the common touch and this made him both an approachable pastor and a credible church guide. There are few bishops today who might be considered his equal in wisdom and genius."[198]

Bernardin was always a churchman and something of a scholar, but people agree that he never lost the common touch. He moved his mother to Chicago, first to the archbishop's residence and then to a home operated and staffed by the Little Sisters of the Poor. He visited with her almost daily. The Felician sister who cooked for him, Sister Mary Lucia Skalka, spoke of the pains he took to make the residence feel like a home. He wanted his house to be neighborly, not a big gated mansion. He wanted flowers—a real garden—out front. He also was not one to stand on ceremony. Instead, he preferred to stop off in the kitchen for small talk or to recommend recipes for some Italian dishes. "Titles never affected him," said Sister Lucia. "He was always a human first."[199] And given the evidence exhibited during the time of his illness and at his wake service and funeral, it seemed that practically everyone in Chicagoland was family.

The cardinal was indeed beloved by many: clergy, neighbors, construction workers, firefighters, cancer patients and more. And then there were the street people. Bishop Gerald Kicanas, then an auxiliary in Chicago, recalled a homeless woman who was obviously heading for him on the street one day. He was sure that she was a panhandler and admitted that he grudgingly let her approach him. When she opened her mouth, it was to say, "Be sure to tell the Cardinal I am praying for him."[200]

Between 1992 and the year of Bernardin's death, it became increasingly evident to Bernardin that there was a need to address polarities among those professing to be Catholic and to tone down some of the rancor that had developed in journalism and ecclesial politics. He crafted a statement, "The Parish in the Contemporary Church" (sometimes also referred to as "The Parish in the Local Church"), which recommended a "both/and" approach on issues. The cardinal appealed to the faithful to be true to doctrine while also being pastoral in their attentions and acts of compassion.[201] It is something he clearly put into practice in Chicago in dealing with AIDS patients. Between 1995 and 1996, Bernardin, still feeling an urgency to address the "liberal versus conservative" or "progressive versus reactionary" labelling, worked with Monsignor Philip J. Murnion of the National Pastoral Life Center and a think tank to discuss questions and controversies regarding the relationship between priests and their parishioners and Catholics among themselves. From a number of dialogues there emerged a statement entitled "Called to Be Catholic: Church in Time of Peril." Murnion identified the work done in that four-year period as the precursor to the decision to make an official launch of the Catholic Common Ground Project and to house it in a new secretariat at the NPLC in New York.[202]

For Bernardin, work on the Common Ground Initiative was unexpectedly disrupted by an accusation of sexual abuse made against him by a former seminarian, then still a teen and, at the time of the accusation, an AIDS patient, Steven Cook. It came in November 1993. As soon as it was received, the cardinal made the accusation public, submitted information to his own sex abuse council (one he had established well in advance of the 2002 crisis and development of the national charter to protect children and youth) and held a press conference. In it, he frankly acknowledged the accusation, indicated his innocence and replied to a reporter's direct question that he had always lived a chaste life and had been faithful to his commitment to celibacy. He said that he would submit to the legal process but would not file a countersuit, despite his innocence. Later, as it became clear that the accusation was dubious at best, Cook recanted and, on February 28, 1994, dropped the lawsuit against Bernardin.

The cardinal resumed an active schedule of episcopal duties, public lectures, attendance at ecumenical and interreligious events—some of them international—and raised his voice against the plague of pornography. In the background, there were rumors that Cook might have been encouraged to make the accusations by someone or another who felt that Bernardin was on the "wrong" side in his positions as a churchman. Bernardin felt that, amid the profound grief and humiliation he had felt, he had drawn closer to the self-emptying of Christ in his passion and particularly related to the Agony in the Garden.[203] When he was relieved of the burden, he felt compassion for Cook, who had allegedly been molested by a priest and was dying of AIDS. Finally, in late December 1994, Bernardin arranged—through Cook's mother in Ohio, officials in the Archdiocese of Philadelphia (where Cook lived) and the rector of St. Charles Borromeo Seminary—to meet with Steven. The young man apologized for the accusation and, though he had been estranged from the Church, wanted the cardinal to say Mass with a few persons present and was anointed by him.

When Bernardin learned in June 1995 that he had pancreatic cancer and a poor prognosis, he said that the new trial was less daunting than the accusation had been. He went through treatments, suffered falls and bone damage and lost weight and height but also enjoyed a period of remission. Meanwhile, all his concerns for God's people and his mission continued. In early August 1996, Bernardin believed that he had a bit more time than he actually had; nevertheless, he felt great urgency to address what he termed "increasing polarization within the Church and, at times, a mean-spiritedness."[204] He became the spokesperson for the launch of the Common Ground Project and the release of its "Called to Be Catholic" statement.

The initiative was both hailed and denounced. Bernardin's last presentation to the initiative urged participants, and Catholics as a whole, to trust the Holy Spirit and work for unifying Catholics—looking at the essentials of the faith and not being occupied with accidentals rather than essentials. Sister Mary Brian Costello, RSM, former superintendent of Chicago's Catholic schools and then the cardinal's chief of staff, remarked on how the cardinal combined an intense work ethic with openness and trust in his colleagues. With others who had worked with him day by day, she made it clear that he had no intention to compromise matters of faith and morals—or any doctrinal matters. Costello noted, "Instead of engaging in conflictual argumentation on women's rights, the Cardinal asked women to assume leadership roles in education, liturgy and divine worship, personnel management, and parish ministry." With a clear allusion to the Common Ground Project, she said, "He trusted that in the final analysis, it was women and men serving collaboratively that would keep this church rooted in ground that was common—and holy."[205]

Those who denounced it were concerned, even rabidly, that dialogue and attempts to reconcile opposing voices might foster compromise of doctrine and might even seem to support the position of dissidents. That, according to the testimony of Cardinal Bernardin and Monsignor Murnion, was far from the intent. As Murnion noted, the initiative was not intended to reframe and water down Church teachings but rather to help Catholics understand the core commitments held by one another. Bernardin was blindsided by the swift criticism of the initiative by some of the Church's highest-ranking clergy who had been privy to the preceding dialogues. That did not dissuade him, however, from standing with them as brothers. Cardinals James Hickey, Bernard Law and Adam Maida were among the line of American cardinals, including Bernardin, photographed shoulder to shoulder in front of the U.S. Capitol in a public witness against partial birth abortion. The show of solidarity occurred one month after their sharp critiques of the Project were issued and just after Bernardin had been awarded the Presidential Medal of Freedom by William Jefferson Clinton.

As Monsignor Kenneth Velo recounted in his homily for the cardinal's Mass of Christian Burial, the cardinal loved, daily prayed and carried with him a copy of the Prayer of St. Francis. "He had the gift of resilience," Velo declared. "He brought light and life," and he recognized that "joy and pardon" went hand in hand. "He knew that it was in pardoning that we are pardoned."[206]

That gift of pardoning was at least part of the story of his final peace. So was that self-emptying he described as he recounted his experience of the accusation. His oncologist, Dominican sister Dr. Ellen Gaynor, observed that the cardinal lived what he preached. "Men and women everywhere have a deep desire to come in contact with the transcendent," he had said. "That is what ordinary people want." As she offered her narrative of the equanimity with which he faced death, Gaynor said that he faced his imminent death with resignation but also with a noteworthy lack of self-concern. Even when he was in much pain, he would pause to speak with patients at the Loyola Cancer Center and indeed extended his visits there so that he could traverse the floors to visit patients he had come to know. "This was a man who actually put on Christ in his own life," his doctor said. "In this man, Bernardin, we experienced the transcendent—we experienced our God."[207]

Given his prominence as well as his passion for justice, it is not surprising that Bernardin had friends and foes—among the faithful and clerics. But here, to many South Carolinians, he remains the man who identified himself as "your brother Joseph" at the Mass of installation in Chicago's Holy

Name Cathedral. Some of the eldest among us remember him as the nice seminarian Joe who worked happily among children at Camp St. Mary's in Okatie, off Route 170 between Beaufort and Bluffton. For others, he is the high school teacher of fond memory, the diocesan golden boy who was a congenial celebrant, an efficient administrator, an articulate spokesman and a thoughtful person. Despite the pomp that surrounded him in later years, when he was the relatively young cardinal and a presumed contender for becoming the first American pope, Joseph Bernardin retained much of the simplicity of his upbringing.

Joseph Bernardin's spirituality became best known in his last years. His reconciliation with Steven Cook was reminiscent of the outreach to and forgiveness offered by St. John Paul II to Mehmet Ali Agca, his attempted assassin. One will never know, but it may have been something Bernardin and the sainted pope spoke of in their phone conversations during the accusation and its aftermath.

As the cardinal undertook his final journey, he penned *The Gift of Peace*. It was a hit with serious Catholics and curious members of other faiths and no faith as it dealt with suffering, the dying process and death. It was a book of hope and triumph, a reflection on how being in Christ supersedes all our doing. One of the ironies and glories was that the cardinal completed the work a mere thirteen days before his death. In the conclusion to that book, Bernardin wrote an introduction to the Prayer of St. Francis. It serves as a kind of Last Will and Testament: "What I would like to leave behind is a simple prayer that each of you may find what I have found—God's special gift to us all: the gift of peace. When we are at peace, we find the freedom to be most fully who we are, even in the worst of times. We let go of what is nonessential and embrace what is essential. We empty ourselves so that God may more fully work within us. And we become instruments in the hands of the Lord.[208]

On November 14, 1996, Joseph Cardinal Bernardin died, but his legacy lives on. The consistent ethic of life that he promoted was largely vindicated with the 1995 publication of *The Gospel of Life* by John Paul II. In that encyclical, the pope clearly and solemnly announced, in union with all the Catholic bishops of the world, that abortion, euthanasia and the killing of innocents are always and everywhere gravely wrong. He also linked to the burgeoning societal "culture of death" a host of sins and crimes against life: capital punishment, human trafficking, oppression of the poor, war, racial and ethnic prejudice and rivalries and damage to the planet's environment. The Common Ground Project did not gain momentum in the United States, but many see in the pastoral practices of Pope Francis an attempt to invite persons with diverse views and commitments to the table. His 2013 encyclical, *The Joy of the Gospel*, promoted encounter and dialogue. Meanwhile, the Catholics of South Carolina celebrate their native son's memory in the Cardinal Bernardin Center adjacent to St. Peter's Basilica in Columbia and the annual Cardinal Bernardin Lectures, hosted by the Religion Department of the University of South Carolina. Most of all, though, so many of the faithful of the Diocese of Charleston warmly remember Joseph as one of their own.

Chapter 14

JOE RILEY AND JEAN TOAL

CATHOLICS IN THE HOLY CITY
AND THE STATE SUPREME COURT

In January 2017, Charleston's forty-year mayor, Joe Riley, and South Carolina Supreme Court chief justice Jean Toal were in St. John the Baptist Cathedral for Evening Prayer. With that Vespers service was a ceremony that awarded them the papal honors. Mayor Riley was named a Knight of St. Gregory and Justice Toal a Dame of St. Gregory. Both recipients were lifelong Catholics and notable political successes. Both were resoundingly pro-life in the inclusive "seamless garment" sense, and both advanced the cause of racial justice in South Carolina. The commendation came from Pope Francis, on the recommendation of Most Reverend Robert E. Guglielmone.

JOE RILEY

The course Joseph Patrick Riley Jr.'s life took came as a surprise to some. He was a descendant of a Confederate soldier and a graduate of The Citadel and thus might have been expected to be a defender of the status quo more than the mover and shaker he turned out to be. What and who he became, however, has transformed the look and the soul of the city of Charleston and forever altered the history of racism in the city and in the state. Some of that may be attributed to the history and signs of his times. Some of it, too, may be credited to his devout practice of the Catholic faith.

The Riley family were devout members of the parish of the Cathedral of St. John the Baptist in Charleston for generations. Archival records reveal that attorney Joseph P. Riley Sr. was consulted about numerous acquisitions of property purchased for the diocese. But that was far from the first family connection. The diocese currently possesses a set of gold rosary beads that the Riley family offered for a fundraiser. A loyal donor selected them, gave his donation and then returned the beads to the diocese. They dated from the nineteenth century. The Rileys were steeped in tradition, so it is no surprise that Mayor Riley graduated from Bishop England High School, The Citadel and the University of South Carolina School of Law (1967).[209]

Joe Riley Jr. had a rich sense of history, but he was also focused on planning for a great future for his beloved city and Church. As far as the city is concerned, he is credited with transforming Charleston into a tourist destination that is lauded worldwide. It has become known as a city of arts and crafts. Whether it is the Gullah-influenced art of Jonathan Green or the sweetgrass baskets crafted by women from Awendaw, the African American culture is touted. Every spring sees a Greek festival in the center of the city. In late May, the Spoleto Festival, an extravaganza of the arts, draws thousands to the city. It would not have become a Charleston tradition had it not been for Joe Riley. And all year-round there are concerts, dramatic performances and art gallery showings that celebrate European, Asian, African, Latino, Native American and general American arts and customs. The drivers of horse- and mule-drawn carriages recount the history of Charleston as riders pass Rainbow Row, the famous old St. Philip's Church, the Catholic cathedral, the Unitarian Circular Church and the homestead of the oleander tea murderess. Visitors are ferried to Fort Sumter, and the elegant—and third consecutive—Cooper River bridge (now Ravenel Bridge) hosts 10k runs.

Joe Riley was elected mayor in December 1975, when he was a mere thirty-two years old but already a six-year veteran of the state House of Representatives. He was practically anointed lifetime mayor by custom and affection, so notable that the Marriott on Lockwood Drive as of 2010 had a wall of photos of Riley at various ages and stages. When Dorothea Benton Frank wrote her regional novels, she was so assured that Joe Riley would continue to be mayor of the Holy City that she simply named him, while the rest of her cast of characters remained fictitious.

Riley rapidly distinguished himself on the state and national stage. He served a term as president of the U.S. Conference of Mayors and, later, on its Executive Committee. He was also the president of the National Association of Democratic Mayors. The National Urban Coalition, the National

Association of Realtors, the Urban Land Institute and the Seaside Institute all awarded him honors for urban leadership. The American Institute of Architects for Public Architecture offered him its Thomas Jefferson Award for "his exceptional leadership and 'Jeffersonian' vision in redefining the promise and, ultimately the future, of our nation and its cities."[210]

From a Catholic perspective, what seems most laudable about the history of the mayoralty of Joe Riley, however, is his steady commitment to racial justice. From the beginning of his time as mayor, he included African Americans in his inner circle of advisors and consultors. Riley early on placed a portrait of Denmark Vesey, alleged leader of a slave revolt, in Charleston's city hall. He was so proactive in matters related to race relations that author and fellow Citadel graduate Pat Conroy could not help but recall that his disparagers nicknamed him "Little Black Joe."[211]

Riley was attuned to crisis. He had led the earthquake- and hurricane-prone city in its recovery after the devastating Hurricane Hugo in 1989, but Hugo was not the first and certainly not the last hurricane he met. His biggest hurricane seemed truly to be the ongoing racial one. After more than twenty years as mayor, Riley continued to campaign for the removal of the Confederate flag from the state capitol as South Carolina saw an upsurge in Ku Klux Klan activity. Riley wrote an opinion piece for *The State*, Columbia's newspaper, that was published on June 17, 1996. In it, he noted that his great-grandfather had been a Confederate soldier who saw battle in Richmond but, after the war, viewed the emblem of the Confederacy this way: "The flag was not to be flown again. For him and for other veterans, it belonged in museums; it had become a part of history." Riley's argument was that it was vitally important to "remove a symbol of division and create opportunities for increased common understanding."

Amid contention over the flag and deeper contention over its offensiveness to the descendants of slaves, Riley finally met the last straw when the state legislature failed to acknowledge Martin Luther King Jr. Day as an official state holiday. On April 2, 2000, Riley led a 120-mile march to the capitol along U.S. Route 176. He invited anyone and everyone to join him, and politicians, business leaders, educators, coaches, college students, children and elders did. U.S. Representative Jim Clyburn, author Pat Conroy and coach Lou Holtz were among those who marched (as reported in *The State*, April 5, 2000). Chris Matthews's MSNBC show *Hardball*, *USA Today* and the *New York Times* picked up the story, noting that Riley had a reputation for being a high-achiever but not one given to dramatic gestures or self-publicity. What activated him and incited him to this march was a cause.

Unfortunately, it was not until the massacre at Mother Emanuel in June 2015 that then-governor Nikki Haley succeeded in having the flag removed altogether from the statehouse. Joe Riley again weighed in on the importance of doing so, and his support of removal of the flag was covered by the *Washington Post*, the *New York Times*, *MSNBC News* and numerous other outlets.

Riley joined the parishioners of Emanuel African Methodist Episcopal Church, numerous Charlestonians and others in the peaceful and prayerful aftermath of the shocking assassination of nine members of that parish by assassin Dylann Roof. Roof had been sure that the shootings would trigger race riots. Riley was sure that such a thing would not happen in Charleston. He joined a throng gathered for a prayer vigil, joined in the singing of "We Shall Overcome" and requested the addition of "What a Friend We Have in Jesus." Riley noted in his reflections offered to the crowd that night that "the gunman's racist beliefs belong in the 'dustpan of failed civilizations,' and that if he thought he could divide the Charleston community he had failed miserably. 'We share one thing in common,' Riley said, 'Our hearts are broken. We have an anguish like we have never had before. In our broken hearts, we realize we love each other more.'"[212] It was one of Joe Riley's last acts as mayor of Charleston, and it revealed for all to see the mettle of the man. One who also observed Riley's gracious leadership was President Barack Obama, who delivered the eulogy at the memorial service for State Senator Reverend Clementa Pinckney, the first victim of the shooting.

Before the honor bestowed on him by Pope Francis and Bishop Robert Guglielmone, Riley had received other ecclesiastical honors. Bishop Robert Baker had already presented him with the Caritas Award and the Catholic Extension Society's Lumen Christi Award, spurred on to nominate Riley for these honors by the clear evidence of his resolute dedication to the pursuit of justice.

Jean Toal

One of those coincidences that cause people to wonder what might have been in the drinking water at the time is the fact that Joe Riley and Jean Hoefer Toal were both born the same year, 1943. Like Riley, Jean Toal attended the University of South Carolina School of Law and was also a groundbreaker in terms of accomplishments and honors. The Hoefer family, German immigrants, settled in Columbia, South Carolina, after the Civil War. Toal's great-grandfather had served as a soldier in the Union army after having enlisted to take the place of an Ohioan who did not desire to serve.[213] Once they moved to Columbia, the Hoefer family became active parishioners at St. Joseph Church, where she resumed membership after a stint in Greenville.

When Jean Hoefer married law school classmate William Thomas Toal, she joined a man who would be the first white lawyer in South Carolina to establish a legal partnership with an African American, their classmate I.S. Leevy Johnson.[214] Jean became a partner in another law firm, the Haynsworth group in Greenville, and then the Belser firm in Columbia. She represented a woman seeking to serve as a state senate page and lost the case. After litigating a variety of appeals for high-stakes cases, she represented the Catawba Nation before the U.S. Supreme Court and won their right to official recognition and to significant land claims in the Piedmont. She distinguished herself as a champion of anti-discrimination causes.[215]

Her political career began in 1974, when she successfully ran for the South Carolina House of Representatives, in which she served for fourteen years. Her first run with the state legislature for the South Carolina Supreme Court was in a three-way race in 1984. In 1985, there was another contest for the court, and she withdrew in order to throw her support to Ernest A. Finney Jr., the first African American named to the court since the post–Civil War era (and father of acclaimed poet Nikky Finney). In late 1986, Toal tried again and was elected to the court, assuming the office officially in March 1988.[216] She was the first woman on the court and in 2000 was elected chief justice—the first woman and the first Catholic to achieve such a distinction. When she reached the required retirement age in 2015, she had served a total of fifteen years as chief justice and a total of forty-one years as an elected official, either in the House or on the court. In the midst of her long career, she also served as president of the Conference of Chief Justices nationwide.[217]

Toal is one of those who defies labels. Because she was a registered Democrat, she was assumed to be liberal. She was indeed a liberal if that means pro-women, anti-racism, interested in championing the rights of underdogs and opposed to the death penalty. Others deemed her conservative because she was openly anti-abortion (and endorsed by right-to-life groups) and tough on claims that pornography enjoyed free speech rights.[218] Overall, Toal's record as a justice is one of high principles and adherence to received law. "When she assumed the bench, she said she would be a strict constructionist in her judicial philosophy, and that she was….Toal certainly was no activist judge making new law."[219] In saying that, however, we also must acknowledge that Toal read the law as serving the rights of all persons and not special interests. Her focus was always justice and equity.

The American Bar Association, South Carolina Trial Lawyers Association and a number of colleges and universities are among those having awarded Toal and extolled her accomplishments. The Church, too, has lauded her as a Catholic woman achieving breakthroughs for women who, in her own lifetime, had been historically barred from the profession and the leadership she assumed. Her Catholicity, though never flaunted, came through in her representation of women and Native Americans, in stepping aside to advance an African American colleague, in her ethic of hard work and honesty and in her unashamed espousal of pro-life ethics. Fittingly, the University of South Carolina School of Religious Studies selected her to deliver the November 2019 Annual Bernardin Lecture. This lecture, hosted each fall by USC, focuses on moral and ethical issues touching contemporary society. Her theme was "The Social Ministry of Joseph Cardinal Bernardin."

Catholics in the Limelight

Riley and Toal have marked—and even epitomized—a new day for Catholics in South Carolina. Once targeted by the Ku Klux Klan, Catholics were shown, in them, to be gifted, responsible citizens. The percentage of Catholics in the state remains just a bit below double digits, even with the influx of northerners, upper midwesterners and Latinos who have swelled the parishes of the diocese. Riley and Toal have shown professional colleagues and voters that they have been wholeheartedly devoted to the common good, the rule of law and the principles of liberty and justice for all. In highlighting them, we also honor all people of faith who have distinguished themselves as good citizens and advocates for the common good of society. As the Second Vatican Council pointed out during the formative young adult years of both Riley and Toal, the role of the lay faithful is to do their part to transform the world so that it better conforms to God's design for it. While Riley and Toal have enjoyed widespread attention, they also represent the many lay Catholics who have reshaped life in South Carolina by good works, professionalism and living faith.

Riley and Toal are noted here for a twofold purpose: first is the high profile they have given to accomplished Catholics in South Carolina; the second is the fact that, in some sense, they represent so many others across the state who have dedicated their lives to God and country. Numerous Catholics can be named as luminaries in their own right. They have played a role in municipal, county and statewide politics. They have made professional contributions in healthcare, law, business, education and social service. Then there are those less well known but who are subtly and powerfully influential by virtue of their character and spiritual strength. They are the ones whom Pope Francis refers to as "the saints next door." Many have excelled in volunteer activities and influenced the cause of life, human rights, literacy, the uplifting of persons with disabilities and direct service to the poor. Their dedication to the general welfare and human dignity are testimonies to Catholicism's belief that the Kingdom of God can be realized to some extent in the present moment—and that is accomplished where truth, charity, grace and peace are the values held dear.

Chapter 15

ANOTHER NORTHERN INCURSION

It's a theme that runs through the history of the region and the diocese. When one looks at the populations, cultures, land and labor that have formed South Carolina, it becomes clear that often, indeed most often, émigrés, opportunists, invaders and retirees have shaped and changed the terrain and the course of events. Even the indigenous peoples, the ones resident for millennia, arrived from elsewhere, probably from a trek across northern Asia and an area that is now the far northeastern territory of Russia. The settlers of Santa Elena, although they may have landed and set out from points south like Havana or Hispaniola, claimed Spain as their homeland. The planters who formed the colony originated in England, Ireland, Scotland, France and Germany, all northern latitudes. The South Carolina militia, whose savvy leaders baffled and routed Redcoats, were, in many cases, men who migrated southward as the American colonies were being established. Sherman's troops, whose destructive sieges during the Civil War necessitated wholesale Reconstruction, were Yankees, as were carpetbaggers who corrupted politics. And the somewhat more nobly motivated industrialists who helped rebuild and refashion the state, newly back in the Union, were also from elsewhere, generally the Northeast. During the last decades of the nineteenth century, vacationers began to find the seacoast an appealing spot for summer recreation—even if they had to arrive on dirt roads or by a short railroad ride from Conway and sleep on the sandy beaches in tents. In the twentieth century and into the twenty-first, more and more people and more and more corporate entities came from

New England, the mid-Atlantic, the upper Midwest and Canada—along with some, like BMW (British Motor Works), from overseas.

Some of the lasting effects of arrivals and incursions from northerly points are the matter of this chapter. For good or for ill, events and episodes recounted here changed the course of history. They show, too, that there are very few in the diocesan and the state census who can claim a southern hemispheric origin—with the exception of some African slaves and their descendants and the more recent arrivals from Central and South America and from South Asia and the Pacific Islands. The American notion of a melting pot civilization is borne out here, and the Catholic sense of one human family, when it is taken to heart, quickly breaks down bias against some obscure "outsider" or other.

THE FIRST NATIONS

How Native Americans first arrived on the American continents, North and South, remains a topic of speculation and folklore. What we do know is that when Columbus arrived, he discovered a New World that was already inhabited. He gradually realized that it was something quite other than India, but this did not prevent him from sending captive "Indians" to Spain—more than five hundred of them—by 1495, with sale in mind. Ferdinand and Isabella ordered Columbus to cease and desist while they deliberated the legality and morality of these proposed transactions, with the result that Columbus and fellow explorers apparently decided to set his native captives to work in the Caribbean to bolster new European ventures in planting and mining.[220]

The question of where these people had come from no more occurred to the explorers and conquistadors than it did to the African slave traders. Much more recent archaeological research suggests that some tribal peoples in the Americas arrived as far back as 10,000 BC and possibly earlier. That would put their arrival before the apparent existence of a famed "land bridge" over the Bering Strait, so the manner of their treks and transport remains a mystery.[221] As Ojibwe anthropologist David Treuer has suggested, Native American creation stories don't offer travel tales or reminiscences of an old country. Rather, they have tribal peoples spontaneously coming from the center of Earth, from a spill from the heavens, from a primal mother or from nomadic wanderings through mystical worlds.[222]

Digs, fossil findings and analyses show that there were once camels here, woolly mammoths and bison.[223] Codes of conduct, clan structures and governing systems developed, along with agriculture, herding, tool-making and the crafting of clothing, pottery and jewelry.[224] Complex languages with no inherent similarity to Indo-European ones developed among them, and a variety of symbols and petroglyphs formed a mode of communication.[225] We have learned some of these things about the First Nations, as aboriginal and indigenous people are commonly called. But the only clues about where they originated come from recent DNA testing of ancient bones. These show commonalities with Asian peoples but also, in some cases, with Europeans. Treuer suggested, "It is quite likely that Europeans migrated into far eastern Asia and mingled with the populations there and that their descendants crossed over into the New World between thirty thousand and twenty thousand years ago."[226] No one knows what continental divisions had yet to take place, what land bridges might have existed or whether something like the seafaring rafts of the early Pacific, made legendary in Thor Heyerdahl's *Kon Tiki*, might have facilitated a very, very long passage. Similarly, no one knows which of the tribal groups might have actually been first. But the general theory is that most, if not all, arrived by northern routes.

By the time Europeans arrived, there were "tawny" native people tending their own vegetable patches and stands of fruit trees.[227] The groups indigenous to the Carolinas and Georgia included those identified as Mississippian, Algonquin, Iroquois, Sioux and Muskegee. These included the Cherokee, Catawba, Edisto and Guale people encountered by early European settlers.[228] The Spanish-speaking and other European arrivals in North America were invaders, as the native peoples came to see them. Once they established themselves, they created what Dunbar-Ortiz has called "a colonialist settler-state"[229] that overtook the First Nations. Aside from the occasional Native American compound or casino and the popularization of dreamcatchers and tom-toms, there are few remnants of these Asia-originated people—except, as noted in chapter 17, in an array of place names.

The British and the Swamp Fox

Tugs of war over the New World ensued in the years after Columbus's discovery. Spain and Portugal drew a line of demarcation that divided South America into their dominions. In North America, Britain and

France squabbled and fought as "proprietary charters" affected what would become the United States and Canada. The charters along the Atlantic coast and the Carolinas were drawn by the 1630s, just a decade after the arrival of the Pilgrims at Plymouth Rock, and by the 1660s, colonies and governors, or lords proprietors, had laid claim to "hundreds of thousands of acres of land."[230]

A passion for self-determination seems to have characterized American colonists and South Carolinians in a notable way. The proprietors exercised considerable administrative authority over many subjects and quickly determined that it was important for each colony to have its own militia—long before the Declaration of Independence was penned. The idea of the "citizen-soldier" was actually supported by the British, who saw it as a way of securing the vast colonial territory. Skirmishes and more serious and deadly conflicts broke out, and in the earlier eighteenth century, Carolina's farmers, horsemen and huntsmen had fought in Queen Anne's War and the Cherokee War. Their experience helped to prime leaders for the militia. Among the seasoned leaders are names that are advertised around the state to this day: Marion, Moultrie, Pickens, Sumter.[231] Of these, Francis Marion, the Swamp Fox, has been the most memorialized and romanticized.

Marion's region of the present state included much of the coast from Charleston to the Pee Dee and into the Midlands as far as Camden and Columbia. Today's guerrilla warfare had a precursor in Marion. Some of his wins over the British were best described as ambushes and raids in which he managed to seize British military supplies and horses, while also taking captives and killing. He reportedly managed to convince some of the Redcoats he captured to switch to the colonists' side. As the war progressed, the savvy of Marion and his men allowed them to navigate seemingly impassable swamplands and survive in blistering heat amid vermin- and insect-infested wilds. With their knowledge of topography and their skill at sneak attacks, Marion repeatedly outsmarted British officers and also local planters who had opted to stay on the Tory side.[232]

While the British were coming and kept coming, Marion, Pickens and Sumter in particular kept launching unconventional attacks and inflicting losses. At Cowpens, they had an imposing victory. Luring the British away from the shoreline communities disallowed the British from capitalizing on their naval strength and forced them to use cavalry and foot soldiers. The American troops gained more strongholds in the Midlands and along the Savannah River; then Marion took control of Georgetown, and militia groups began to squeeze the British-occupied Charleston. Major General

Nathanael Greene finally secured Charleston in 1783—two weeks after a contingent that included Benjamin Franklin, John Adams, John Jay and Henry Laurens had signed the Treaty of Paris, which ultimately broke the last hold of the British over the soon-to-be named United States.[233]

Sons born in South Carolina, military men from other areas of the colonies, slave labor—sometimes forced, sometimes voluntary—and British captives who let their loyalty to the Crown lapse all helped win the war for independence. It took some fifteen years, but a constitutional republic emerged, and southern and northern colonies alike joined forces and sent representatives to the Continental Congresses. Moultrie, Pickens and Sumter gave their names to forts, towns and counties. Francis Marion gave his to a town, a county, a national forest and a man-made lake that, ironically, covered his family plantation near Eutawville.[234] John Gordon remarked that Pickens came from Pennsylvania and, later, Virginia, and Sumter was from Virginia, where he was born to newly arrived British parents. Both, it seems, were "part of the large internal migration down the 'Virginia Road' from Pennsylvania that helped carry people into the backcountry of both Carolinas and Georgia."[235] Henry Laurens sent his son, who died in battle, to Switzerland for his education,[236] and Laurens himself was quite a cosmopolitan figure, who initially decried the abusive treatment of poorer immigrants and of slaves but made a fortune selling them.[237] Nathanael Greene and his troops were dispatched southward by General Washington. Marion was born in South Carolina in the French Huguenot locale then called, as Edgar says, "French Santee."[238] As much as the soil and spirit of South Carolina possessed these men, they had in common European and northern colonial roots.

The Civil War, Reconstruction and Beyond

There is no doubt that the outbreak of the Civil War pitted North against South. However, that was not an entirely new phenomenon. During the American Revolution and the first decades of the new nation, both parts of the country worked together while continuing to disagree over matters of sovereignty and slavery. As the abolitionist movement grew, disagreements became more vitriolic, and compromise was the only route to dealing with slavery when new states were admitted to the Union. The word *Yankee* became a contemptuous epithet, and as described in chapters 6 and 7, the devastation that wracked the state after the Civil War entrenched contempt.

So, too, did the Republican Party, the party of Lincoln—an irony in what is now so heavily a "red state." The era of Reconstruction, while it served just causes for the newly freed slaves, also invited racketeers. Carpetbaggers arrived from the North, intent on gaining political leverage and also profiteering from civic projects. Institutions were repaired or rebuilt, but the urge to return to the Old South set in as soon as federally enforced inclusion of freed slaves in business ventures, selling crops, voting and holding office was loosened in the late 1877. While some areas that staked their economic success on planting and harvesting recovered, many areas suffered soil exhaustion. Textile mills, paper mills and other industries began moving in. With the departure of some of the freed slaves for urban areas like New York, Philadelphia, Detroit and Chicago, the need for a labor force was pressing.

There were railroads and bridges to be built and factories to be constructed or upgraded, and there were new mercantile and service industries emerging. One route to getting necessary laborers began within three years of the end of the Civil War. John Wagener, who had enticed German nationals to settle in Walhalla in the Upstate, became mayor of Charleston and shortly thereafter was named the state's first "commissioner of immigration." He created a pamphlet entitled *South Carolina: A Home for Immigrants*, which Archie Vernon Huff reported was published in German, Danish, Swedish and Norwegian, along with English. Wagener's intent was to create a working class of "an intelligent, thrifty, white population" from Europe or the northern United States.[239] Wagener specified the national origins he desired, but he did not specify anything about the religious faith of the laborers he hoped for. He simply wanted able-bodied workers.

Wagener's wish clearly came true, but many other influences were also brought to bear on the future of the state and the Church—and the resources of both—as the decades ahead unfolded and centuries turned. Each area of the state underwent remarkable transitions in population and conversions of economy in the twentieth and twenty-first centuries. The next chapter, with sections headed by the names of the Catholic deaneries of the bicentennial era, describes some of those changes, including the state's mixture of massive population drift and the persistence of backwater communities.

Chapter 16

THE HUBS OF THE DIOCESE

E ach deanery is named for a population center, an area with a history that stretches beyond its borders. But each deanery also includes obscure towns and villages, areas dominated, perhaps, by the major centers yet, at the same time, unique in terms of their stories and their inhabitants. Denmark, for example, sits in a stretch that belongs to the Columbia deanery, but its location makes that a toss-up. Despite that it has a college—Voorhees—any Catholics in Denmark would attend church at St. Theresa in Springfield, a mission church served by Orangeburg's Holy Trinity. It would not be surprising for Catholics in Denmark to feel underserved, if not invisible—a minority if there ever was one. And yet, the Catholics of Denmark live in a state where vibrant life can be found and parishes can prosper. In looking at the hubs, the deanery centers, of the Diocese of Charleston today, we may also get a glimpse of the circumstances and developments affecting the Catholics in and around those hubs.

AIKEN

The Aiken deanery includes a variety of small towns and rural areas like Gloverville, the site of one of the active Catholic Charities outreach centers; McCormick; Edgefield, whose name is associated with a unique style of pottery; Greenwood, site of Lander University and Piedmont Technical

College; Murphy Village, the locus for the Irish Travelers; and North Augusta, one of the communities, like Aiken, most economically affected by the development of the Savannah River nuclear facility. Aiken itself is an old community, tracing origins to the Westo, Savanna and Chickasaw tribes who engaged in the fur trade. Some (the Westo tribe, certainly) also engaged in the African slave trade.[240] The nineteenth century saw the city boom as railroads connected it, via Hamburg, to commerce. A German immigrant, Henry Schultz, built a toll bridge across the Savannah River and developed a wharf, a steamboat company and a bank for the region, which became a successful exporter of cotton.[241] After the setbacks caused by the destruction of rail lines toward the end of the Civil War, Aiken gradually recovered and became, at times, a center for canal-building, rail transportation, agricultural production, cultural performances and the equestrian installations that mark it today.

Part of the Aiken area's history includes involvement in research and testing related to the development of atomic weapons. It was nothing like the scale of Tennessee's Oak Ridge, but Aiken County, particularly the town of Ellenton, was involved in nuclear research and nuclear fuel refinement. During the post–World War II arms race, it fell victim to land purchase and land condemnation to construct the Savannah River Plant,[242] now known as the Savannah River Site. Despite what would seem to be an attraction for engineers and technicians, from the 1920s and 1930s on, Aiken became a destination for northerners and globetrotters, especially celebrities seeking winter warmth—among them Fred Astaire; the Whitney family of New York's famed Whitney Museum; the Duke and Duchess of Windsor, the former king Edward VIII and his wife, Wallace Simpson; and graduates of the Juilliard School of Music.[243] Steeplechase racing became a feature of the area—and now the impetus for the Aiken Thoroughbred Racing Hall of Fame and Museum.

In terms of its Catholic history, Aiken's parish church, St. Mary Help of Christians, dating its foundation in 1853, worshiped at a site that fell victim to high winds in 1878[244] but was rebuilt and extended its service to Blackwell and beyond. Among projects initiated by Aiken pastors and sisters was the formation and continuation of schools. These included St. Angela Academy in Aiken, established by the Ursuline sisters in 1900, shortly thereafter taken on by the Sisters of Charity of Our Lady of Mercy in 1906, when the Ursulines rejoined others in their order residing in Columbia.[245] Bishop Northrop agreed to assume the outstanding debt on the academy, and the school went on.[246] Later, when Emmet Walsh was bishop, "a vocational and crafts school" was opened in 1940 in Horse Creek Valley (also sometimes called Midlands Valley) under the guidance of the Sisters of Our Lady of Christian Doctrine.[247]

As of the last census, the Aiken area had a population distinctly less Hispanic/Latino than much of the rest of the state, but Aiken itself is close to one-third African American, which includes the historically rooted St. Gerard Catholic Church, which was initially identified as a mission of Orangeburg, thanks to Redemptorist initiative in 1942.[248] Chapter 8 tells a bit of its tale of survival.

BEAUFORT

Beaufort County and the Beaufort deanery—which includes Allendale, Colleton, Hampton and Jasper Counties—includes both notably affluent and notably depressed areas. As mentioned from the outset of this book, Beaufort lays claim to early settlement and was likely the first regularly used worship space in South Carolina and much of La Florida. It also rapidly ascended to leadership in planting and exporting—with indigo, cotton, fruits and vegetables creating wealth but also entrenching slavery. Catholics were in Beaufort from the earliest times, and they bought or brought slaves with them. They also relied on cultural foundations first in Spain and France and then Ireland and the British isles, like so many others of the famed South Carolina plantation owners. The city was chartered in 1711, so it is truly an icon of the Old South and the Carolina Sea Islands. Bluffton, with a one-square-mile Old Town, was inhabited by planters, slaves and a mix of other people who settled the area in the eighteenth century. It was officially founded in 1852. Annexation of once outlying areas has buttressed both the population and the acreage of Bluffton. Some surrounding areas, such as Hilton Head, incorporated in 1983, developed in the latter twentieth century. Gullah-Geechee people, the descendants of freed slaves, have long inhabited the area but are, in many cases, afflicted by lack of formal documents to prove title to their family properties.

Waves of newcomers to both the city and county of Beaufort came with the establishment of Parris Island and the Marine Corps Air Station and, later, the development of Hilton Head and Bluffton as envied vacation and retirement venues. The Pinckney family influence on the development of Catholic life in the area has been recounted in chapter 5. Much of the founding or expansion of parishes and missions in Beaufort, Bluffton, Hilton Head, Hardeeville, Ridgeland, Walterboro and St. Helena Island is attributable to the arrival of northerners interested in golf and a warm climate. What was said of Charles Fraser's profitable ventures on Hilton Head, undertaken in the late 1950s and 1960s, is telling:

> *When development began on Hilton Head, virtually everything started from scratch. Electricity and telephone service had to be brought in. New roads had to be laid out and paved. In a way, it was fortunate that there were few buildings, fot that allowed planners to develop communities in a logical fashion. It was fortunate for Hilton Head that some of those early planners were visionaries who saw the island's beauty and were determined to preserve it.*[249]

Opportunistic or not, Fraser and his colleagues did not exactly start with nothing, since the islanders included people steeped in Gullah traditions, plowing with the help of marsh tackies descended from small Spanish horses and at peace with a make-do culture. There were also early hunting and fishing expeditions and some land buy-ups by northerners who were accomplished bankers, scientists, merchants and other professionals.[250] Then the boom came.

An outcome of the growth of Hilton Head was the urgent need to establish a second Beaufort County parish there. An interesting note in Muller's history concerns the bishop of Charleston. Ernest Unterkoefler loomed large physically and historically. He is most often noted because of his participation in every session of the Second Vatican Council and his efforts to bring the spirit of the council to the Diocese of Charleston. He also played a vital role in desegregation and was known as a civil rights activist. In the midst of those more solemn notes is one lighter one. Muller attributed to him the opening of their new church at an existing eatery, with the result that locals called it "The Church of Crazy Crab" or "The Holy Crab."[251] Muller's story—verified by Monsignor Martin Laughlin, one of two vicars general for Bishop Robert Baker and, from 2007 to 2009, administrator of the diocese—is that the restaurant temporarily became a place of worship. The future parishioners of St. Francis by the Sea used the Crazy Crab restaurant for nearly four years while their church was being planned and built. The growth of Hilton Head, championed by Charles Fraser and friends, also meant the growth of Catholicism. And even though the new parishioners were for the most part not southern-born, they readily adopted the practical—and occasionally unconventional—problem-solving capacities of Catholics of the diocese. Their choice of a worship site became a part of local humor and oral history.

The early development of what is now the Beaufort deanery was minimal compared to what has ended up becoming, as of recent estimates, a population of more than forty thousand on the island alone. Growth on the barrier islands beyond Beaufort—St. Helena, Dataw, Harbor, Hunting and Fripp Islands—is similarly dynamic, but as yet without population growth comparable to that of Hilton Head. A similar phenomenon is breaking out in Jasper County, which includes much of Sun City, as plans for construction of Latitude Margaritaville are realized and properties are being sold to grow what is hoped to be an expansive community for residents ages fifty-five and up in Hardeeville. This will, without doubt, necessitate massively expanded local parishes or a new one altogether.

In some sense, author Pat Conroy can take partial credit and partial blame for the fate of some of the Lowcountry area that he prized and memorialized. His burial at Penn Center, after a Mass of Christian Burial at St. Peter's, Beaufort, is a fitting symbol of his care and concern for the Gullah culture and the future of the long-term residents of the sea islands—a concern reflected in his first professional job, teaching on Dafuskie Island, which was the basis of his first successful book, which was made into a feature film. His creative nonfiction account of his teaching year, *The Water Is Wide* (1972), was adapted by 20th Century Fox as the movie *Conrack* (1974). For some, Conroy glorified his preferred locale in that and subsequent books, and he can be said to have helped attract a considerable number of visitors who eventually decided to stay.

CHARLESTON

The richly historic "Holy City" is known for its church steeples, its bounteous plantations and gardens, its carriage rides, Fort Sumter, the famed Rainbow Row, the Battery, The Citadel, an array of sporting and cultural events and the ill-fated first submarine, the *Hunley*. Charleston has survived battles, fires, earthquakes and hurricanes over the years and to this day experiences significant street flooding with regularity. It is the seat of the diocese as well as of the Charleston deanery. Its first bishops include, of course, the famed John England, Ignatius Reynolds and Patrick Lynch, the Irishman who arrived in South Carolina as a not quite two-year-old, who spanned the pre—

and post–Civil War eras and relied on confreres in urban areas and across the seas to help rebuild his beleaguered diocese.

As previously mentioned, the successor of Bishop Patrick Lynch was Bishop Henry Pinckney Northrop, a native son of South Carolina and a childhood convert to the faith. Rome educated, he served briefly in New York City after his ordination in Rome and then was assigned to parishes in Charleston and eventually to oversight of the Vicariate of North Carolina. He assumed the office of bishop in 1883. Bishop Northrop continued the energetic efforts of Bishop Lynch to rebuild and build new, both in the city of Charleston and in various areas of the state. Repairs to churches, rectories and other diocesan facilities were still underway when a massive earthquake hit Charleston in 1886.[252] The OLM-operated St. Francis Xavier Infirmary, opened in 1882, also was in need of repair in the aftermath of the earthquake.

It was not just churches and health facilities that needed repair or renewed building. In Charleston proper and locales around the state, there was pressure to open Catholic schools. Construction of buildings was one thing, but access around the state was another as an age of transportation and industrialization was being born. Railroads were being built, often by workers enticed from Ireland.[253] As a result, both northern industrialists and new immigrants were influencing the development of civic communities and the requirements of the diocesan church. Statewide, as well as in Charleston proper, construction workers were required as brick buildings became preferred over vulnerable wooden ones; securing buildings with the earthquake bolts pointed out by every carriage driver in Charleston to this day required workers savvy in new methods of installation.

While all this was going on, historic St. Mary's in Charleston and the cathedral were simultaneously being rebuilt and importing paintings, stained-glass windows and statuary from Europe.[254] Rental of temporary parish sites, construction of new churches and schools and rearrangements in the care of orphans continued with diocesan leadership.[255] The Sisters of Our Lady of Mercy relocated their motherhouse to give more space to house orphans, and the City of Charleston agreed to provide financial assistance for the boys and girls who were among the orphans in the sisters' care. Around the state, the continuing influx of Irish workers was followed by the arrival of Italian immigrants primed to work as stonecutters and in phosphate mines. Lebanese Catholics of the Maronite rite appeared in Georgetown as the twentieth century opened, and not long thereafter, other Lebanese families came to Charleston and later to Columbia and other areas of the state.[256] Many of them were merchants, and the second generation produced medical professionals, lawyers and entrepreneurs with a variety of interests. Father Joseph O'Brien, later known as Monsignor or "Doc" O'Brien, originally from the Diocese of Scranton in Pennsylvania and a scholar from the International Catholic University of Fribourg in Switzerland, arrived in the diocese charged with the mission of starting a Catholic high school.[257] Thomas McQueeney has recorded the story of his gifts and his personal legacy to Catholic education in *Holy Water of Charleston: The Compelling Influence of Bishop John England and Father Joseph L. O'Brien*. The book was produced in preparation for the Centennial of Bishop England High School, celebrated in 2015.

As the twentieth century progressed, a line of bishops guided the construction of more and more churches, schools, healthcare facilities and social outreach institutions. The Greater Charleston area became a magnet for tourists interested in sunny beaches, the rich history of the region and the arts. While U.S. Navy installations decreased in the latter twentieth century, freighters larger than urban apartment buildings arrived in the Charleston port. In the twenty-first century, cruise ships began to dock in Charleston and set out for the Bahamas, Bermuda, Puerto Rico and other Caribbean destinations. The scent of the paper mill on the Cooper River fills the air when the wind blows city-ward, and new industries like Boeing have built extensive facilities and employed personnel from far and wide. The forty-year mayoralty of Joe Riley (noted in chapter 14) has had lasting impact on the financial, industrial and cultural status of the city and vicinity. Colleges have expanded their enrollment, and technical training facilities have bolstered a population prepared with skills to serve new needs. The long-lived St. Francis Xavier Hospital has been sold, under the leadership of Sister Bridget Sullivan, OLM, to the Bon Secours Health System. Bon Secours constructed a new hospital in West Ashley, Bon Secours St. Francis, and merged the downtown hospital with Roper to become Roper St. Francis, giving Charleston two hospitals with a Catholic history. Populations in Mount Pleasant and on Daniel Island have boomed and brought new technological industries and sporting events to the area. Charleston has become a tourist destination, rated first in the nation in the *U.S. News & World Report* lineup of the "Best Fall Vacations," posted in August 2019.[258] The Charleston deanery, to be sure, is replete with both southern charm and an increasingly urbane, sophisticated population. But it also includes outlying areas like Wadmalaw Island and Edisto Island, areas where, in the first case, there is no Catholic church and, in the second, where current construction is replacing a mission church that seemed a notch above a Quonset hut.

Columbia

For some South Carolinians and some Catholics, Columbia is the best place to gather people who don't care to drive from Hilton Head to Rock Hill or from Anderson to Myrtle Beach. To others, the capital city is simply the urban area with the tallest buildings and the hottest summers—hot enough for teachers to demonstrate that one can literally fry eggs on the sidewalk—and hope that children will not attempt to walk barefoot on cement or macadam on those hottest days.

Columbia is inevitably associated with the state executive, legislative and judicial offices and all their collateral entities, as well as the University of South Carolina. Museums, news media centers and corporate facilities cover the map of the city. Parks and the conversion of an old mill district into the downtown Vista area have attracted sightseers and business persons on break. The 1980s addition of upper decks to the Williams-Brice Stadium and the 1990s upgrade of the airport have accommodated hundreds of thousands of residents and area guests.[259] There are other colleges there, too, along with those making up USC. Allen and Benedict are historically black. Columbia International University offers biblical and pastoral studies as well as management and other courses. Columbia College retains its reputation as an undergraduate school for women, while its postgraduate programs are co-ed. Then there is the large military presence. Fort Jackson has brought in an endless stream of army recruits, military personnel and their families.

Columbia is rich in Catholic schools, with four elementary ones, and Cardinal Newman School, which, as a secondary school, has been lauded for its quality, inclusion and both academic and athletic successes. Columbia is, of course, also the site of the diocese's only basilica and the revered birthplace of Joseph Cardinal Bernardin, who is memorialized there in a number of ways.

As a Catholic deanery, the city of Columbia, with its multiple Catholic churches and schools, is the center, but it also includes some smaller and lesser-known areas with their own rich histories and their own peculiar concerns. Urban sprawl from Columbia affects areas like Irmo and Chapin to the west and Blythewood to the north and slightly east. Summerton, off I-95, remains a less affluent area, as does Springfield, accessible by roads verging off from Bells, Denmark, Erhardt and other small communities north of I-95 and far west of I-26. St. Mark's in Newberry, a good forty miles north and west of Columbia, features Newberry College and the old opera house in what has to be deemed a quaint but struggling downtown area. Its mission churches in Joanna and Laurens are actually in the Greenville deanery. But Columbia itself is the preferred site for all sorts of statewide and diocesan-wide events, largely because of its central location and its accessibility from converging interstate highways. It has hosted diocesan conferences, ordinations, celebrations and catechetical and diaconal formation classes for years. One of the two vicars general for the diocese, Reverend Monsignor Richard Harris, resides and pastors there. Columbia itself, no matter how deep its stake in history and certain relics of the Confederacy, is subject to the influences of diverse cultures and both Western and Eastern religions. The fact that the three largest ecumenical and interreligious groups—the Fellowship of South Carolina Bishops, the South Carolina Christian Action Council and Interfaith Partners of South Carolina—gather regularly there attests to that.

The British philosopher John Locke proposed key ideas about the nature of the polis, thereby influencing the drafters of the Declaration of Independence and in 1669 helping to craft the Fundamental Constitution of Carolina.[260] His influence persists, particularly in the legislative halls of the capital city. Statecraft is inevitably in the blood of residents of Columbia, who are surrounded by the signs and symbols of government and politics. Also in the blood of many is the memory of the Civil War and the wreckage it made of the city. In a number of ways, the recovery of Columbia and its current thriving give ways to a special civic pride in the city. Columbia has also found ways to attract major industries and service providers. Corporate executives of Blue Cross and Blue Shield, Bank of America at its Gervais Street Center and Colonial Life (linked with Unum US and Unum UK) are among the leaders from elsewhere who have influenced helped to shape the future of the state. Many of them hail from points north and, in making the South their own, have linked with local professionals to produce an increasingly cosmopolitan city. For the farther reaches of the deanery, professional offices providing health, educational and legal service; chain stores; technological industries; agribusinesses; and such things as deer processing plants or poultry farms and plants are among the entities that have provided employment for area residents and newcomers.

GREENVILLE

From plantations and textile mills to intentional leadership in education and the arts as the twentieth century progressed, Greenville has become an area of diversified industries, technical and technological expertise and a variety of ventures in transportation and healthcare.[261] South Carolina Educational Television claims Greenville as the site of its founding in 1963. Downtown Greenville has spent forty to fifty years adapting to new needs, new tastes and new opportunities. The result is that the city has refashioned itself into a pedestrian-friendly and tourist-friendly area of shops, walking spaces, hotels and restaurants. Today's Greenville proudly hosts a stream of visitors and corporate heads. BMW, Michelin and Clemson International Center for Automotive Research have strong entities in Greenville, as do Bon Secours Health, Proterra, Caristrap International and Sealed Air.

The area is rife with memorable events and personalities. Two contrasting yet complementary ones, however, illustrate how influences from far afield and from very close to home have helped to shape Greenville's current image. In 1991, Edvard Tchivzel was touring the United States with the USSR Symphony Orchestra. In the midst of a stint conducting the Greenville Symphony Orchestra, he, traveling with his wife and children—a rarity for Soviet artists and musicians—was invited to dinner. The group made a whimsical visit to Chuck E. Cheese. Tchivzel made quiet mention of his desire to stay, and his host realized that he wasn't just speaking fondly of the child-friendly pizza and game venue. She connected with higher ups at Immigration and Naturalizaion who arranged for him and his family to give the hovering Soviet KGB the slip. The family succeeded in moving to Greenville, with arrangements for political asylum. By 1999, Maestro Tchivzel had become a U.S. citizen and the director of the Greenville Symphony, a position he has held through 2019. A story that sounds like one appropriate to the New York or the Los Angeles Philharmonic has been recounted over and over.[262]

Another local story is the rise of a South Carolinian who has become an acclaimed biotech entrepreneur and a regular incisive reporter on Mike Switzer's daily brief on ETV radio, the "South Carolina Business Review." John "Swampfox" Warner is cofounder of Concepts to Companies and founder and CEO of Accessible Diagnostics, which has developed medical screening systems that employ smartphones and smartwatches to track and convey medical information to primary care and other physicians and veterinarians. He regularly advances all manner of entrepreneurship and takes a special interest in biomedicine, bioagriculture (producing pharmaceuticals, for example), biotechnology and the use of social media to advance progress. Warner, a Greenville native, has noted that life science industries in South Carolina have become a $11.4 million industry in the state.[263] Like Tchivzel, Warner's religious commitments are not widely publicized, but he has been known to post not only political commentary but also observations from activist Baptists. Warner's fans and allies include Catholic mayors and council members from the Lowcountry.

Tchivzel and Warner are ranked among Greenville's star cizens. On a less publicized level, we might also point to those who have influenced the profile of Catholicism. Greenville's pastors have included, and do so to this day, theological scholars, dedicated educators, skilled homilists and community builders. They have supported Catholic schools, reached out to area campuses and encouraged parishioners in their dedication, piety and innovation. Christian LeBlanc, from St. Mary's, Greenville, has developed a conversational and interactive catechetical text used with middle school students developing familiarity with sacred scripture. Liz List from St. Mary Magdalene has championed the cause of inclusion for autistic children and children with other disabilities. Like Christian LeBlanc, she has educated parishioners and catechists from across the diocese. The deaneries' directors of religious education, youth ministers, principals and other parish ministers, along with all the active parish volunteers and prayer teams, have sparked life and growth in an increasingly cosmopolitan area of the state. These faithful people are a few examples of those who have effected positive change and enhanced the Catholic community.

In terms of overall Catholic presence, the city of Greenville includes three Catholic parishes with schools and a large, highly regarded private Catholic middle and secondary school; the immediate area also includes one of the two fastest-growing parishes in the state, St. Mary Magdalene in Simpsonville, plus additional parishes and mission churches. Greenville deanery's expanse includes aforementioned missions served from Newberry and others, along with the campuses of Clemson University, Furman, Wofford, University of South Carolina Upstate and Converse College, all served by Catholic campus ministry on a local or regional basis. One of the ironies of the area is the fact that Bob Jones University, with a world-class art collection, has what is likely to be the vastest holdings in Catholic art not only in the state but also in most of the South. Unfortunately, it has to date been the least ecumenically engaged for campus ministry and other purposes. A recent development, however, narrated by Diocesan Secretary of Communications and Public Affairs Michael Acquilano, is its interest in joining Catholics and other evangelicals in efforts to buttress and expand Miracle Hill Ministries in Greenville, which serves homeless men, women and children.

One can hardly mention the deanery without its attraction for devoted Clemson fans. It is hard to drive on interstates 85, 385 and 185 during football season without seeing orange paw decals, orange tiger tails and all manner of Clemson symbolism decorating cars and places of business.

In other matters, Greenville and Greer host, respectively, a new Hispanic/ Latino mission church and a Vietnamese parish. Mission churches in Easley, Gaffney, Union and Walhalla serve small but fervent groups of Catholics. Each and all have been affected by the mix of longtime Catholics, new converts and people entering the area and the region for business, educational or cultural purposes, some from abroad.

MYRTLE BEACH

Bikers, Canadians and families with a yen for surf, amusement rides, boardwalk and all-you-can-eat lobster join Myrtle Beach's regular and irregular population every year. The regular residents are used to the closures of some beach grub eateries and tattoo parlors and don't much miss them. What they and the off-season visitors do enjoy are the things that always seem to be there: Market Square; shops and outlets; hospitable convention venues; shows at the Carolina Opry, Alabama Theater, Pirates Voyage, Broadway at the Beach or the House of Blues, which looks like a living metal corrugation or Tin Pan Alley turned upright; helicopter rides; and the inevitable zip-lines. There are playlands for children and golf courses for youth and adults.

The Myrtle Beach deanery is far more than sand and surf, however. It includes distinctly rural areas like Kingstree, Lake City and Bennettsville; small, colorfully historic communities like Florence, Dillon or Darlington; the Georgetown steel and paper mills; and Conway, booming with the rapidly growing Coastal Carolina University. But Myrtle Beach holds a special interest, and because it is in some ways a South Carolina icon, its history has had a ripple effect on the state and the diocese.

Since the late nineteenth century, the Grand Strand—as it had been dubbed by the 1940s—has been a destination for travelers and vacationers. The earliest of them traveled by carriage or the early Fords, and those who wanted to make an overnight or more of it had to bring their own tents and cooking paraphernalia. By 1901–2, there was a hotel and, for commuters, wooden bathing pavilions for those who dipped into the ocean and were too sandy to board trains to Conway. Early on, Myrtle Beach was referred to as "New Town," in contrast to the "Old Town" and seat of Horry County, Conway.[264] By the 1920s, roads had improved as the automobile gained currency, and cottages began to dot the beach town. Dress-up clothes were de rigueur: white shirts and ties, plus summer straw hats for the gents and dresses for the ladies.[265] The popularity of dancing and musical performances by jazz bands—including African American groups—ratcheted up the influx into the beach area. By the 1930s, despite the 1929 stock market crash and the Depression, there were advertisements in New York City and Miami touting Myrtle Beach as an ideal location "halfway between the two cities."[266] What that meant was that people not native to the state drove its growth and economy, such that by 1938 it was formally incorporated as a city.

From 1948 through 2006, the Myrtle Beach Pavilion was both landmark and legend. It was "a reinforced concrete structure that could withstand anything, including winds up to 150 miles an hour"[267]—winds, in other words, verging on a Category 5 hurricane. A destination for local dances as well as widely popular shows, the Pavilion hosted beauty pageants, wrestling matches, singers, acrobats, comics and bingo games, while outdoors there were tennis tournaments and parades. The Pavilion gets credit for popularizing the shag, the state dance. New roads, like the improved Kings Highway, U.S. 17 and Route 501, attracted more and more people into the area—to settle or to visit and spend. By 1961, there was a Can-Am festival, which brought Canadians regularly and may get credit for the regularity to this day of the arrival of vehicles bearing Ontario license plates as weather turns frigid in the northern climes. For Christians, an Easter Sunrise service became an annual event just outside the Pavilion,[268] while for Catholics, St. Andrew Church in Myrtle Beach grew steadily from the 1946 parish for all of Horry County to, by the late 1950s and early 1960s, a distinguished larger church with a parish school. St. Andrew's found itself by the end of the twentieth century celebrating Masses on Easter at the Convention Center or the Palace Theater to accommodate tens of thousands of Catholics.[269] In the twenty-first century, Myrtle Beach continues to grow as it builds anew or expands townhouses, medical facilities, entertainment venues, beachfront hotels and shopping areas beyond Market Square, as well as widens its highways. It has a new Catholic school, St. Elizabeth Ann Seton High School, graduating its first senior class in 2020—just in time for the bicentennial of the Diocese of Charleston.

From roller coasters to neon dazzle, the home base of the Myrtle Beach deanery has flourished, in large part, due to floods of people from the northern United States and Canada who have found a home or a vacation spot there. This is not to downplay the importance of places like Georgetown, which is among several locations posting a claim for the first celebration of a Mass in the state (thanks to suggestions that Vasquez D'Allyon initially landed on Winyah Bay), but it does show that while there was a St. Mary's in 1899 and Bishop Lynch's home parish in Cheraw in 1842, the scattered Catholics did not gain much numeric strength until the city of Myrtle Beach came to dominate the area.

ROCK HILL

Rock Hill is a city that can tend to get short shrift, as it is distant from the prime city of the diocese and also the smallest deanery in terms of the number of parishes and missions that it encompasses. For that reason, it will have somewhat more extensive coverage here. The city has an interesting history and presence in its own right, but it can tend to be overshadowed by its close neighbor, the city of Charlotte, North Carolina. The Charlotte skyline is marked by tall buildings, and the city itself is home to headquarters of Bank of America, the eastern region of Wells Fargo and a number of other significant corporate entities. Charlotte attracts sports enthusiasts to football games thanks to the Carolina Panthers, NASCAR races and basketball with the Hornets. Roller coasters and the varied amusement park features of Carowinds draw crowds, and boating and fishing opportunities at nearby Lake Norman attract year-round residents and seasonal visitors. It is not surprising, then, that the Charlotte Metropolitan Area, climbing toward a population of 3 million, spills over into Rock Hill. A convergence of interstate highways means that what was once the province of the Catawba tribe and early Carolinian homesteaders has become a deanery of diverse influences and multiplex cultures.

Rock Hill, however, is considerably more than a steppingstone to Charlotte. Centuries ago, it was a destination for settlers and, for other travelers across the states, a stop on what was called the "Great Wagon Road."[270] The Catawbas, the people indigenous to the area who were skilled in hunting and agriculture, had established a route for trade. Simply being on a roadway (no matter how rutted and primitive the early roadways might seem) meant that various buyers and sellers and providers of services made their way into the area. For decades, the area had abundant cotton fields. By the early twentieth century, there were at least eight cotton mills operating in the area, and there were sawmills processing the lumber, mostly from felled tall pines, coming in from more southerly points in the state. As twentieth century progressed, one woman interviewed by historians Beard and Lee noted that the town, in her early life, had its furniture stores, building and loan associations, a large printery and shops. But, she recalled, gradually there were more and more "outsiders coming in." Among them were President and Mrs. William Howard Taft, who spent some time in an upstairs suite in a home owned by a trustee of Winthrop College.[271] Chain stores like Woolworth's and McCrory's began to appear as radios, autos and central heating became more commonplace. A local citizen named John Gary Anderson started manufacturing luxury cars in 1915. His hope was that Rock Hill would turn itself into Detroit's rival. Apparently, his downfall happened before the stock market crash of 1929, likely because he disdained assembly lines.[272]

In the post–World War II years, housing developers came, and international groups were attracted to the city's Tech Park as mills began to close. Another major player in Rock Hill's history, though, is Winthrop University. Begun in Columbia as a normal school, a training ground for public school teachers, it transformed itself into Winthrop College and relocated to Rock Hill in 1895. The intent of the Normal College had been to make education available to female students of modest means. When it moved to Rock Hill, it continued that tradition while also expanding curricular offerings. One of the revered longtime residents of Rock Hill, Mrs. Addie Stokes Mayfield, declared that "Winthrop *made* Rock Hill, and Rock Hill made Winthrop." She was a Winthrop graduate who appears to have played a notable role in her husband's payroll business.[273]

Winthrop today is a coeducational university with a diverse student body enrolled in liberal arts, business and finance, technological, educational, environmental, theater and sports programs. It supports numerous extracurricular activities and service projects and has an active campus ministry program. Its current student body numbers more than six thousand. Its expansive campus is home to resident and day students. The names of campus buildings, past and present, honor key figures in South Carolina history. In the late 1920s, a female student might well have lived in Catawba Dormitory.[274]

Two civil rights struggles have affected Rock Hill. One involved the Catawbas, who had ceded land by treaties to colonial leaders and, as they understood it, to King George III in 1760 and 1763. They were to have retained hunting rights in many areas of the then colony and 144,000 acres of land, concentrated particularly in the Waxhaw (Lancaster

County) region.[275] During the American Revolution, they were persuaded to side with the Patriots. Unfortunately, they found it necessary to flee into Virginia—probably as far as Roanoke and Danville—when Charleston and Camden were overrun by the British, and the British threatened severe retribution to those who had aided and abetted the revolutionary army's cause. Many returned to their South Carolina reservation after the British surrendered, but by 1840, there were few surviving Catawbas; what became known as the Treaty of 1840 (or the Treaty of Nations Ford) handed their 144,000 acres over to South Carolina, with promises of payment—a historic debt that was never paid.[276]

Catawbas lived on, and some served in the Confederate army and, much later, in the U.S. military; Catawba children were educated at Christian mission schools, a school arranged by Indian agents, and other facilities. Various attempts were made to set things right via state and federal appeals over a number of decades. As mentioned in chapter 14, Jean Toal played a role in the Catawbas' litigation. A settlement was finally achieved in 1993, when the U.S. Congress agreed to recognize tribal rights and establish land acquisition, economic development and education trusts (according to HR 2399, with Senate amendments). The value of the settlement is cited as $50 million, with an additional cession of 3,000 acres to supplement the 630 reserved for the tribe (as of 1993). After this Congressional resolution, issues regarding medical bills, property claims and education costs continued to be contentious.[277] By any account, the Catawba tribe made some gains as a result of the Settlement Act of 1993, but it by no means restored their 144,000 acres.

The second civil rights issue was, of course, segregation. The desegregation of St. Anne School is noted in chapter 11. Rock Hill itself was the locus of a number of protests and picketings in the early 1960s. As the stories of lunch counter sit-ins, "kneel-ins" at segregated churches and a period of civil unrest in the city are retold, the names of a number of peacemakers and personages who served as voices of reason recounted. Among them is Brother David Boone, CO, a member of the Rock Hill Oratory.[278]

When Brother David died on November 5, 2017, he was eighty-four years old. Numerous tributes to him came from leaders of the larger civic community, the black community and adults who had known him in their childhood as an advocate on their behalf. Mayor Douglas Echols called him a "great humanitarian"[279] for his advocacy of human rights to all, for equitable education and for working across color lines and religious lines on behalf of the common good. In November 2019, another Oratorian,

Father Henry Tevlin, was honored as Brother Boone had been—with a plaque placed on Rock Hill's Freedom Walkway. Father Tevlin was the pastor of St. Mary's who drove a van that transported the first children to integrate St. Anne School when it braved the taunts and threats of those opposed to integration.

A number of the parishes in the Rock Hill deanery are staffed by Oratorians, while diocesan priests cover other parishes and missions. The boom in growth in the area has affected the churches in Fort Mill, Indian Land (Lancaster), Lake Wylie and Rock Hill proper, as well as St. Anne School. On a weekend in 2008, St. Anne typically recorded a few over eight hundred parishioners attending Mass. In 2018, there were more than six thousand people registered in the parish.

Outside the city of Rock Hill, Fort Mill's St. Philip Neri Church actually boasts the largest number of parishioners in the deanery, with more than 8,300 registered in the parish in 2018. Named for the founder of the Oratory, the population moving into Fort Mill has been able to support a move from the parish community's first sites of worship in the early 1990s: a Lutheran church in Lake Wylie and a then a Methodist church's fellowship hall. By 1998, the construction of a parish center was complete. It offered worship space, offices and rooms used for religious education and youth ministry (using the Lifeteen model) and a locus for family life ministry. One of the unique features of the parish is its Italian festival, complete with cannoli and wine tasting. This certainly celebrates the heritage of the Oratory's patron saint while it also honors the heritage of a founding pastor. Within ten years, the growing parish needed to build a new sanctuary, and this was dedicated in 2013. As St. Anne Catholic School expanded from its long-standing early childhood and elementary education center in Rock Hill into the secondary level, it quickly needed additional space. St. Philip Neri became the new campus for the high school students in 2017.

Lake Wylie's All Saints Church now enrolls roughly 2,500 parishioners, while Our Lady of Grace in Indian Land was approaching 2,000 as of 2018. Harking back to the area's history, the Indian Land parish's mailing address is Waxhaw Highway, pointing to the name of a tribe other than the Catawba once making a home in the neighborhood. The other parishes of the deanery vary widely in size. There are Divine Savior in York with nearly 900 parishioners and St. Catherine in Lancaster with not quite 750. St. Michael Mission in Great Falls may see a little over 50. Mass attendance in the whole deanery, as recorded over a ten-year period, has held steady, although in some churches it has doubled, in another quadrupled and in still another multiplied six times. Proximity to Charlotte—with its business, educational and recreational opportunities—has prompted new construction and an influx of residents. While the Rock Hill deanery is more compact geographically than some others, it is clearly affected in such a way that considerable growth can reasonably be projected. Meanwhile, ministry goes on, and the population that has been there for generations mixes gifts, talents and customs with new arrivals, whether they are from Vietnam, Brazil or Pennsylvania.

CLOSING REMARKS ON ORIGIN STORIES

Native born or not—tribal peoples originating from Asia and, likely, the area of the Bering Strait, slaves' children and their descendants, southern gentlefolk and generations of plantation and seafaring families—it seems quite clear that if one goes back far enough, those who have affected the history of South Carolina and its seven deaneries arrived from somewhere else. In recent times, an increasingly diverse population has been swelled by a northern incursion from the United States and Canada, along with Europe, as cultural events and multinational corporations have transformed life in the state.

While identifying with the state of South Carolina and the Diocese of Charleston is often as much a matter of affinity as it is one of birth place or arrival, it has to be said that migrations and incursions are part of all of human history. That history is wrapped, for believers, in the grander scheme of salvation history. And salvation history is understood to be God's design that celebrates all of creation as good and reveals God's will to dispense plentiful redemption. To borrow a phrase used occasionally by Bishop Robert Barron, the important outcome of all growth, onslaught and change—including that experienced by the state of South Carolina and the Diocese of Charleston—can and must be, for the believer, an "invasion of grace."

Chapter 17

THE ONE AND THE MANY

A MULTIETHNIC, MULTIRACIAL DIOCESE

The Church credits its identification as "catholic" to St. Ignatius of Antioch, a second-century martyr and Father of the Church. This universality has sparked missionary efforts across all the centuries of the Christian era and has also pressed on Catholic Christians the need to find ways to evangelize and accommodate converts to the faith. Over the centuries, geniuses of inculturation like Saints Boniface, Patrick, Cyril and Methodius, the Jesuit Matteo Ricci and then some of the early religious in the Americas have found ways to respect the language and customs of people as they were being Christianized. America has, from the beginning, had a reputation for being an immigrant country, and the Catholic Church has been notable for its adaptations and service to immigrants from numerous ethnic groups. It also has taken pains to respect the devotions, traditions and cultures of longtime Catholics who have come from various regions around the world. In the past, many of those immigrants were western or eastern European. Today's immigrants come from other nations and peoples, but the impetus to serve and preserve is mighty. That is clearly true in the Church of the Diocese of Charleston.

Father Michael Okere, pastor at St. Martin de Porres in Columbia, occasionally offers Mass in Igbo, one of the languages of Nigeria. At St. Mary Magdalene in Simpsonville, one may regularly come upon a Sunday or vigil Mass in Spanish, Polish or Tagalog. St. Anne in Florence also adds Tagalog to its liturgical languages. In Columbia, at St. John Neumann, there is Mass in Korean, while four parishes celebrate Mass in Vietnamese: St. Thomas in North Charleston, Our Lady of La Vang in Greer, St. Anne in Rock Hill and St. Andrew in Myrtle Beach. If it's Portuguese that one needs, St. Andrew in Myrtle Beach or Immaculate Conception in Goose Creek can meet that need. And at least forty-six parish and mission churches in the diocese offer Spanish Masses every weekend.

Linguistic variety is a necessary thing. One's core language, the language of love, is typically the first language a human being has spoken. No matter how many languages a person might have command of, there is always a root one that most easily speaks to and about God. Latin Masses are offered in the diocese too, most regularly at Prince of Peace in Taylors. For some, Latin is their first Church language, and it carries a kind of mystical reverence that no other language does. So the Church of Charleston makes a mighty effort to meet the needs of the faithful—the point being that the Lord might do what is offered to seeker and sinner in the prophet Hosea: "lead her into the desert and there speak to her heart" (Hosea 2:14).

Statistics only begin to tell a story. In the past few years leading to the bicentennial, the percentage of Catholics in the Charleston diocese who are considered European American, by family ethnic origins, is more than 75 percent. The Hispanic/Latino population is between 16 and 20 percent, with an admission that a number of Spanish-speaking Catholics practice the faith but do not officially register in their parishes. The Vietnamese Catholic population is roughly 2.5 percent, the African American and African Catholic population approximately 2 percent and the combined Filipino, Korean and Pacific Island Catholic count a little over 1 percent. Native American Catholics and part Native American persons make up less than 1 percent of parishioners.

The numbers vary from year to year, and parish personnel do not always find it possible to make an accurate accounting of ethnic and racial origins among their members. Whether or not the numbers reported to the diocese are numerically accurate, there is evidence that a variety of national and racial groups occupy the pews of our churches and missions. The national trend is and has been for greater and greater diversity among American Catholics. As a result, the United States Conference of Catholic Bishops has laid a great emphasis on honoring this multicultural makeup of the Church.

Energy from the USCCB and the Diocese

Mar Muñoz-Vivoso, who serves as executive director of the Secretariat of Cultural Diversity in the Church with the United States Conference of Catholic Bishops, has hailed the exhortation on youth issued by Pope Francis in 2019. She noted that in *Christus Vivit! (Christ Lives!)*, the Holy Father cited numerous examples of young saints and urges commitment to the Gospel, which is forever young. Poking through the exhortation, one finds that the saints and beatified figures whom the Holy Father invokes as models for youth indeed come from Asia, Africa, Europe, South America and North America—and start with the Blessed Mother in the Holy Land. She noted, "I especially appreciated the diversity of ethnic backgrounds, geographical locations, and time in history in which these young saints lived."[280] It has been clear for years that the Church in the United States is keenly aware of its increasing cultural diversity. In recent years, the USCCB has sponsored workshops on "Building Intercultural Competence for Ministers," and in April 2013, the diocese sent a delegation of diocesan leaders to the Southeast Pastoral Institute (SEPI) in Miami to participate in the training.

With an impetus for greater attention to intercultural understanding and ethnic ministries, Bishop Robert Baker in 2002 established the Office of Ethnic Ministries, led by Kathleen Merritt from offices in Greenville. Initially, the office's activities included Hispanic Ministry, the Office of Black Catholics and Vietnamese Ministry. As the diocese was realizing exponential growth in Hispanic presence, Hispanic Ministry was established as a separate office in 2012. The head of that office was added to the diocesan curia on the secretary level in 2014. The Office of Ethnic Ministries has added staff and now has added to Vietnamese ministry Asian and Pacific Islanders, which includes Korean and Filipino Catholics. Native American Ministry was added in 2012. As director, Kathleen Merritt has said, "The Office is committed to organizing ways for the Church as a whole to celebrate its ethnic diversity as a strength of the Church. We are focused on bridging the gap between those in the mainstream culture and those who feel marginalized from the Church because of ethnic or cultural differences." She added, "Diversity and inclusion training initiatives are also a component of the Office."[281]

NATIVE AMERICANS IN THE DIOCESE

The names alone assert the Native American origins of South Carolina. Counties are named Oconee, Saluda and Cherokee; rivers and lakes bear names like Catawba, Edisto, Waccamaw and Kiawah. Towns from Seneca to Yemassee, Awendaw to Cheraw, all can be traced to the Native Americans who were here before Spaniards and Frenchmen landed or the British crafted a colony.

In Monsignor Richard Madden's history of the diocese, he referred to missions of Father Sebastian Montero and Juan Rogel to Native Americans in the 1560s and 1570s. The locations of outreach to members of the Orista tribe and at least one other seem to have been Santa Elena and Anderson County.[282] Missionary presence, or at least Catholic presence, touched Aiken County, near the Savannah River, even earlier. Some of Hernando de Soto's exploratory party came upon a tribe who made them offerings of "a dagger, an axe, and a rosary."[283] In 1606, Bishop Juan de las Cabezas Altamirano arrived in the Southeast "to confirm some 2,000 natives, some of whom came from Carolina."[284] Franciscan friars and Jesuit priests were among those who continued missionary travels and presence at sites called *visitas*. More than a century and a half later, Father Aloysius Folchi, who worked avidly with African American Catholics, initiated visits to the Catawbas of York County and was invited to return by William George, the chief of the tribe. When Folchi left in the late 1870s to join the California missions, the priest resident in Charlotte, Father J.J. O'Connell, reached out, but without the success that Folchi had anticipated.[285]

What seems to have happened with Native Americans in general and Native American Catholics in particular in the Diocese of Charleston is what transpired all over North America. Some who had converted held on to their faith and passed it to ensuing generations. Many lost their Native American identity as their names were anglicized and they intermarried with European Americans, African Americans and Latino Americans. In the midst of these blendings, various religious identities were adopted. The latter years of the twentieth century and the early years of the twenty-first, however, found many Americans avidly pursuing their ancestral roots. Whatever their tribal origin, many with Native American ancestry have taken pride in the canonization in 2012 of Saint Kateri Tekakwitha, commonly known as the Lily of the Mohawks, and one of the patron saints of ecology.

As of a census of parishes in 2018, there were parishioners around the state who identified themselves as Native American. The largest number in one mission is Hampton's St. Mary's, where thirty-eight claimed native origin. The Church's commitment to the First Nation people of the Americas has led to several initiatives in the diocese.

Bishop Robert Baker, formerly the ordinary of this diocese, released a historical novel, *Cacique*, authored with Tony Sands, shortly before he left to lead the Diocese of Birmingham in Alabama. It tells a story of Franciscans and Florida's tribal people. The Office of Ethnic Ministries hosts St. Kateri days and Catholic Native American Heritage celebrations; it also has had men and women, one a chieftain, in tribal dress at its annual Christmas day telecast for Fox Greenville. The office has also encouraged South Carolinians' participation in, and sent representatives to, the annual National Tekakwitha Conference. Springbank Eco-Spirituality and the Arts Center—operated outside Kingstree by Dominican sisters, sisters from other religious congregations and an ecumenical board—offers retreats and sabbaticals. Contemplative Catholic spiritual traditions and Native American rituals are featured there.

Hispanic/Latino Presence

While statistics show nearly one-fifth of South Carolina's Catholics claiming Hispanic/Latino heritage, there are anecdotal reasons to believe it to be much higher. The bishop has long observed that in many locales, more than half the young people being confirmed are Hispanic, and diocesan-wide youth ministry, available in English-speaking or Spanish-speaking modes, has a highly visible presence of Hispanics. There is also the fact that regularly attending Spanish-speaking Catholics are not always registered parishioners, as mentioned earlier. Some are wary of giving identifying information, even to the Church, in a time when immigration is a hot-button topic and law enforcement officers are rumored to have overstepped boundaries, even on church properties. Also, not all parishes are able to track or even estimate the racial and ethnic backgrounds of their parishioners for their annual reports to the diocese. Then there is also the case of migrant workers, who join in the activities of local parishes for seasons but are sporadic as their places of employment move up and down the Atlantic seaboard.

The Office of Hispanic Ministry, under the leadership of Vicar for Hispanic Ministry Father Teo Trujillo and Secretary for Hispanic Ministry Dr. Gustavo Valdez, developed a Pastoral Plan for Hispanic Ministry

2015–2020, "Together in Christ," or "Juntos en Cristo." It is the fruit of a yearlong consultation around the diocese. In its historical notes, the first observation it makes is that the Oblate Sisters of Providence, cited here in chapter 8 for their ministry to the African American community, actually undertook exploring the prospectus for Hispanic ministry in the diocese in 1964. They were soon joined by the OLM community and the Sisters of St. Mary of Namur, along with priests—Father Michael Kaney and another known only as Father Tornero—with a concentration on offering a summer school for migrants and providing outreach to migrant camps. By the late 1970s and into the 1980s, Hispanic ministry grew around the state, and people from South Carolina participated in training with Southeast Pastoral Institute (SEPI) and also the Second National Pastoral Hispanic Encounter (*Encuentro*), which was spearheaded by then-archbishop Joseph Bernardin. In 1990, Bishop Thompson appointed layman Juan Carlos Gomez to serve as diocesan director for Hispanic ministry; after a hiatus in leadership, Bishop Baker, in 1999, named a new director, Sister Guadalupe Stump, RSM, and began appointing priests as vicar for Hispanic ministry. "Sister Lupe," as she was called, held the position until ill health overtook her. Dr. Gustavo Valdez is her current successor.

A number of initiatives rapidly developed. The central office for the ministry was set up in Columbia, while each deanery retained its own coordinators with its own schedule of meetings of parish leaders. A leader for Hispanic youth ministry was appointed in 2009, as were a coordinator of communications and a coordinator for adult faith formation. In short order, a Hispanic radio station (Revive.fm) and a rigorous catechetical program for training in pastoral ministry, the Spanish School of Faith, was set up, the latter in the spring of 2015. Hundreds of Spanish-speaking Catholics have participated in this formation program and have been awarded certificates at the conclusion of the three-year training period. Additionally, an increasing number of aspirants and their wives have participated actively in the diocese's diaconate formation program, while bilingual Hispanics have been accepted into seminaries.

As with any ethnic ministry, Hispanic ministry is committed to maintaining families' faith traditions and expressions. As a result, a growing number of parishes have become very familiar with the roses and Aztec costumes and depictions of St. Juan Diego that accompany the Feast of Our Lady of Guadalupe, now patroness of the Americas. The late Advent *posadas* proceed to open the doors to Christmas, and some parishes offer a dramatic Passion play and Stations of the Cross in the Spanish language or in a bilingual offering. Most English-speaking Catholics now know something about Diá de Muertos (Day of the Dead) and Cinco de Mayo celebrations. Some understand the religious significance of the presentation of three-year-old girls and of quinceañeras. Parish missions are conducted in English and Spanish, and *Emaus* retreat programs are repeated, with good participation.

Many of these observances are distinctive to Mexican Catholics, but it must be noted that the Hispanic/Latino population of the diocese includes Guatemalans and other Central Americans, along with Argentinians, Ecuadorans, Venezuelans, Colombians and others. At the same time that traditions are honored and preserved, the goal of the Office of Hispanic Ministry is stated thus: "The Hispanic Ministry Pastoral Plan 2015–2020 has the *mission* to help the Hispanic community become fully integrated in the life of the Church as they grow in the understanding of the Catholic faith and holiness….In communion with the mission, this Pastoral Plan has the *vision* of helping the Hispanic community in the process of being integrated with the English speaking community." In collaboration with the Catholic Schools Office and Superintendent Sandra Leatherwood, Hispanic ministry has worked to encourage greater enrollment of Hispanic/Latino students in Catholic schools, and the diocese has sponsored several gatherings of principals and others to facilitate this goal.

African American Catholic Heritage and Celebrations

Considerable background on African American Catholic history in the Diocese of Charleston has appeared in chapter 8 of this work. In addition to the matter of parishes and schools, it is important to note the various programs and initiatives the Office of Ethnic Ministries has sponsored and fostered.

Along with special black history and devotional days that take place around the diocese, the annual diocesan Black Catholic Heritage Day is a well-attended event that has drawn such luminaries as Bishop Edward Braxton of Belleville, Illinois, as keynoters. Bishop Braxton's pastoral letter of December 2016, "The Racial Divide in the United States," has been a continued cause for meetings and material for reflection around the diocese. For Black Catholic History Month in November and Black History Month in February, there are special activities planned by the office. A five-year plan, "Living Like Saints: A Pastoral Plan and Resources for the

Evangelization of African Americans in the Roman Catholic Diocese of Charleston 2013–2018," has guided activities and new efforts. To continue the energy of that plan, the office has subscribed to the 2017 National Black Catholic Congress adoption in 2017 of a "Pastoral Plan of Action" for African American Catholics. In July 2019, Bishop Guglielmone appointed a new assistant director for African American Evangelization in the person of Sister Roberta Fulton, SSMN. A monthly newsletter gives an update on events and celebrations around the state, and the site also offers links to historical essays and provides links to various websites and YouTube® features on black history and African American Catholic activities.

The Office of Ethnic Ministries follows the lead of National Black Catholic Congress, while it also develops its own initiatives and strategic plans. The five-year plan for this diocese, which focused on the years 2013–18, identified pillars of action for African American outreach. These pillars have ongoing implementation: (1) promoting holiness of life, (2) cherishing life and dignity of the human person, (3) walking with the saints, (4) engaging in parish life and evangelization, (5) being faith-informed, (6) sustaining schools in historically African American neighborhoods, (7) reaching out to the next generations, (8) promoting Church vocations, (9) getting married and staying married and (10) promoting the social apostolate. New programs and plans are underway, and as part of the bicentennial celebration, the Office of Ethnic Ministries joined the College of Charleston to host a gathering of and dialogue with black Catholic theologians from academic institutions from across the country in October 2019. The bicentennial has brought on a broad-based effort to bringing the national impetus to local.

The Irish Travelers

St. Edward Church in Murphy Village, near North Augusta, South Carolina, is located in a place unlike any other in the state. It is a tinker settlement, birthed among a group that came to the United States in the later 1840s, the time of the famed Irish potato famine that caused 1 million or more people to die of starvation. Irish immigrants fled to this country, and some of them—the ones known as tinkers, travelers and even "white gypsies"—crisscrossed the country for decades.[286] They were peddlers and repairmen who carted their whole families in horse-drawn wagons. The Travelers who came to the North Augusta area were ministered to by Father Joseph

Murphy, who was the pastor at Our Lady of Peace Church in the 1940s. A parish church intended for their use was dedicated in December 1964 by the administrator of the diocese, Monsignor Joseph Bernardin, shortly before the arrival of Bishop Unterkoefler.[287]

The Travelers are a unique group practicing the Catholic faith that is their heritage but adopting only some contemporary ways of life. In terms of trade, the Travelers are characteristically nomadic,[288] so for much of the year they travel from town to town repairing roofs, selling flooring materials, painting houses and barns, doing road work and general handyman labor. They return to their settlements (such as the one in South Carolina or another in Texas), where their lifestyle can only be described as clannish. Arranged marriages persist. Because the children are engaged so young, there are always legal concerns. Not surprisingly, the Department of Social Services has launched occasional investigations to ensure that children are receiving proper schooling and are not in underage marriages, which would be considered a form of abuse or exploitation. Elizabeth Blanchet, a roving photographer, found herself greeted with suspicion when she made a visit to Murphy Village in 2018. She did receive hospitality from two women, however, and was allowed to photograph some of the mansions that the Travelers have constructed, as well as a mobile home or two that persist on the poorer side of the commune. Blanchet also photographed statuary representing the Blessed Mother and angels that adorn homes and yards.[289]

While the diocese has provided a parish church and pastors since the 1960s, there has not been a formal ethnic ministry to the Travelers. Some send their children to Our Lady of Peace Catholic School in North Augusta, and a few Traveler women have helped staff the school. Others may homeschool. Overall, Blanchet is among the many who find the Irish Travelers of South Carolina to be an overtly religious but generally very "reclusive" group—much more so, she says, than the Travelers she has met and photographed in the United Kingdom. She also noted that the Travelers can readily revert to their own language, Cant, which Brendan Koerner described as a mixture of "Gaelic, English, Greek, and Hebrew," thus inaccessible to outsiders.[290]

A Vietnamese Parish

As standoffish as the Travelers can be, the Vietnamese Catholics of South Carolina are warm, publicly engaged and involved in both parish and diocesan ministry. As mentioned earlier, four parishes—two in the Piedmont and two in the coastal area—regularly offer Masses in Vietnamese. In Greer, in the Greenville deanery, Our Lady of La Vang Church was dedicated in November 2016 by Bishop Robert E. Guglielmone. The site of a former Baptist church, Our Lady of La Vang is a place where celebrations feature children in colorful scarves, drumming and the appearance of decorative paper dragons, similar to ones many citizens associate with the Chinese New Year.[291]

Vietnamese Catholics arrived in many areas of the United States during and after the war that racked their nation and the United States for years. By the early 1980s, Masses in Vietnamese were being celebrated in the diocese in North Charleston, Greenville, Anderson, Rock Hill, Walhalla and Lexington, as well as in family homes. It took more than thirty years for the parish in Greer to develop, but that did not deter Vietnamese families from celebrating their historic faith.

At one time part of French Indochina, Vietnam is now officially a Communist nation. The number of Vietnamese Catholics has always been small, but their faith has its roots in the work of missionaries who arrived in their land in the sixteenth and seventeenth centuries. In the United States, many Vietnamese arrived as refugees, and several thousand of them or their descendants live in South Carolina. Many of these are Catholics, loyal to a hard-won faith that estimates it lost more than 130,000 to martyrdom in Vietnam from the early seventeenth through the later nineteenth centuries.[292] The more than 1,500 Vietnamese Catholics in the diocese have annual celebrations either on parish or diocesan level. Two major feasts occur in the month of November, that of Our Lady of La Vang, celebrated on November 22, and that of the Vietnamese martyrs, celebrated on November 24 in memory of those who died for their faith. Along with these November dates marked by Vietnamese Catholics in the diocese, they also maintain the long-standing custom of processions and presentations of flowers during the month of May, which is dedicated to Our Lady. Those born in Vietnam cherish the ways in which many villages honored Mary in that month, and the statues they bear are ones depicting her in the familiar garb of Our Lady of La Vang.

Michael Tran, who is of Vietnamese heritage and serves as assistant director for the Office of Ethnic Ministries in the diocese, oversees ministry to all Asian and Pacific Islanders in the Diocese of Charleston. In 2018, the office published a booklet entitled "Love Drives Us to Do This: The History of Vietnamese Catholics in South Carolina," in a bilingual (English and Vietnamese) edition.

Filipinos, Koreans, Pacific Islanders and Other Immigrants

As noted earlier, there are now Masses regularly celebrated in Tagalog, a dominant language of the Philippines, and Korean at several places in the diocese. The Office of Ethnic Ministries supports special religious and festal activities from these diverse people.

The recent shift in origin of newcomers to the Diocese of Charleston always stands in the background of a long history of reception of immigrants. As has often been said, America is a nation of immigrants, and the Catholic Church has been home to immigrants for all of America's history. Sometimes there were ethnic conflicts and rivalries. At other times, one immigrant group welcomed and cooperated with another. The Spanish settled briefly at Santa Elena and came into conflict with indigenous tribes. The Irish and the French landed in Charleston, and it was not without stress. Monsignor Madden's history noted that an early fracturing and even interdict at old St. Mary's in Charleston took place when the archbishop of Baltimore (who was then also shepherding the Carolinas and Georgia) sent a French priest, Father Joseph Picot de Cloriviere, to replace Father Simon Gallagher, an Irish priest.[293] When there was an influx of Italian immigrants in Charleston in the 1870s, "the sons of sunny Italy" staged a St. Joseph Day celebration that started at the Hibernian Hall and ended with a speech by an Irish pastor.[294] That was because they had yet to acquire a chaplain or guest priest of Italian ancestry and needed a physical space to host their event. Annals of the diocese show that, over the years, more Italian, Irish and then Lebanese and Czech (Bohemian) immigrants arrived to work as stonecutters and in phosphate mines, mills, mercantile endeavors and railroad and tunnel projects. In every case, the Church of Charleston struggled to minister to these varied groups. When they lacked resources or clergy, somehow the people found a way to pass the faith on to a next generation while they continued to pray for priestly presence. They also had an avid interest in celebrating, as best they could, the customs and devotions of the old country—including praying and singing in their original language even as they were becoming Americanized.

It is that balance of cherished traditions and new initiatives that the Office of Ethnic Ministries and the diocese have taken pains to uphold.

Chapter 18

THE FRANCIS PHENOMENON AND THE TWENTY-FIRST CENTURY

The two papal dramas of 2013 were the resignation of Pope Benedict XVI in February and the election in March of an Argentinian successor, Cardinal Jorge Bergoglio. A little after the lunch meal at the bishop's residence on Broad Street in Charleston, members of the diocesan curia were preparing to leave at the conclusion of their meeting on March 13 when Don Glover, the bishop's chef and frequent caterer of diocesan events, came in to say that there was about to be a papal announcement. The group made its way to a parlor, turned on the television, watched the replay of the tell-tale white smoke over the Sistine Chapel and awaited the announcement, "Habemus papam: We have a pope." In short order, the figure in white cassock and zucchetto appeared, and his new name was announced: Pope Francis. He was the third consecutive non-Italian elected to the papacy, and he appeared both slightly stunned and in need of a few moments to collect himself. He asked the crowd to bless and pray for him.

Born to an Italian family who had immigrated to Argentina, Cardinal Bergoglio was a Jesuit who, in his life before novitiate and seminary, was known to enjoy the tango and, as an adult, remained an aficionado of literature, had served as a teacher and administrator and was a personality distinguished by a down-to-earth style and a dislike for pomp and circumstance. Not long after the public announcement, he went to his hotel to pay his conclave bill and determined that he really did not want to live in isolated splendor in the papal apartments but to retain quarters, reportedly two rooms, at the Domus Sanctae Marthae next door.

Like every Catholic in the world, Bishop Guglielmone and the members of the curia had little idea as to what to expect of this fascinating new pope.

His Style

Pope Francis has sprung for pizza parties for the homeless and selected cardinals from places that never boasted any. Bishops and archbishops from places like Huehuetenango, Guatemala; Rabat, Morocco; Managua, Nicaragua; Ouagadougou, Burkina Faso; Abidjan, Côte d'Ivoire; and Yangon, Myanmar, are now in the College of Cardinals and lined up to be among the next papal electors. Typical of his colorful expression, Francis cautioned the first twenty cardinals he appointed that their role should not go to their heads as overindulgence in grappa might. He charged them with keeping fixed on the cross of Christ.[295] The pope from South America has made it a point to enact what theologians like Karl Rahner and Walbert Bühlman had predicted in the mid- and later twentieth century: the likelihood that the Church of the third millennium would be dominated—and potentially converted from lethargy—by people of faith from those nations considered Third World, the vast majority of them from the Southern Hemisphere.

At the annual Holy Thursday feet-washing, Pope Francis has deliberately chosen men and women, convicts and street people, Catholics and persons of non-Christian faiths, to be recipients of his ministrations—in keeping, it seems, with Christ's Gospel message that one should invite the poor, the blind and the lame to banquets, those who could not repay.

Phrases from his encyclicals and exhortations on joy and holiness have been oft repeated: reminders to clergy that the confessional is not a "torture chamber" and admittance to sacraments not a "tollhouse"[296] and cautions to the faithful that they not come across like "mummies in a museum," treasuring a stale old faith,[297] and that pessimists and "sourpusses" are a poor advertisement for the Gospel.[298] He invited all to respond to the call to holiness with joy, humor and a simplicity that both recognizes and aspires to become one of the "saints next door."[299] Pope Francis is more comfortable riding city buses than in limousines, and he has made it clear that sanctity is accessible to all. The call to holiness, as attested by the pontiff, includes a love of life, a love of people and a love of sea, earth and sky. His personal example and his exhortation have affected the people of the Diocese of Charleston and the manner in which the Church sets priorities and communicates.

In both his style and his substance, Pope Francis seems to be living out a declaration that St. John Paul II made in his first encyclical, *Redemptor Hominis: The Redeemer of Man*, issued in 1978, and repeated a number of times in his writings: "The human person is the way for the Church."

HIS SUBSTANCE

Pope Francis has neither the charismatic theological and philosophical genius of St. John Paul II nor the scholarly care and reserve of Pope Benedict XVI, his two immediate predecessors. What he does have, however, is a vigorous and highly articulate commitment to pressing the importance of a vibrant and real faith life that prizes encounter. Contrary to some of the media iconography of Francis, he is far from a maverick in terms of his theology. His writings reveal how grounded in Catholic tradition and scripture he is and has been. What is different is his style of delivery and his emphasis.

The Primacy of Faith

The very first encyclical of his papacy, *Lumen Fidei*, issued amid the Year of Faith proclaimed by Pope Benedict for 2013 (on the fiftieth anniversary of Vatican II), was clearly dependent on materials Benedict himself had begun to amass for an encyclical. It is, at the same time, also distinctly that of Francis. In speaking of faith, Pope Francis emphasizes past and future, seeing and hearing, receiving and unifying. Relationality and reason together converge in faith in "the real Jesus."[300] The pope makes it clear that faith presumes and rests on objective truth and that subjective truth claims, where one person's truth differs from another's willy-nilly, not only make no logical sense but also make faith impossible. Thus, Pope Francis speaks of how the risen Christ offers light and life and proves not only God's ongoing presence and involvement "in this world" but also "God's reliability."[301]

For Francis, obedience to truth and contemplation of Christ make church membership and attendance vital. The Church provides, he says, "equilibrium, the space needed to sustain." The Church, through its magisterium—its teaching role—also provides guidance for the project of theology as St. Anselm long ago described it: "Faith seeking understanding." Faith, Francis teaches, is and must be passed on and nurtured and therefore is inherently relational, familial—with creedal beliefs, sacraments, the moral life and prayer essential to growth in love. In defining the person of faith, the religious person, Pope Francis speaks of one who can see with the eyes of Christ and thus "see signs of God in the daily experiences of life," including the events of the natural world and the mysteries of the cosmos.[302] Seeing with the eyes of Christ assumes, however, that one also sees with the eyes of a community of believers while also knowing that the unexpected may appear at any time on the horizon. Pope Francis calls the religious person "a wayfarer," one who is always ready "to find the God of perpetual surprise" amid the firm foundation of revealed truth and a life of grace.[303] Francis teaches that Christian faith counts on respect—respect for truth that simultaneously arises from and translates into respect for family life, respect for all humanity and respect for the created world.

The imperative to strengthen faith and the community of faith has certainly been heard in the diocese, as new energy has been given to evangelizing, publicly celebrating faith and ushering into parishes a variety of retreat and renewal programs like Christ Renews His Parish, *Emaus* (among the Hispanic community), Stephen Ministries, Formed (an online faith development resource) and many more.

Another gesture of Pope Francis profoundly affected the diocese. While he entered onto the world stage amid a Year of Faith and made very clear his commitment to all the core tenets of faith, barely two years later he announced an Extraordinary Year of Mercy, beginning on Divine Mercy Sunday in 2015. The pope who took pains to reassure those focused on orthodoxy also wanted to highlight the Church's commitment to pastoral care. Before that, however, he paved the way with the apostolic exhortation *Evangelii Gaudium* (*The Joy of the Gospel*) closing the Year of Faith.

The Work of Evangelizing

It is in *The Joy of the Gospel* that Francis takes up some cajoling and chiding. It is very clear that he sees the Church's essential mission to the margins as sometimes easily overlooked, particularly when the faithful become protective and self-absorbed. He issues a challenge to evangelizers to "take on the 'smell of the sheep'" and to attend to engagement in the real lives of real people.[304] He counsels that those who teach and preach must be attentive to the situations in which people live the totality of their lives and that their mission must be holistic, committed to "the integral promotion of each human being," excluding no one.[305] By word and deed, Pope Francis demonstrates that spreading the Gospel in this day and time is every bit as messy—and sometimes risky—as it was in the time of Jesus. Religion isn't private, and what Americans refer to as "preaching to the choir" is something Francis challenges the Church to eschew. Outreach to the poor and otherwise disadvantaged and works of justice must be linked to evangelization. Occasional "small personal gestures," what Pope Francis terms "a kind of charity à la carte," cannot suffice. Living "from the heart of the Gospel" is "being in the heart of the people," Francis tells us.[306] Evangelizing is truly a Marian act, born of the kind of maternal care the Blessed Mother offered to St. Juan Diego as she revealed herself, *La Morena*, as Our Lady of Guadalupe, says Pope Francis.

In the Diocese of Charleston, deliberation has continued as Marian devotions have been coupled with pro-life action and ethnic celebrations. Evangelization plans undertaken in parishes and service organizations have also emphasized the mixture of proclaiming the faith with healing wounds and tending needs.

The Path of Mercy

The path of mercy is one of the ways in which the Gospel spreads. People see genuine goodness in others and receive its benefits. As a celebration of the fiftieth anniversary of the conclusion of the Second Vatican Council, Francis called for a year dedicated to mercy. In the bull *Misericordiae Vultus* (*The Face of Mercy*), Pope Francis inaugurated a year of special invitations to the faith, interreligious encounter, opportunities for sacramental reconciliation, pilgrimages and indulgences all conditioned on "opening our hearts to those living on the outermost fringes of society."[307] The Kingdom of God requires Christians to be missionary disciples, as Pope Francis often says, and being missionary means linking our efforts to convert hearts and move souls with definite steps taken to improve the practical lot in life of all of God's children. That means that believers engage in both spiritual and corporal works of mercy. The pope specified the time from December 8, 2015, the Feast of the Immaculate Conception, to November 20, 2016, that year's celebration of the Solemnity of Christ the King, as the Year of Mercy.

In terms of spiritual works of mercy, Francis asked dioceses around the world to designate pilgrimage sites and offer plenary indulgences connected with pilgrimage, prayer and penance. In the Diocese of Charleston, nine pilgrimage sites were named: the Cathedral of St. John the Baptist, St. Michael in Murrells Inlet, St. Anthony in Florence, St. Gregory the Great in Bluffton, St. Peter in Columbia, St. Mary in Greenville, St. Mary Help of Christians in Aiken, the Oratory in Rock Hill and the Shrine of Our Lady of South Carolina, Our Lady of Joyful Hope, in Kingstree. Each of these created or designated a "holy door" through which pilgrims would pass. The whole idea, as advanced by Pope Francis and, in turn, by the bishops, was to offer forgiveness on a grand scale to souls suffering the pain of remorse.

The other segment of the year of mercy was the emphasis on encountering those on the margins and taking steps to relieve their sufferings. Thus it was not and is not surprising to hear Francis speaking out passionately on behalf of refugees and condemning both personal selfishness and the strongly isolationist tones of current politics.

Ordinary parishioners and diocesan personnel alike have been particularly moved by the constant emphasis on the underserved and the neglected issuing from Pope Francis since the conclave of cardinals elected him. Kathy Schmugge—who has served for a number of years as director of family life for the diocese, pro-life activist and champion of outreach to women suffering post-abortion trauma—has personally encountered Pope Francis at the canonization of Saints John Paul II and John XXIII in April 2014. In his homily at the joint canonization, Francis had noted how each Holy Father had looked on the wounds of Christ and found hope and joy in them. She related the concrete effect this observation, along with the previous example and exhortation from Francis, had on her:

> *Walking from St. Peter's, I saw a beggar whose legs were twisted and he had disfiguring tumors on his face. My sister later mentioned that he looked like he had leprosy. I knew he needed more than a few coins, so without reservation, I reached down and hugged him. I wanted him to know that his wounds were beautiful and his life mattered. He never raised his eyes, but I could see that he was crying. I know that I would never have thought to do this if it had not been for the homily and Pope Francis' frequent example of modeling Christ who goes out looking for the sheep and doesn't mind smelling like his sheep.*[308]

When Pope Francis speaks about evangelization and mercy, he expressed concern about what he terms "spiritual 'desertification'" in modern life.[309] But he is also, as it turns out, just as strongly worried about environmental desertification, climate change and the degradation of the planet.

Care for the Earth

It was St. John Paul II who named Saint Francis of Assisi the patron saint of ecology. Over several decades, bishops' conferences around the world had sounded the alarm over abuses of land and sea and raised concerns about the wastes wrought by rampant consumerism and acquisitiveness. The bishops of the Philippines in *What Is Happening to Our Beautiful Land?* (1987) had gone so far as to identify ecological concerns as "the ultimate pro-life issue." When John Paul released *The Gospel of Life* in 1995, he identified abortion, euthanasia and all killing of innocents as the gravest of sins against life, while also naming other sins like human trafficking, abuse of the poor and environmental damage as being both symptoms and outcomes of the what he called the fearsome reign of a "culture of death." Pope Francis issued the encyclical *Laudato Si'* (*On Care for Our Common Home*) on Pentecost Sunday 2015.

The issuance of an entire encyclical on ecological issues was not without controversy, but it was also not without precedent, given the concerns already voiced by the pope's predecessors and fellow bishops of the world. From the outset, the Holy Father wields a double-edged sword. He begins by quoting the God-praising and creation-affirming "Canticle of the Sun," a famous prayer of Saint Francis of Assisi. Then, in a quick turn, he laments what he terms humanity's "irresponsible use and abuse" of the natural world. Here, listed in bullets, are calls to action from His Holiness as the search for some remedy ensues. People of good will ought to, in summary:

- take an honest look at how present choices and actions affect the future of the earth;
- acknowledge that carelessness and greed have damaged the world of nature and deeply hurt the poor;
- confront the compelling evidence that climate change is happening and that it is likely that we will be faced with people who will become environmental refugees;
- recognize that access to clean, fresh water is a human right and not a commodity for marketing;
- preserve biodiversity, especially by caring for the health of the Amazon and Congo River Basins;
- respect the interconnections and interdependence among species, human and nonhuman;
- realize that urban sprawl and 'round-the-clock technology both tend to isolate us from nature and depersonalize and desensitize us;
- hear God's call for personal conversion, civic action and what His Holiness calls "a cultural revolution" that will resist what previous popes and bishops have called a "culture of death";
- focus on the needs of families and the living conditions needed to foster well-being;

- renounce wastefulness, selfishness, overconsumption and demands for instant gratification;
- engage in a vigorous quest for non-polluting, renewable sources of energy;
- exercise responsible citizenship by working to build societies dedicated to human persons, human dignity and wise stewardship of our God-given gifts.

Pope Francis makes it clear, in line with magisterial voices before him, that wise use of the goods of planet Earth is a moral imperative. There is also a healthy eco-spirituality to embrace. Pope Francis makes it clear that beauty is essential for the human soul. If we were to translate his notes into South Carolina terms, we would find him reminding us that we delight in the Atlantic coast, the farm fields of the Midlands, the sandhills and the rich rise of the Piedmont into the Blue Ridge, all of which soothe spirits and raise minds and hearts to God.

But like St. Francis, the pope reminds us that the poor are entitled to life, flourishing and bounty. The Holy Father decries the way in which contemporary culture can prize progress and creature comforts and still affect beloved landscapes so that they "look more and more like an immense pile of filth."[310] Worse, he cautions against evading the truth about how overconsumption and clear-cutting and waste contribute to sickness and death. For South Carolinians, then, it isn't just the armadillo and deer kill bloodying roads. It's also the wheeze and wobble of folks who live in the rusted-out trailers and rotted shacks off parkways and interstates. And it's the children who work fields and sweatshops and drink polluted water halfway around the world who suffer from our affluence as they are paid a pittance to produce our disposable goods. He notes that there is a necessary, God-ordained link between "the cry of the earth and the cry of the poor."[311] Humans are responsible for care of God's good earth, and they also bear blame for damages to it and carelessness about the lives of one another.

In the Diocese of Charleston, there has not been a massive ecological movement, but there certainly have been a number of ways in which individuals and institutions have been promoting conservation and preservation, especially in recent years. When projects for building churches and schools have been presented to both the diocesan Building and Renovations Commission and government agencies, energy efficiency has been a priority. So, too, has preservation or remediation of wetlands and provision for appropriate landscaping. Recycling is part of the institutional culture. Children and youth have been engaged in cleanup campaigns and have also been introduced to tree planting, garden tending and beautification projects, especially as STEM (science/technology/engineering/math) programs and their variant STREAM (science/technology/religion/engineering/arts/math) projects have entered their schools. Parish volunteers don fluorescent green jackets to pick up litter on roadsides. And a number of religious education programs and lay associations have held study sessions on Catholic environmental ethics in general and *Laudato Si'* in particular.

Pope Francis emphasizes that a truly Catholic spirituality will praise God with and in all of creation. But it will also call us to repentance for harms done. There is, he avers, "a true ecological debt" that "exists, particularly between the global north and south."[312] Repentance will lead contrite hearts to renew and reform. Simplifying our lives and spending more time in thankful contemplation should not only bring more personal peace but also help heal and preserve the planet. The pope invites people of prayer to ask the Blessed Mother "to enable us to look at this world with eyes of wisdom."[313] For our Holy Father, eco-spirituality is biblical, traditional, Franciscan and Marian. Most of all, it is devoted to making the good we have received better for handing on.

Love and Family

In the midst of national and international upheavals concerning the understanding of gender, intimacy, marital love and family, Pope Francis hosted a synod on the family and, in 2016, issued the Post-Synodal Exhortation *Amoris Laetitia (On Love in the Family)*. While strongly upholding the understanding of marriage as a loving bond between a man and a woman open to bringing forth new life, the exhortation also takes note of numerous pastoral concerns. The sacrament of matrimony remains an indissoluble commitment and a gift whereby the couple minister to each other. For the integrity of the sacrament, good spiritual and practical preparation is imperative, and education for "responsible parenthood," a phrase often used since the papacy of St. Paul VI, is a church obligation. Since families continue to be understood as "domestic churches," they are owed support in catechesis, counseling and practical means to prevent families' affliction with "discrimination, poverty, exclusion, and violence."[314]

The synod acknowledged the common experiences of family breakdown and divorce and admitted that sometimes separations are necessary to protect a spouse and children. It also spoke to the pressure brought to bear on people of faith to recognize homosexual "marriages," now legal in many societies. To this it simply responds that churches should not be put in situations where assistance to the poor or to their clients is conditioned on acceptance of gay marriage, given Catholic understanding of God's will for families and human society resting on monogamous heterosexual unions and stable family units. Dealing with death, family disruptions and tragedies, such as those caused by addiction, are matters people of faith need to be engaged with. So, too, does the education of children for good citizenship and for coping skills. The latter requires what the pope calls "patient realism" and "ethical formation."[315] In addressing the escalating prevalence of indulgence in pornography and sexual libertinism, the synod advocates for well-thought-out and solidly values-based sexual education programs.

A number of representatives of the Diocese of Charleston and family members of parishioners and diocesan staff attended the World Meeting of Families in Philadelphia in September 2015. Those attending were devoted to preserving both health and a sense of the sacred as they supported this pro-life and pro-family gathering. Dr. Michael Martocchio, interim secretary for evangelization and education for the diocese as of this writing, was one of those attendees. With his wife and three young daughters, he traveled to the World Meeting. He was doubly moved by the pope's demeanor throughout the visit and by the power of his message. Martocchio noted the pains Francis took to meet with victims of sexual abuse, immigrants and impoverished children as he advocated for religious liberty and spoke of the family. "All the love God has in himself, all the beauty God has in himself, all the truth God has in himself, he entrusts to the family," Martocchio remembered the pontiff saying.

Martocchio was impressed, too, with the very practical awareness of the pope. The pope alluded to what Martocchio recalled him describing as "the headaches and the flying dishes of marriage," noting that love in the family is incarnated in a less than ideal world. Francis, following the insights of many catechetical leaders who have noted that the *abuela*, the grandmother, is often the beacon of religious light for children, made it a point at the conference—and a point Martocchio keenly has internalized—that families are called to take "special care…for children and grandparents, who link one in the present to God's creative love exercised in both the past and the future. Connecting the generations within our families is a real way of participating in God's work of salvation history."[316]

While much of the World Meeting emphasized upholding the importance of Church teaching and strengthening family life, it also was very honest about the fracturing that has occurred in life ethics and the understanding of marriage and family. In his written reflections, the Holy Father emphasizes the importance of providing pastoral care. He urges ministers and the faithful to find means, one way or another, of keeping doors and lines of communication open so that people in situations that don't align with Church teaching might at some point find their way back. He declares, on the basis of long-held understanding of factors mitigating personal responsibility and freedom, that "it can no longer be simply said that all those in any 'irregular' situation are living in a state of mortal sin and are deprived of sanctifying grace....Saint Thomas Aquinas himself recognized that someone may possess grace and charity, yet not be able to exercise any one of the virtues well."[317] In keeping with his delicate balance of adhering to traditional understanding of God's will for the human race and to the call of mercy, Pope Francis counsels that the whole Church is charged to recall this guiding principle: "The Bride of Christ must pattern her behavior after the Son of God who goes out to everyone without exception. She knows that Jesus himself is the shepherd of the hundred, not just of the ninety-nine. He loves them all. On the basis of this realization, it will become possible for 'the balm of mercy to reach everyone, believers and those far away, as a sign that the kingdom of God is already present in our midst.'"[318] Again, Pope Francis appeals to mercy, to grace and to tenderness. All of these, of course, are essential to a life of holiness.

Holiness and Wholeness

Every Catholic theoretically would like to think that some day he or she will be among the multitude celebrated every November 1, All Saints' Day. The desire to be a saint, however, is not something often spoken of in terms of everyday life. No matter how good one's religious education may be or may have been, there is a tendency to think that holiness is somehow inaccessible to people living ordinary lives. Pope Francis has attempted to disabuse people of that kind of thinking.

Gaudete et Exsultate: Rejoice and Be Glad, the 2018 Apostolic Exhortation subtitled *On the Call to Holiness in Today's World*, includes some less well-known references. Francis invokes the memory of old heresies and gives them contemporary application. He cautions against excessively intellectualizing faith, as well as succumbing to what Protestant critics term "works righteousness." Having all our theological concepts in order is no more saving—and no holier—than thinking that piling up good works earns us credits toward a spiritual diploma.

What Francis is most interested in—and what he most advises—is that genuine holiness is wholesome, holistic, humble in the earthy sense and joyful. Holy people embrace and live the Beatitudes and unashamedly go "against the flow...counter to the way things are usually done in our world."[319] Holy people are unimpressed by worldly standards of success and understand that advocating and acting on behalf of "the innocent unborn...the poor, those already born, the destitute, the abandoned and the underprivileged, the vulnerable infirm and elderly exposed to covert euthanasia, the victims of human trafficking, new form of slavery, and every form of rejection"[320] are both an expression and evidence of holiness.

Holiness requires hospitality, not a remote disengagement from the travails of the world. Being in the world but not of it, as the Savior phrased it, seems to be the key, as Francis urges against the temptation to be taken in by the pleasure-seeking and the acquisitiveness fostered by materialistic, secular cultures.

The models of holiness he offers are an interesting array. Some—like Saints John Chrysostom, Augustine, Thomas Aquinas, John of the Cross and Ignatius Loyola—are predictable. Others are lesser known: Blessed Maria Gabriella Sagheddu, a Trappistine committed to Christian unity; St. Teresa Benedicta of the Cross, earlier known as Edith Stein, the Jewish scholar and convert executed by the Nazis; Cardinal Francis Xavier Nguyên van Thuân, imprisoned by Communists in Vietnam for thirteen years; and a line of female saints who are doctors of the Church. Francis reminds the faithful that persecution and martyrdom are always possibilities for those who pursue holiness and hold fast to the core of Christ. Somehow he always returns to mercy and care for the least of the brothers and sisters. "Holiness," Francis insists, "is not about swooning in mystic rapture"[321] but is hands-on and willing to get mussed and grubby.

A passion for life, boldness for the sake of the reign of the Lord and an accessible holiness are marks of the new evangelizer and the saint of the day. The combination of emphasis on evangelization and holiness has inspired several leaders in the diocese to consider means of implementing new resources and train personnel for the new evangelization. If some of these truly have their intended effect, they may offer the most appeal to disaffected youth. That disaffection has been a cause for alarm, as there are persuasive studies indicating that as many as 80 percent of young people under the age of twenty-five have left the practice of the Catholic and other Christian faiths.

The Living Christ and Vibrant Youth

On the Solemnity of the Annunciation in 2019, Pope Francis issued *Christus Vivit: Christ Lives,* an exhortation responding to the Synod on Youth, which preceded it. It is addressed to youth but also to "the entire people of God." From the outset, Francis focuses on the aliveness of Christ, the fact that his earthly mission was conducted while he himself was a young adult and that there is and must be an everlasting newness about the faith and its expressions in Church and in the world.

Deacon Jerry White, director of youth, young adult and campus ministries in the diocese, commented that "Pope Francis over and over has said that the youth are not the future of the Church, but they are the NOW of the Church! They must be invited and welcomed into the life of the Church and called to share their gifts. He said at World Youth Day in Panama that Jesus is not a passing fad but, instead, the one offering an invitation to youth 'to live out your love in a practical way' and thus open a 'gateway for the Holy Spirit to give us a new Pentecost for the world and for the Church.'"[322]

When it comes to young people, Pope Francis urges an emphasis on relationality amid a solid foundation in faith. He speaks of the importance of a listening Church and recognizes that among the sins and failings of the official Church have sometimes been inattentiveness to the young that has alienated them. These sentiments match exactly testimony offered by those engaged in youth and young adult ministry. Francis recognizes, and urges those in ministry to respond to, the fact that young people are affected simultaneously by many cultures. They live in a global society, and social media invite them into numerous spaces, while they are also faced with a danger that Francis notes several times: the danger of "ideological colonization."[323] Worldwide, the Holy Father expresses concern that the secular opinions of the Western world are exported across the globe—and perilously tied to economic and educational assistance. The pope urges young people to develop their own identities, become firm in Christlikeness and Christian values and to resist the temptation to adopt every trend that comes along—especially as regards sexuality, marriage, family life and social justice.

He borrows from Venerable Carlo Acutis, a computer geek who was devoted to the rosary and the Eucharist. In the lead-up to his death at age fifteen from leukemia, he developed a website devoted to a catalogue of Eucharistic miracles that encouraged followers to create a traveling display. Pope Francis quotes a compelling insight of Carlo and uses it as a counsel to his contemporaries: "Everyone is born as an original, but many people end up dying as photocopies."[324] A balance of individuality, friendship, family and intergenerational relationships is what Francis urges youth and those who befriend them and minister to them to help create. He emphasizes encounter over mere indoctrination, inclusion and accompaniment.

With great confidence in young people, their energies, capacities and devotion, Francis focuses on the need over and over to flip the ongoing search for an answer to the question "Who am I?" to "For whom am I?"[325] This will happen only if there are living models of those who have found how to "remain online" with Jesus.[326] Deacon White speaks of the imperative to activate the occupants of our pews to move out and find ways and means to "developing intentional disciples." As the risen Christ walked with the two on the road to Emmaus, the faith is about going out, journeying and joining with others on the way.

Pope Francis Affecting the Diocese

Every papacy affects the life of the People of God both intrinsically and extrinsically. Papal statements and appointments, the bishops' *Ad Limina* visits, years of faith and global celebrations all call for a response. The papacy of St. John Paul II—given his high visibility, his wide popularity and his visit to South Carolina—certainly left lasting marks on the diocese and on people's perceptions of the faith and their actions on behalf of life and family. Even as a frail elder, St. John Paul II held an indescribable appeal to young people, whose chant, "John Paul II, we love you," continues to echo. Pope Benedict XVI, though a less magnetic personality, has been seen as a heroic figure, and his works, both the encyclicals and the three-volume *Jesus of Nazareth* series, were the subject of study by deacons, diaconal aspirants and parish groups as they appeared in print.

In various ways, the Catholic faithful, their parishes and diocesan offices likewise have taken direction from Pope Francis. His papacy has especially colored the lead-up to the bicentennial celebration of the Diocese of

Charleston. Outreach to the poor has energized works operated by religious communities and their lay associates, Catholic Charities and individuals who volunteer with Habitat for Humanity, the St. Vincent de Paul Society and numerous other charitable organizations. Catechetical and ministerial formation programs and ethnic ministry strategies have been developed to promote evangelization and to raise both awareness and action in the realm of missionary discipleship. Family life ministries have widened their programming to include not only regular pro-life activities but also ministry to those suffering from post-abortion grief and those facing unexpected pregnancies. They have also fostered formation of parents. The diocese in 2019–20 is offering additional counseling, healing ministry and renewal programs to those who have been affected by the sexual abuse crisis and scandal. Youth ministry, campus ministry and young adult ministry have reached out with holistic programs to help young people find a genuine home in the community of faith and to understand and internalize that faith effectively. Ethnic and ecumenical ministries sponsor events and gather people with an eye to improving harmonious relations among a diversity of peoples, and Catholic schools have made noteworthy strides in including persons of diverse backgrounds and abilities in their student count. The spiritual life of the faithful is being nurtured by days of recollection, retreats and increased opportunities for spiritual direction, at the behest of Bishop Robert Guglielmone and with investment of diocesan funds.

In a state marked by hyper-development, Pope Francis's environmental admonitions have perhaps gotten less traction than his other messages about passionate evangelization, real-life holiness, protection of family life and care for the poor. He has, however, made a mark in very personal ways, and as noted, people have become more and more aware of the ravages caused by overconsumption and wastefulness.

Dr. Michael Martocchio has been assisting Deacon Jerry White in developing strategies to assist parishes in their own work of evangelization. Deacon White envisions the development of what he terms Paul and Timothy movements: one to provide guidance, organization, resources and training on behalf of the diocese and the other to develop teams to bring the new evangelization home—to parishes and their mission churches and the surrounding area. They are heeding the call to "go out to the peripheries," as Francis frequently admonishes, and to engage in relational ministry. With inspiration and implicit affirmation from Pope Francis, whom he has seen at World Youth Days and during a pilgrimage to Rome, Deacon Jerry has continually sought out and implemented new ways of evangelizing. He is ever rallying young people and has pressed for personal, parish and diocesan commitments of time, talent, treasure and technical know-how to enliven evangelization. His long-standing development of youth to serve on an E-team (his savvy youth evangelization team) and his formation of the sought-after Diocesan Missionary Team of six or seven young adults ministering to peers and near-peers, embarking on its fifth year as the diocese turns two hundred, are examples par excellence of the very much alive ministry that Pope Francis envisions.

Whether one has the enthusiasm for Francis of Jesuit Sean Salai, whose book *What Would Pope Francis Do?* focuses on conversion and action among young people, or the tentativeness about Francis of Ross Douthat, whose *To Change the Church* suggests that the Argentinian pope has sometimes sown confusion, it is without question that Pope Francis has challenged Catholics' assumptions, customs and actions. His basis in the tried-and-true is also widely open to the new and to God's surprises, as he has repeatedly called them. Salai has one way of summing it up: "If St. John Paul II was the diocesan bishop who strengthened the institutional Church against Communism and Benedict XVI was the theology professor who gave us beautiful insight, then Francis is the Jesuit novice master sending all of us on mission."[327]

"Grace acts in history," says Pope Francis.[328] He reminds us that God uses our abilities and insights but that God's action far surpasses our capacities. Self-reliance may be a long-hailed American virtue, but dependence and interdependence are key to living the Christian life and also refining our capacity "to see the real and possible steps that the Lord demands of us at every moment, once we are attracted and empowered by his gift."[329]

In other words, the diocese and its missionary disciple population are challenged to celebrate a graced history while they also make history.

Chapter 19

BISHOPS, BISHOPS AND MORE BISHOPS

CHALLENGES AND OPPORTUNITIES

From John England to Robert Guglielmone, the Diocese of Charleston has had, among its thirteen bishops, men of varied backgrounds, diverse abilities and interests and different styles of leadership. Each bishop of Charleston has faced unexpected challenges and opportunities. In meeting these, each has left a legacy that has, in one way or another, shaped what is canonically deemed the "local Church," currently the Church of the whole state of South Carolina.

The first bishop of Charleston was an immigrant from Ireland, John England, 1820–42. Others were from outside the Carolinas: from Kentucky, Ignatius Reynolds, 1843–55; from Maryland, William Russell, 1916–27, and John Russell, 1950–58; from Ohio, Paul John Hallinan, 1958–62; from New York, Francis Reh, 1962–64, and Robert Guglielmone, 2009–present; from Pennsylvania and Virginia, Ernest Unterkoefler, 1964–90; from Pennsylvania, David Thompson, 1990–99; and from both Ohio and Florida, Robert Baker, 1999–2007. One was born in Ireland but arrived in South Carolina as an infant and was ordained for the Diocese of Charleston: Patrick Lynch, 1857–82. Others were native sons of South Carolina: Henry Northrop, 1883–1916, and Emmet Walsh, 1927–49. Bishop Reh served a mere two years in the diocese, while Bishops England, Lynch, Northrop, Walsh and Unterkoefler surpassed the twenty-year mark.

A bishop does not single-handedly determine the destiny of a diocese or the disposition of its souls, but he certainly sets an apostolic tone, exercises governance and makes decisions that affect massive numbers of people and have ripple effects far into the future. The bishops of Charleston have lived through slavery and tolerated it and, later, ended segregation in Catholic institutions. They have purchased properties and built churches, schools, social service missions and chanceries. They have ordained priests and assisted at the ordinations of other bishops. One of them, Ernest Unterkoefler, was among the first in the United States to ordain permanent deacons. The bishops have seen to it that catechetical programs were designed and that curricula for both religious education and Catholic schools were developed and updated. They have confirmed hundreds and hundreds of youth and welcomed catechumens and candidates into full communion with the Church. They have accepted former clergy who have converted from other Christian faiths into ordained ministry. They have called synods and promulgated policies. And over the decades, they have promoted increased diversity of backgrounds and life experiences among clergy, Catholic school student bodies, parish and diocesan employees and leaders and clients served.

From the very beginning of the diocese, the bishops of Charleston have also forged relationships with civic leaders and with an ecumenical array of ministers, preachers, bishops and interfaith leaders. As far as lay empowerment is concerned, they have consulted and sometimes confronted trustees and councils and, particularly in the post–Vatican II era, swelled the ranks of lay ministerial leaders and established programs for their formation in the faith. They have faced crises, particularly the scandal of clergy abuse of minors and misconduct on the part of clergy, employees and volunteers. They have comforted mourners after the deaths of soldiers, firefighters, children and victims of hate crimes. The bishops have led Corpus Christi processions through the streets, extended services to women with problem pregnancies and provided post-abortion counseling for those who have come to feel the pain of that choice. They have stood with the homeless and sat with prisoners. And they themselves have faced accusations and responded to them—whether these were false claims about the Church itself or more personal ones. They have borne the burden of office and relied on grace to carry them through. A more expansive list of highlights of the episcopal ministry of each is found in Appendix A.

Along with the intra-Church matters to which they have had to attend have been a plethora of local, national and international stresses. The Civil War and its lead-up, World War I, World War II, the Korean War, the War in Vietnam, the Gulf wars and the ongoing threat of terrorism have all worn on the faithful and clergy. Financial crashes and crises have undermined personal, family and corporate incomes and also stressed diocesan resources.

Racial and ethnic conflicts have tainted our cities and towns, and gun violence has wrought havoc on our citizens and tested our resolve to conquer all with love. Outbreaks of disease—yellow fever in the nineteenth century, a flu and polio epidemics in the twenteith and the coronavirus pandemic of the twenty-first have taken lives and afflicted the whole body of believers and their neighbors. Natural disasters have affected the diocese through the terms of all of the bishops: hurricanes, fires, an earthquake, tornados, floods and more. All of these have damaged homes and businesses, churches and schools, some irrevocably. And all of them have required Catholic prayer, muscle and money to restore both temporal and spiritual goods.

Amid a multiplicity of challenges, the bishops of Charleston have had to pray and trust that the Holy Spirit was guiding them and their widespread and diverse diocese. At one time, helping Catholics keep the faith in a bastion of Protestantism was the burning issue. As the diocese celebrates its 200th anniversary, developing strategies for helping people encounter Jesus and spurring on a new evangelization reaches top priority. The bishops of the latter twentieth and the twenty-first centuries have faced an increasingly secularized and often hedonistic culture—one in which the attrition of practice of the faith among youth and young adults has sounded an alarm. Thus, the invitation of Pope Francis to focus on relational ministry and to spread the "joy of the Gospel" in extraordinary ways is incumbent on the ordinaries of the diocese—its bishops. So it is on the people of faith who fill the pews of parishes with eleven thousand members on their rolls and mission outposts with twenty-five regular attendees.

Whoever the next bishops of Charleston may be, they will find a complex South Carolina history and culture and, in its midst, pockets of resilience and deep devotion. They should expect to find, among the diverse peoples of the diocese, something of what John England found in the first month of his episcopacy. He mentioned that two women named Mrs. Thompson, one younger and one older, were ever ready to offer gracious hospitality and would surely be found worthy of the "great merit [that] is due before God for preserving the faith in this country."[330] We know nothing about their personal histories, and the only reference to them is a passing one in a bishop's little diary. But they typify the saints we celebrate on All Saints' Day: the ones who have never been canonized but whose lives and almost instinctive charity have touched and enhanced the life of the Church. The people of the Diocese of Charleston understand well that their bishops exercise par excellence Christ's role as prophet, priest and king but that, by virtue of baptism and in response to God's grace, they must too.

Chapter 20

WHAT IS, FROM WHAT WAS

W hen Bishop England began to traverse his still sparsely populated diocese, it measured close to 145,000 square miles, and travel from one area to another could require a long ride along the coast by boat or a multi-day trip by stagecoach or on horseback.[331] His jurisdiction expanded even more when he was appointed to oversee the Republic of Haiti for several troubled years. The current Diocese of Charleston is itself quite extensive, measuring, by its own report, 31,200 square miles. Both the Diocese of Charleston and the Diocese of Raleigh claim a census upward of 200,000 registered in parishes but estimate that there are just as many or more unregistered, eighty to one hundred times as many as required ministry and mercy when John England landed in Charleston Harbor. This chapter examines what has become of the regions at one time or another governed by the bishop of Charleston.

HAITI

A slave rebellion that raged from 1791 to 1804 broke Haiti from being a colony in the hands of France, a nation that was itself writhing through a revolution in the shadows of the guillotine and massive blood-letting, a revolution that continued as Haiti wrested itself free. Anti-clericalism was as much alive in Haiti as in France, perhaps fueled by missionaries or resident priests who always seemed accommodating of whatever social and political structures were the status quo, and then fired up further as chaos and want beset the new nation. By 1832, some of that anti-clerical or anti-religious spirit seemed to be fading, and the Vatican was apprised that the Haitians were interested in establishing "a concordat" with Rome.[332]

In 1832, John England was asked to assist in "a restoration of peace and a re-establishment of religion" in the new republic that was, in reality, a dictatorship.[333] From 1832 to 1837, Charleston's bishop made voyages back and forth from South Carolina to Haiti and temporarily got a coadjutor bishop, William Clancy, to assist him. Neither one succeeded in "bring[ing] the government and the Holy See to an acceptable compromise." The tasks this bit of ecclesiastical diplomacy entailed put Bishop England under suspicion of being a closeted abolitionist.[334] So, too, may have an ordination he celebrated, in hopes of smoothing relations with Haiti.

The first man of color ordained by an American bishop was one George Paddington, a Santo Domingo–born and well-educated gentleman described by England as a "mulatto." Paddington was ordained to ministry as a sub-deacon in 1836 by England's coadjutor and then ordained, according to some accounts, deacon and priest by Bishop England, later in 1836 or 1837.[335] Paddington was assigned to Haiti, but his time there was short-lived; he eventually came to the States and settled into ministry in St. Louis.[336]

Bishop England was relieved to be released from oversight of that island nation by 1837. The travel back and forth was both treacherous and exhausting.[337] Haiti eventually made peace with Catholicism. By 1861, Port-au-Prince was made its own archdiocese. The archdiocese embraced several dioceses. Though geographically not widespread, Haiti included dioceses in Les Cayes, Jacmel, Anse-à-Veau et Miragoâne and Jérémie. At present, there are two archdioceses, Cap-Haïten and Port-au-Prince, and eight dioceses, the four mentioned plus Fort-Liberté, Hinche, Les Gonaïves and Port-de-Paix. The island nation, which has long suffered relentless poverty—and a devastating earthquake in 2010— was visited by Pope St. John Paul II in the fifth year of his papacy, 1983. Current statistics suggest that there are between 6 and 6.4 million Catholics among a national population of more than 11 million in the parishes and missions of the collective dioceses and archdioceses.[338]

SAVANNAH

The majestic white Cathedral of St. John the Baptist is one of Savannah's iconic landmarks and a stop on every tourist trolley and bus. One might be inclined to think that it took its name from the cathedral of its mother church in Charleston, but it actually has its origins in a church formed by French immigrants. Some of them were fleeing the same Haitian revolution that broke relations with the Catholic Church. Others were fleeing France in the same time period, the late eighteenth century, when the Reign of Terror was afoot[339] and it was clear that the revolutionary cry of "liberty, equality, fraternity" did not apply to Catholics. The French parish name, Saint Jean-Baptiste, eventually lent its name to Savannah's grand cathedral.

The Diocese of Savannah, then comprising all of the state of Georgia and parts of eastern Florida, was divided from Charleston in 1850, with Francis X. Gartland, an Irishman, named as its first bishop. Even with Atlanta later split from it, Savannah remains a large diocese with a population of roughly seventy-seven thousand Catholics served by seventy-nine parishes and missions spread across seven deaneries.[340] Some of the churches are large, architecturally brilliant ones like the cathedral. These would include churches like Most Holy Trinity in Augusta, Holy Family in Columbus, St. Joseph in Macon and more.

Others churches and missions are notably small and humble. St. Ann Mission in Alapaha, on its website, describes its first facility as a "little log cabin church" on the property of the farm owned by a Murray family, and its current membership worships in a church very similar to the Pinckney family chapel that became St. Andrew in Bluffton (described in chapter 5). St. Mary Magdalen Mission in Buena Vista is the size of a modest family home, and Our Lady of Guadalupe in Glennville resembles a double-wide. That is not meant in any way as a critique but more to attest to the fact that the divisions of the diocese that was once part of a larger Diocese of Charleston still can lay legitimate claim to being mission territory.

NORTH CAROLINA, BEFORE THE DIOCESE OF RALEIGH

As Reconstruction was unfolding and the wreckage of so much of his diocese consumed his energies, Bishop Patrick Lynch urged Rome to separate North Carolina from the Diocese of Charleston. In 1868, the request was granted, and all of North Carolina became the Vicariate Apostolic of North Carolina under the administration of Bishop James Gibbons, who came to reside in Wilmington. In 1872, Bishop Gibbons became bishop of Richmond and in 1877 archbishop of Baltimore; he was named a cardinal in 1886. The future fourth bishop of Charleston, Henry Pinckney Northrop, served as vicar apostolic shortly before the death of Bishop Lynch. During the time that North Carolina remained a vicariate, a priest known as the "Tar Heel Apostle" busied himself among the mission areas of the state. This priest, Father Thomas Frederick Price, was a native North Carolinian. In 1911, he and Father James Anthony Walsh traveled to meet with Pope St. Pius X and gained approval on the Feast of Saints Peter and Paul for the mission society they desired to bring into being, the Catholic Foreign Mission Society, more commonly known as the Maryknoll Fathers and Brothers. With significant home mission experience, Father Price was among the three priests who, in 1918, were the first Maryknoll missionaries to China. He died the following year in China, at the age of fifty-nine. In 1920, the Maryknoll Sisters were formed with the same spirit and inspiration, the outgrowth of a women's lay volunteer movement.[341] The Vicariate of North Carolina continued between 1872 and 1924 under the leadership of several episcopal administrators until the establishment of the Diocese of Raleigh in 1924.

THE BAHAMAS

Shortly before the first shots were fired that began the Civil War, Bishop Patrick Lynch received a request from the Holy See to assume jurisdiction of the Bahama Islands. Conditions of travel and the outbreak of the war made it virtually impossible to provide ministry there, but in 1863, Father Leon Fillion of Charleston, "who was not a citizen and would not be held in case of capture, ran the blockade to Nassau" and spent some time visiting as an emissary of the bishop.[342] It is not clear how long his sojourn on the islands lasted, but on a return trip, amid the war, his vessel took cannon fire, both outside Nassau and also offshore from the Isle of Palms, South Carolina. Fillion and the other passengers safely disembarked from the ship, which appears to have been beached deliberately, and the captain set the ship afire, likely to prevent it from being looted or seized. Father Fillion lost some possessions, but he and his shipmates did not lose their lives.[343]

Very little is known of the diocese's charge of the Bahamas until the appointment of Charleston-born Henry Northrop. Before he was officially installed as bishop of Charleston and while he was still administrator of the

Vicariate of North Carolina, he visited the Bahamas. Seeing the circuitous route the post-Reconstruction years required—through Florida to Cuba and then to the islands—he asked that other provisions be made for the pastoral care of the Bahamas.[344] In 1885, the islands were transferred to the Archdiocese of New York and long remained so. In 1929, a Prefecture Apostolic of the Bahamas was created, and once an episcopal legate was in residence, oversight from New York was suspended; then, in 1941, the Vicariate Apostolic of the Bahamas was created. In 1960, the Diocese of Nassau came into its own, and it became an archdiocese in 1999, claiming fifty-one thousand Catholics by 2016. The archdiocese includes Bermuda and the Turks and Caicos and is a member of the Antilles Episcopal Conference.[345]

Raleigh

In 1924, just five years after the death of the "Tar Heel Apostle" and cofounder of Maryknoll, Pope Pius XI formed a diocese that included all of North Carolina. Still a numerically small mission diocese, it was expansive geographically, only about four thousand less in square mileage than Georgia's original Diocese of Savannah—that is, fifty-four thousand square miles compared to Georgia's nearly fifty-eight thousand.[346] Raleigh today has a bishop who was born in Colombia, South America, Luis Rafael Zamara, formerly an auxiliary bishop in Atlanta, and a diverse Catholic population. Its more than 110 parishes and missions serve an increasing number of Hispanic, African and Asian Catholics.[347] Like South Carolina, the diocese also has areas and neighborhoods where retirees from other parts of the United States have settled because of the attraction of the warmer climate, the golf communities, the Atlantic seacoast and various equestrian and auto racing opportunities.

Like the Diocese of Savannah, the Diocese of Charleston, the Diocese of Charlotte and the Archdiocese of Atlanta, the parishes and missions vary in their history and size. Some, like St. John the Baptist Church in Roanoke Rapids, retain a relatively compact, tasteful structure built in the 1930s and have added service to a mission church in Halifax, North Carolina, which was founded in the late 1880s.[348] Both vigil and Sunday Masses there are celebrated in English and Spanish. St. Anthony of Padua in Southern Pines is small by city standards, but it livestreams vigil, Sunday and weekday Masses every day but Friday to a parish membership of more than one thousand families. Originally founded in 1885, it was the only parish in the Sandhills region, and it served only twenty people. Thirty years later, it was joined by a mission and then (twenty years later) by a new parish in Pinehurst (a hub for affluent golfers) and, in 1935, by a new parish in Southern Pines, an African American one, Our Lady of Victory. The two merged, at the insistence of Bishop Vincent Waters, to integrate the two local parish communities in 1961 and constructed a new, modern church in the mid-1970s.[349] The churches in Roanoke Rapids and Southern Pines contrast with each other but also with more massive churches, like the Basilica Shrine of St. Mary in Wilmington or Saint Raphael the Archangel in Raleigh, which boasts four Jesuit priests on its roster of clergy.

With a growing population, the Diocese of Raleigh continues to expand, and if any diocese of the province were to subdivide once again, it would likely be Raleigh—which indeed it did in 1971.

ATLANTA

In 1956, Georgia's statewide Diocese of Savannah was split and the Diocese of Atlanta was founded. The first bishop was Francis Edward Hyland, who led the new diocese from 1956 to 1962. Bishop Hyland, originally a priest of the Archdiocese of Philadelphia, had been auxiliary bishop of Savannah before his appointment to Atlanta. Ill health prevented him from assuming a new office, namely that of archbishop, after 1962, and he died in 1968 at the age of sixty-six.[350]

If it had remained simply a collection of pleasant rural churches like St. Anthony in Blue Ridge and Good Samaritan in Ellijay, interspersed with the occasional stately, well-attended one like the Basilica of the Sacred Heart in Atlanta, it might have taken longer for it to become an archdiocese. But as Atlanta began to grow into a hub for interstate highways, air travel, international news, major-league sports and other industrial and commercial ventures, it clearly was a city on the move.[351] Becoming an archdiocese made it the head of a province, which then included the Dioceses of Savannah, Charleston and Raleigh. When it became an archdiocese in 1962, Paul J. Hallinan, bishop of Charleston for a mere four years, was named its archbishop. Not long after, in 1964, the young Monsignor Joseph Bernardin, with whom Hallinan had worked, became auxiliary bishop of Atlanta after a very short stint as administrator of the Diocese of Charleston in the interim between the departure of Bishop Francis Reh to serve at the North American College in Rome and the arrival of Bishop Ernest Unterkoefler.[352]

The archdiocese serves 1.2 million Catholics in 104 parishes with twenty-five schools (eighteen parish or diocesan, seven independent). While all of the dioceses of the province offer Mass in a number of languages, Atlanta includes several not as frequently mentioned: American Sign Language, Indonesian, Chinese, Haitian Creole, Igbo and Croatian among the thirteen its various parishes cite.[353]

Atlanta has also sparked interest among those working with the inner-city poor and those otherwise marginalized. As a result, Cristo Rey Atlanta, founded in 2014, exists as part of a network of Cristo Rey schools devoted to serving an ecumenical and interreligious body of students "of limited economic means" in a strong academic curriculum that is tied to work study experiences, Catholic values and civic service.[354]

In June 2019, Sister Mary Prema Pierick, general superior of the Missionaries of Charity, the community founded by St. Teresa of Kolkata, visited the sisters from her community who had been serving in Atlanta for a quarter of a century. They currently operate the Gift of Grace House for women suffering from AIDS.[355]

Archbishop Wilton Daniel Gregory[356] was the sixth archbishop of Atlanta and the third of African American descent, following Eugene Marino and James Lyke, OFM. These appointments, while significant in themselves, also have had huge symbolic import, showing that the Church is one in the new South of the civil rights and post–Vatican II eras. The Bernardin connection seems significant in at least two of the appointments of Atlanta's archbishops. James Lyke was auxiliary bishop of Cleveland, while Bernardin was archbishop of Cincinnati, and both had prominence in arenas of social justice. Wilton Gregory was an auxiliary bishop in Chicago while Bernardin was cardinal archbishop there.

Archbishop Gregory served Atlanta from 2005 to 2019 and during that time opened a new pastoral center and oversaw the hosting of numerous events. Prior to his arrival in Atlanta, while he was bishop of Belleville, Illinois, he served as president of the United States Conference of Catholic Bishops as the clergy sex abuse scandals began to unfold. During his tenure, the bishops set about the business of drafting the *Charter for the Protection of Children and Young People*, which set up new strictures and methodologies in parishes, schools and dioceses across the country with an eye to detection and prevention of the abuse of children and other vulnerable persons. In 2019, Gregory was appointed archbishop of Washington, D.C., which puts him in an even higher-profile ecclesiastical position and is seen as a gesture of healing on many levels.

CHARLOTTE

The most recent of the dioceses founded from the original Diocese of Charleston is that of Charlotte, established in 1971. It is a diocese of nearly 300,000 Catholics, ninety-four parishes and missions and twenty thousand square miles of territory. Its fourth bishop, Peter Jugis, is a native son and Charlotte-educated. His education in Rome and at the Catholic University of America secured him a licentiate and a doctorate in canon law. Bishop Jugis was ordained a priest by St. John Paul II at St. Peter Basilica in Rome in 1983, a rare distinction.

As in the other dioceses of the Southeast, Charlotte has seen a significant rise in Hispanic/Latino and Asian Catholic population, and the churches and missions of the diocese vary widely in size, history and provenance.

Charleston has the Basilica of St. Peter in Columbia, Raleigh has the Basilica Shrine of St. Mary in Wilmington and Atlanta has its Basilica of the Sacred Heart of Jesus right in the see city. The Diocese of Charlotte is distinct in that it has two basilicas: the Basilica of St. Lawrence in Asheville and the Basilica of Our Lady Help of Christians in Belmont. All of these are minor basilicas. In order to be designated a basilica, the edifice itself has to have some historic significance and noteworthy artistic and architectural character. It also has to be a locus of liturgical celebrations, with a special quality of Eucharistic liturgies, especially on solemnities, and also occasions of recitation of the Divine Office. The basilica should be a place of evangelization too. Each of the basilicas in the Atlanta Province has these characteristics, and the Diocese of Charlotte celebrates its special place among them.

In addition to the basilicas, the Diocese of Charlotte has the very typical mixture of elegant old parish churches and small missions. In Charlotte, the churches with ethnic connections are more far flung, but a glance into the history of some of the churches highlights the special populations they serve. St. Mary in Greensboro claims African American roots, while St. Peter Yu in the same city serves a Korean population. St. Benedict the Moor in Winston-Salem is a historically African American parish, while the parish church of Our Lady of Guadalupe in Cherokee is built with Native American symbolic design and is located on a Cherokee reservation. The latter notes that its unique seven-sided church was built in 1966, "426 years after the first missionaries brought the word of Christ among the Cherokee as they accompanied DeSoto's expedition into the wilderness."[357] St. Margaret of Scotland is an appropriate name for the parish in Maggie Valley, in the

Smoky Mountains, given the large numbers of Scotch-Irish who settled in the Smokies, the Blue Ridge and the Appalachians. And in Boone, the church named St. Elizabeth of the Hill Country harks back to the Visitation of the Virgin Mary with Elizabeth, but it also is fitting for a parish in the hills that also serves students at Appalachian State and hosts some of the concerts offered by Mountain Home Music.[358]

Having two basilicas is one of the remarkable facts about the Diocese of Charlotte. Another is having the only Catholic college in the Province, Belmont Abbey (described in chapter 11). A third—and probably the most noted—is the fact that, as of 2017, St. Matthew Church in Ballentyne, North Carolina, was determined to be the largest Catholic Church in the United States, with a population of more than thirty-five thousand parishioners.[359] The parish has a main campus, where six vigil and Sunday Masses are celebrated, and also a south campus in Waxhaw, where four vigil and Sunday Masses are offered. A look at the parish bulletin reveals that the parish has something for everyone—liturgical celebrations, prayer groups and devotions, service activities, faith formation for all ages, small group activities, social events and a parish staff and support group list that takes up a page—and includes four priests, six permanent deacons, one sister, numerous lay leaders and indicators of counseling services and social work ministry.[360]

Eastern Rite Churches

Distributed across the three states that were once the Diocese of Charleston, there are not only ethnically identified parish communities but also a number of Eastern Rite Catholic churches. The websites of the several dioceses and the Archdiocese of Atlanta cite the presence of Maronite, Melkite and Syro-Malabar churches, typically serving, respectively, people originating from Lebanon, the general Syriac-Arabic Mideast and India. Byzantine rite Catholics and Greek Catholics sometimes identify their churches as Ukrainian or, occasionally, as Ruthenian. All of these are in full communion with Rome and are not to be confused with the Orthodox churches. Catholics share many common roots and certain sacramental privileges with the Orthodox, but the Orthodox remain apart from full union with the Chair of Peter.

Chapter 21

BEYOND THE 200TH

The state of South Carolina and the Diocese of Charleston have lived through triumph and tragedy. Slavery and segregation have dogged its history, and the beatings and lynchings of the antebellum and post–Civil War eras helped to birth the Orangeburg massacre of the 1960s and the Mother Emanuel shootings of 2015. Bishops who bought and held slaves have been succeeded by bishops who recruited and incardinated African and African American priests, religious and laity to pastor parishes, serve as deacons and lead diocesan offices. The rubble left by Sherman's troops has given way to what historian Walter Edgar has called "New South boosterism" and an economy fueled by technological start-ups, auto and airline industries and large-scale tourism. Catholics have endured scandals of pedophilia and misconduct, and some of these have stripped clergy of their freedom as well as their clerical status. Sadly, both a native son who became a cardinal and the bishop who planned the bicentennial endured false accusations leveled against them. The Church of the diocese has been visited by canonized saints and has doubtless raised up nameless ones who are celebrated every All Saints' Day.

Meanwhile, the faithful stay on. Two of the major themes of St. John Paul II energize so many persons and so many activities in the diocese. The call to build a "culture of life" has resulted in annual marches, ministry to women and girls with problem pregnancies and to those who have lived to regret their abortions. Legislative action and outreach centers have looked to the needs of persons with learning differences and disabilities and those living in unrelenting poverty. Catechetical programs, youth and young adult ministry, Catholic schools and adult faith formation, renewal and retreat offerings have responded to the call to a "new evangelization" and have strategized to counter the increasing secularization of society. Pope Francis has elaborated on and expanded the reach of these calls. The reach to the margins has extended to the unchurched—and sometimes the unwashed. It also demands a call to collaboration. Working with Christian brothers and sisters in many places achieves an ecumenical abundance of generosity, and building relations with the broader community fosters new respect and understanding among people of many faiths.

No matter what spins around them, Catholics in the Diocese of Charleston are called repeatedly to recognize the risen Lord in the midst and to be the face of Christ for those they meet in the work world and the marketplace—and they respond with surprising grace and gusto to that call.

Pinchas Lapide, a Jewish theologian and ethicist who wrote of the impact of Saint Francis of Assisi, once characterized his legacy as a spirituality of small steps. The Catholics of the diocese, known or unknown, have at times taken huge, perilous leaps and at other times have trod slowly and timorously into the new. The promise of the future of the diocese is built on solid rock. That rock is, of course, the Lord, who is acclaimed as rock and salvation, as well as the rock of Peter and all those other rocks that, like the ballast that has cobbled old port city streets, endures and endures.

Highlights Regarding
the Bishops of Charleston

John England, 1820–1842,
First Bishop of Charleston

- Established and consolidated a new diocese; built the first cathedral (a wooden one), the Cathedral of Saint Finbar; and formulated a diocesan constitution.
- Exercised a vigorous sacramental and preaching ministry across three states.
- Published an English-Latin missal for popular use and a catechism and in 1822 inaugurated the first Catholic newspaper in the nation, the *United States Catholic Miscellany.*
- Met with President James Monroe and then–secretary of state John Quincy Adams and made a historic presentation to a joint session of Congress on the compatibility of Catholicism and democracy.
- Founded a religious community of women, the Sisters of Our Lady of Mercy, and invited Ursuline sisters to serve in the diocese.
- Opened a seminary and Catholic schools for girls and for free black children, as well as a free school for the poor.
- While assenting to Church condemnation of the slave trade, tolerated existing slavery and advocated for religious education and other training for enslaved and free Africans.
- For a time served as vicar general for St. Augustine and eastern Florida and became apostolic delegate to Haiti.

Ignatius A. Reynolds, 1844–1855, Second Bishop of Charleston

- Continued to erect parishes and appoint pastors and circuit riding priests.
- Reduced diocesan debt and raised funds for a cathedral that would replace the wooden one.
- Laid the cornerstone for the new cathedral in 1850 and completed the cathedral of Saint John and Saint Finbar in 1854.
- Organized an effort to collect and publish five volumes of Bishop England's writings.
- Petitioned to have the diocese divided, with the result that the Vatican established the Diocese of Savannah, for the state of Georgia, in 1850.

Patrick N. Lynch, 1858–1882, Third Bishop of Charleston

- Was the first South Carolina native son to serve as bishop.
- Negotiated the return of the Ursuline Sisters of Cincinnati (including his blood sister, Mother Baptista) to the diocese after a hiatus in their service.
- Was given jurisdiction over the Bahama Islands.
- Supported secession from the Union on a states' rights basis but also, it appears, on the basis of his family's experience of slaveholding while also advocating for humane treatment of slaves.
- Went on a mission to Rome at the behest of Jefferson Davis but presented himself to Pope Pius IX for an *ad limina* visit without presenting the Confederate credentials he had carried with him.
- Was pardoned by President Andrew Johnson and allowed to return after professing allegiance to the United States government.
- Took action to restore ruined parishes and other sites in Charleston and Columbia and spent himself raising funds and making presentations to benefit his war-torn diocese.
- Established St. Peter's Church in Charleston for freed slaves.
- Advocated for the separation of North Carolina from the Diocese of Charleston and succeeded in having it named an Apostolic Vicariate.
- Attended the First Vatican Council, 1869–70.

HENRY P. NORTHROP, 1883–1916, FOURTH BISHOP OF CHARLESTON

- Continued and completed Bishop Lynch's plans to renovate and rebuild the new cathedral and dedicated it to St. John the Baptist in 1907.
- Focused on healthcare and education and built Catholic schools, girls' academies and the first Catholic high school (Bishop England High School, 1915); with the aid of St. Katharine Drexel, established schools and parishes for black Catholics.
- Blessed the efforts of the OLM sisters as they established St. Francis Xavier Infirmary, the first Catholic hospital in the diocese.
- Welcomed the Knights of Columbus to the diocese, which laid a foundation for important works of service and financial support.
- Opened twenty new parishes and missions.

WILLIAM T. RUSSELL, 1916–1927, FIFTH BISHOP OF CHARLESTON

- Established new Midlands, Lowcountry and Upstate parishes.
- Provided for ministry to troops in South Carolina training camps during World War I.
- Was appointed, with three other bishops, to oversee the newly founded National Catholic War Council, later known as the National Catholic Welfare Council, the National Council of Catholic Bishops and, now, the United States Conference of Catholic Bishops.
- Started the Diocesan Council of Catholic Women, which linked with the National Council and enacted charitable and material support to the works of the diocese.
- Welcomed the Oblate Sisters of Providence, an African American community, to minister at a number of locations in the diocese.
- Approved the construction of an expanded and updated St. Francis Hospital in Charleston.

EMMET M. WALSH, 1927–1949,
SIXTH BISHOP OF CHARLESTON

- Supported the faithful through the Great Depression and World War II.
- Invited the Sisters of the Poor of St. Francis to the diocese to open a Catholic hospital in Greenville and encouraged other groups of women religious to open Catholic hospitals in Columbia, Rock Hill, York and Dillon.
- Started summer programs in religious education that developed into Camp St. Mary's in Okatie in 1929 and Camp St. Anne's outside Caesar's Head in the Piedmont thereafter.
- Initiated and dedicated new parishes and schools.
- Welcomed a vigorous preacher, then-monsignor Fulton J. Sheen, to the dedication of the rebuilt Sacred Heart Church in Charleston, destroyed by a tornado in 1939.
- Continued to invite men's and women's religious communities to serve in the diocese, with the Oratory of St. Philip Neri arriving in Rock Hill in 1935 and the Trappists (Order of Cistercians of the Strict Observance) to Mepkin in 1949.
- Departed from the diocese when appointed to serve as coadjutor of the Diocese of Youngstown, Ohio.

JOHN J. RUSSELL, 1950–1958,
SEVENTH BISHOP OF CHARLESTON

- Oversaw a spurt in the growth of the Catholic population in the Charleston, Columbia and Greenville areas in the years after World War II and during and after the Korean War.
- Established new Catholic schools in response to the postwar baby boom.
- Was the presiding bishop when St. Anne's in Rock Hill became the first Catholic school in the diocese to be fully integrated—in 1954, coinciding with the U.S. Supreme Court decision in *Brown v. the Board of Education*.
- Reestablished a diocesan newspaper, the *Catholic Banner.*
- Opened a diocesan chancery at 119 Broad Street, moving it from the lower level of the bishop's residence.
- Welcomed the Order of St. Clare (the Poor Clares) to Greenville.
- Was transferred to lead the Diocese of Richmond, Virginia, in 1958.

Paul J. Hallinan, 1958–1962,
Eighth Bishop of Charleston

- Oversaw a diocesan synod, in which Father (later Cardinal) Joseph Bernardin served as secretary.
- Moved toward fuller integration of the Catholic schools and emphasized its importance in a pastoral letter in 1961.
- Presided over the diocese as preparations for the Second Vatican Council were underway.
- Continued to establish new schools around the diocese, including Cardinal Newman School in Columbia.
- Was appointed the first archbishop of Atlanta and thus head of the province in February 1962.
- Had the newly installed Bishop Joseph Bernardin serving as an auxiliary in Atlanta.

Francis F. Reh, 1962–1964,
Ninth Bishop of Charleston

- Attended and participated in the Second Vatican Council.
- Initiated fuller integration of the Catholic schools in the diocese and was in touch with the Attorney General of the United States Robert Francis Kennedy on civil rights matters.
- After the shortest term for a bishop in the diocese, was appointed rector of the North American College in Rome.

Ernest L. Unterkoefler, 1964–1990,
Tenth Bishop of Charleston

- Attended all sessions of the Second Vatican Council both before and after his appointment to Charleston.
- A known civil rights activist, mandated the completion of full integration of all Catholic parishes, schools and organizations.
- Closed several traditionally black Catholic parishes and schools in the hopes of accelerating integration but with the unexpected

effect in some cases of weakening solidarity in the black Catholic community.

- Implemented liturgical and other ecclesial reforms promulgated by the Second Vatican Council.
- Became known for advancing ecumenical relations in the state.
- Was among the first to establish a program of formation for the permanent diaconate and to ordain permanent deacons.
- Hosted St. Teresa of Kolkata and Pope St. John Paul II during their visits to the diocese in 1982 and 1987, respectively.

David B. Thompson, 1990–1999, Eleventh Bishop of Charleston

- Began assisting in post–Hurricane Hugo recovery throughout the diocese.
- Convoked and promulgated the pastoral plan for renewal designed by a diocesan synod, which began with listening sessions that included numerous laity, religious and clergy in 1991 and concluded with a document that had garnered a high level of consensus.
- Renamed the diocesan newspaper the *New Catholic Miscellany*, reflecting its roots in the paper established by Bishop England; restored its offices to Charleston; and garnered an award from the Catholic Press Association as its publisher.
- Established several new parishes and missions and new Catholic schools in Beaufort County (St. Peter and St. Francis by the Sea) and between Horry and Georgetown Counties (Murrells Inlet, formerly Garden City).
- Developed and strengthened programs to promote adult faith formation and lay ecclesial ministry training.
- Placed heavy emphasis on the social mission of the Church and ecumenical outreach.

Robert J. Baker, 1999–2007, Twelfth Bishop of Charleston

- Established new Catholic schools and laid initial plans for two new Catholic secondary schools.
- Encouraged ethnic ministry outreach, particularly to African American, Native American, Hispanic and Vietnamese Catholics.
- Accelerated recruitment of priests from South and Central America, India and the Philippines and Africa to serve parishes and ministries in the diocese.
- Initiated structural repairs to the cathedral and the building of the long-awaited bell tower.
- Promoted catechetical conferences (Fire at the Beach, later called On Fire with Faith) targeting adult religious educators.
- Honored lay and consecrated religious for Catholic leadership.
- Was appointed bishop of Birmingham and installed in 2007.

Robert E. Guglielmone, 2009–, Thirteenth Bishop of Charleston

- Promoted formation in faith for diocesan and parish employees and established a new diocesan office to implement that goal.
- Raised funds, engaged in planning and oversaw construction of two new Catholic secondary schools—one in Ridgeland and one in Myrtle Beach—a new Cardinal Newman School in Columbia and a new Pastoral Center with chapel and conference hall to replace the downtown and West Ashley chanceries and provide space for diocesan meetings, faith formation and special events.
- Reconstituted the curia to include more representation of Hispanic ministry and temporalities.
- Encouraged and saw a significant increase in applications to seminary studies and training for the permanent diaconate.
- Forged strong relationships with the Collaboration for Ministry Initiative, gathering women religious annually for spiritual enrichment and grant-seeking for outreach programs across the diocese.
- Sought and secured additional religious women and men for service in the diocese.

- Engaged in ecumenical activities with the Fellowship of South Carolina Bishops and gave strong support to the South Carolina Christian Action Council.
- Initiated a $60 million capital campaign in preparation for the celebration of the bicentennial of the diocese, with proceeds supporting parishes and specific diocesan initiatives.

Appendix B

PARISHES AND MISSION CHURCHES,
2019–2020

Listed Alphabetically by Location

City or Town	Parish or Mission Name	Founding Year
Abbeville	Sacred Heart	1885
Aiken	St. Gerard	1943
	St. Mary Help of Christians	1853
Allendale	St. Mary Mission	1922
Anderson	St. Joseph	1868
	St. Mary of the Angels	1943
Barnwell	St. Andrew	1831
Batesburg-Leesville	St. John of the Cross	1959
Beaufort	St. Peter	1846
Bennettsville	St. Denis Mission	1942
Bluffton	St. Gregory the Great	1932 (founded as St. Andrew Church, renamed in 2000)
Blythewood	Transfiguration	1998

City or Town	Parish or Mission Name	Founding Year
Bonneau	Our Lady of Peace Mission	1922
Camden	Our Lady of Perpetual Help	1914
Chapin	Our Lady of the Lake	1978
Charleston	Blessed Sacrament	1944
	Cathedral of St. John the Baptist*	1821
	Church of the Nativity	1959
	Sacred Heart	1920
	St. Joseph	1966
	St. Mary of the Annunciation	1789 (the first established parish in the Carolinas and Georgia)
	St. Patrick	1837
Cheraw	St. Peter	1842
Chester	St. Joseph	1854
Clemson	St. Andrew	1940
Columbia	Basilica of St. Peter	1821 (named a minor basilica in 2018)
	Our Lady of the Hills	1972
	St. John Neumann	1977
	St. Joseph	1948
	St. Martin de Porres	1935
	St. Thomas More	1953 (initially a University Center, it was named a parish in 2014)
Conway	St. James	1945
Daniel Island	St. Clare of Assisi	2014
Darlington	St. Joseph Mission	1959
Dillon	St. Louis	1943

City or Town	Parish or Mission Name	Founding Year
Easley	St. Luke Mission	1994
Edgefield	St. Mary of the Immaculate Conception	1856
Edisto Island	Sts. Frederick and Stephen Mission	1979
Florence	St. Anne	1940
	St. Anthony	1872
Folly Beach	Our Lady of Good Counsel	1950
Fort Mill	St. Philip Neri	1993
Gaffney	Sacred Heart	1955
Georgetown	St. Mary, Our Lady of Ransom	1899 (now includes St. Cyprian, founded 1951)
Gloverville	Our Lady of the Valley	1954
Goose Creek	Immaculate Conception	1976
Great Falls	St. Michael Mission	1953
Greenville	Our Lady of the Rosary	1952
	San Sebastian Mission	2012
	St. Anthony of Padua	1939
	St. Mary	1852
Greenwood	Our Lady of Lourdes	1920
Greer	Blessed Trinity	1974
	Our Lady of La Vang	2015
Hampton	St. Mary Mission	1955
Hanahan	Divine Redeemer	1956
Hardeeville	St. Anthony Mission	1923

City or Town	Parish or Mission Name	Founding Year
Hartsville	St. Mary, the Virgin Mother	1941
Hilton Head Island	Holy Family	1966
	St. Francis by the Sea	1984
Joanna	St. Boniface	1949
Johns Island	Holy Spirit	1939
Johnsonville	St. Patrick Mission	1979
Kingstree	St. Ann	1947
Lake City	St. Philip the Apostle	1952
Lake Wylie	All Saints	1983
Lancaster	Our Lady of Grace	2017 (originally Our Lady of Grace Mission, Indian Land)
	St. Catherine of Siena	1948
Laurens	Holy Spirit Mission	1961
Lexington	Corpus Christi	1978
Loris	Church of the Resurrection Mission	1975
Manning	St. Mary, Our Lady of Hope	2002
Marion	Church of the Infant Jesus Mission	1967
McCormick	Good Shepherd	1964
Moncks Corner	St. Philip Benizi	1965
Mount Pleasant	Christ Our King	1971
	St. Benedict	1999
Murphy Village	St. Edward	1964
Murrells Inlet	St. Michael	1976
Myrtle Beach	St. Andrew	1946
Newberry	St. Mark	1956
North Augusta	Our Lady of Peace	1948

City or Town	Parish or Mission Name	Founding Year
North Charleston	St. John	1929
	St. Thomas the Apostle	1966
North Myrtle Beach	Our Lady Star of the Sea	1964
Orangeburg	Holy Trinity	1917
Pageland	St. Ernest Mission	1990
Pawleys Island	Precious Blood of Christ	1985
Pickens	Holy Cross	1965
Ridgeland	St. Anthony	1963
Rock Hill	St. Anne	1919
	St. Mary	1945
Santee	St. Ann	2004
Seneca	St. Paul the Apostle	1995
Simpsonville	St. Elizabeth Ann Seton	1972
	St. Mary Magdalene	1989
Spartanburg	Jesus, Our Risen Savior	1979
	St. Paul the Apostle	1883
Springfield	St. Theresa Mission	1916
St. Helena Island	Holy Cross Mission	1969
Sullivan's Island	Stella Maris	1845
Summerton	St. Mary Mission	1914
Summerville	St. John the Beloved	1898
	St. Theresa the Little Flower	1984
Sumter	St. Anne and St. Jude	1838 (St. Jude, founded 1938, combined with St. Anne)

City or Town	Parish or Mission Name	Founding Year
Taylors	Prince of Peace	1976
Union	St. Augustine	1967
Walhalla	St. Francis Mission	1917
Walterboro	St. Anthony	1917
	St. James the Greater Mission	1882 (traditionally known as Catholic Hill, Catholic Cross Road, Ritter)
Ward	St. William	1895
Winnsboro	St. Theresa	1851
Yonges Island	St. Mary	1911
York	Divine Savior	1938

*Founded as Cathedral of St. Finbar. Renamed Cathedral of Saint John and Saint Finbar and consecrated in 1854. Following a massive fire, there was a pro-cathedral on Queen Street. Cathedral of St. John the Baptist was consecrated in 1907.

In South Carolina, there are also Catholic communities of other Catholic rites:

- Blessed Basil Hopko Mission, Byzantine Eparchy of Passaic, Conway, SC
- Byzantine Catholic Mission/Community, Byzantine Eparchy of Passaic, Fort Mill, SC
- Holy Cross Eastern Catholic Mission, Eparchy of St. Josaphat of Parma, Blythewood, SC
- Mother of God Eastern Catholic Mission, Eparchy of St. Josaphat of Parma, Greer, SC
- St. Rafka Maronite Catholic Church, Eparchy of St. Maron, Greer, SC

Appendix C

CATHOLIC SCHOOLS, PRESENT AND PAST

Listed Chronologically

1822	Philosophical and Classical Seminary and Boys' School, Charleston	Closed 1851
1830	The Academy of Our Lady of Mercy for Girls, Charleston	Closed 1929
1835	Free Black Children School, Charleston	Closed 1836 (reopened 1841–48)
1835	Ursuline Academy, Charleston	Closed 1847
1837	St. Mary's Free School for Girls, Charleston	Closed 1906
1847	Classical Institute, Charleston	Closed 1850
1852	St. Mary's Collegiate Institute, Columbia	Closed 1859
1852	Ursuline Academy, Columbia	Closed 1938
1854	Academy of Immaculate Conception, Columbia	Closed 1865 (various locations post–Civil War)
1858	Ursuline Academy, Columbia	Burned 1865 (relocated to Valle Crucis, belonging to Bishop Lynch)

1863	Academy of St. Joseph, Sumter	Closed 1929
1872	St. Peter's Parochial School, Columbia (moved to new building 1992)	
1874	Cathedral Parochial School for Boys, Charleston	Closed 1878
1874	Parochial School for Girls, Charleston	Closed 1878
1878	Central Catholic School for Boys, Charleston	Closed 1886 (due to earthquake)
1878	St. Peter's Parochial School, Charleston	Closed 1917 (merged with Immaculate Conception School, Charleston)
1887	St. Patrick's Parochial School, Charleston	Closed 1965
1887	St. Mary's Parish School for Boys, Charleston	Closed 1893 (merged with Immaculate Conception School, Charleston)
1887	Ursuline High School, relocated from Valle Crucis	
1887	Cathedral School, Charleston	Closed 1990
1887	St. Joseph School, Charleston	Closed 1954
1898	St. James the Greater, Catholic Cross Road, Ritter	Closed 1960 (moved and became St. Anthony Catholic School, Walterboro)
1900	St. Angela's Academy, Aiken	Closed 9th through 12th grades and incorporated lower grades into St. Mary Help of Christians 1988
1900	St. Mary's School, Greenville	
1900	Sacred Heart Academy, Greenville	Closed 1933
1903	Immaculate Conception School, Charleston (with St. Peter's)	Closed 1973 (high school merged with Bishop England, 1968)

1915	Bishop England High School, Charleston	
1920	St. William Catholic School (Mine Creek), Ward	Closed 1944
1930	Sacred Heart School, Charleston (merged with Cathedral School, 1990)	
1936	St. Martin de Porres Catholic School, Columbia	
1937	Oratory High School for Boys, Rock Hill	Closed 1943
1938	Ursuline High School, Columbia accredited; became coed, late 1940s	Closed 1957 (became diocesan school, renamed Catholic High School of Columbia)
1941	St Paul the Apostle, Spartanburg	
1944	Christ the King/Holy Trinity School, Orangeburg	Closed 1998
1948	St. Jude Elementary School, Sumter	Closed 1993
1948	St. Euphrasia Training School, Batesburg	Closed 1967
1949	Blessed Sacrament School, Charleston	
1949	St. John Catholic School, North Charleston	
1949	St. Gerard School, Aiken	Closed 1972
1950	St. Mary's Parochial School, Georgetown	Closed 1968 (merged with St. Cyprian's, Georgetown)
1950	Stella Maris School, Mount Pleasant (Sullivan's Island Parish)	Closed 1971 (merged with Christ Our King, Mount Pleasant)
1951	St. Mary the Virgin Mother, Hartsville	Closed 1981

1951	St. Cyprian School, Georgetown	Closed 1991 (St. Mary's, Georgetown, included)
1951	St. Anthony of Padua School, Greenville	
1951	St. Anne Catholic School, Rock Hill	
1954	St. Peter's Elementary School, Cheraw	Closed 1969
1954	St. Anne Catholic School, Sumter	
1954	St. Joseph Catholic School, Columbia	
1955	St. Mary Help of Christians School, Aiken	
1955	Our Lady of the Rosary Catholic School, Greenville	
1955	St. Joseph/St. Anthony, known as St. Anthony by 1956, Walterboro	Closed 1992
1956	Our Lady of Peace, North Augusta	
1956	St. Andrew Catholic School, Myrtle Beach	
1956	St. Anthony Catholic School, Florence	
1957	Catholic High School of Columbia, formerly Ursuline High, Columbia (relocated and renamed Cardinal Newman School in 1961)	
1959	St. Jude High School/Central High (1984), Sumter Catholic (1994)	Closed 1997
1960	Nativity Catholic School, Charleston	
1960	Divine Redeemer Catholic School, Hanahan	
1961	Cardinal Newman School, Columbia (relocated to a new campus, January 2017)	
1963	St. Jude Boarding School for Girls, Sumter	Closed 1970

1967	St. Joseph Catholic School, Anderson	
1971	Christ Our King/Stella Maris Catholic School, Mount Pleasant	
1985	St. John Neumann Catholic School, Columbia	
1987	Summerville Catholic School, Summerville (shared by area parishes)	
1991	Charleston Catholic School, Charleston (shared by six parishes)	
1991	St. Peter Catholic School, Beaufort	
1993	St. Joseph Catholic School, Greenville (private Catholic school)	
1996	St. Francis by the Sea Catholic School, Hilton Head	
1999	St. Michael Catholic School, Garden City (now Murrells Inlet)	
2000	St. Francis Xavier High School, Sumter (private Catholic school; reverted to St. Anne/St. Jude in 2017)	
2004	Prince of Peace Catholic School, Taylors	
2007	St. Gregory the Great Catholic School, Bluffton	
2009	Holy Trinity, Longs (moved to Our Lady Star of the Sea, North Myrtle Beach, post-hurricane in 2018–19)	
2013	John Paul II Catholic School, Ridgeland	
2016	St. Elizabeth Ann Seton, Myrtle Beach	

Notes

Preface

1. John England, *Works V*, 422, quoted in Carey, *Immigrant Bishop*, 134.

Introduction

2. Bishop England quoted by John Gilmary Shea, *Life and Times of the Most Rev. John Carroll, Bishop and First Archbishop of Baltimore*, available at https:// books.google.com.
3. O'Brien, *John England, Bishop of Charleston*, 7.

Chapter 1

4. Spieler, *Beaufort, South Carolina*, 13.
5. Rhyne, *Chronicles of the South Carolina Sea Islands*, 148.
6. Spieler, *Beaufort, South Carolina*, 11–12.
7. Madden, *Catholics in South Carolina*, 1.
8. Rhyne, *Chronicles of the South Carolina Sea Islands*, 148.
9. Spieler, *Beaufort, South Carolina*, 11–12.
10. Lyon, *Santa Elena*, i.
11. Christopher Allen, lecture at Santa Elena Museum, March 24, 2018.
12. Information for this paragraph was drawn from display boards at the Santa Elena History Center, Beaufort, viewed March 24 and April 6, 2018.

13. National Park Service, American Latino Heritage, "Charlesfort–Santa Elena, Port Royal, South Carolina," https://nps.gov/travel/Charlesfort_Santa_Elena.
14. Manucy, *Menéndez*, 86.
15. Ibid., 43–45.
16. Ibid., 55.
17. Ibid., 97.
18. Madden, *Catholics in South Carolina*, 2, 4.
19. John Buescher, "America's First Mass," http://www.catholicworldreport.com/2014/05/13/americas-first-mass.
20. Ibid.
21. Allen lecture, n.8.
22. *Catholic Diocese of Charleston*, 72–73.

Chapter 2

23. Buchanan, *Catholicism in the Carolinas and Georgia*, 11.
24. Ibid., 15.
25. Ibid., 16–17.
26. Ibid., 22, 26; Madden, *Catholics in South Carolina*, 10.
27. Madden, *Catholics in South Carolina*, 8.
28. Buchanan, *Catholicism in the Carolinas and Georgia*, 18–19.
29. Ibid., 23–24.
30. Ibid., 22.
31. Madden, *Catholics in South Carolina*, 14–15.
32. Ibid., 10–11.
33. Buchanan, *Catholicism in the Carolinas and Georgia*, 56–61.
34. Ibid., 31–33.
35. Ibid., 34.
36. Robert Hayden, "Middle Passage," available to the public online from www.poetryfoundation.org.
37. Jeffries, preface to Jeffries et al., *Teaching Hard History*.
38. Christy Clark-Pujara, "Rhode Island's Revisionist History," in Jeffries et al., *Teaching Hard History*, 38–39.
39. Buchanan, *Catholicism in the Carolinas and Georgia*, 136.
40. Ibid., 69.
41. Madden, *Catholics in South Carolina*, 1.
42. Ibid., 2.
43. Ibid., 3–5.
44. Ibid., 5.

45. Ibid.
46. The information in this paragraph is recorded in Madden, *Catholics in South Carolina*, 17–18, 21.
47. Ibid., 25.
48. Information on the Gallagher to Cloriviere era is found in Madden, *Catholics in South Carolina*, 25–27.
49. Ibid., 29.

Chapter 3

50. Joseph Kelly, "Charleston's Bishop John England and American Slavery," Project Muse, muse.jhu.edu/login?auth+0&type+summary&url=/journals/new_hibernia_review/v005/5.4kellyhtml, quoted in McQueeney, *Holy Waters of Charleston*, 39, n.27.
51. England, *Diurnal of the Right Rev. John England*, 3–5.
52. Ibid., 25.
53. O'Brien, *John England, Bishop of Charleston*, 47.
54. Heisser, "England, John."
55. O'Brien, *John England, Bishop of Charleston*, 69.
56. Cudahy, *From Blackmoor Lane to Capitol Hill*, manuscript edition.
57. England, quoted in Cudahy, *From Blackmoor Lane to Capitol Hill*.
58. Ibid., 125.
59. Carey, *Immigrant Bishop*, 163–67.
60. Ibid., 163.
61. Madden, *Catholics in South Carolina*, 49.
62. Ibid.
63. Ibid.

Chapter 4

64. Dunsky, *Fire and Forgiveness*, 5, 7.
65. Ibid., 19, 23.
66. Ibid., 28, 33.
67. Nancy Stockton, "Mother Mary Baptista Aloysius (née Ellen Lynch); A Confederate Nun and Her Southern Identity," in Spruill, Littlefield and Johnson, *South Carolina Women*, 1:214ff.
68. Ibid., 1:217.
69. Mother Baptista quoted in Stockton, "Mother Mary Baptista Aloysius," 222.

70. History panel entitled "Bishop John England, Our Founder," in Sisters of Charity of Our Lady of Mercy Heritage Room, at the Motherhouse, May Forest, James Island, South Carolina, and at www.sistersofcharityolm.org.

71. Much of this information has been gleaned from the congregation's website, from displays at the OLM Heritage Room and from interviews with Sister Anne Francis Campbell, OLM, on September 23 and October 2, 2019.

72. McQueeney, "A Reach Out to Others: Sister Mary Joseph Ritter," in *Sunsets Over Charleston*, 96–103.

73. McQueeney, *Sunsets Over Charleston*, 97.

74. Ibid. Additional information provided by Erika Plater, director of the Our Lady of Mercy Community Outreach, Johns Island, South Carolina.

75. This narrative of the establishment of Providence Hospital in Columbia and the efforts of the Sisters of Charity of St. Augustine was shared by Sister Nancy Hendershot, CSA, at the annual Collaboration for Ministry Initiative gathering in Myrtle Beach on November 3, 2019. She remarked that their ministry in Columbia led the sisters to make personal acquaintance with the Bernardin family and also noted that the grandson of the Younginer family is Deacon Michael Younginer, who serves at St. Peter Church in Columbia.

76. McNamara, *Sisters in Arms*, 644.

77. Downey, *Trappist*, 16.

78. This information is readily available at https://poorclaresc.com.

Chapter 5

79. Powell, *Back Over Home*, 2, 4.

80. Ibid., 27 ff.

81. Edgar, *South Carolina*, 250.

82. Powell, *Back Over Home*, 101.

83. Ibid., 102.

84. Ibid., 107.

85. Ibid., 117, 124.

86. Ibid., 116.

87. Found in typed family "Recollections" offered upon the Golden Jubilee of St. Andrew Church.

88. This information is found in an e-mail exchange between Reverend H. Gregory West, then pastor of St. Gregory the Great in Bluffton, and diocesan archivist Brian Fahey, May 16, 2007. Father West had numerous conversations with members of the extended Pinckney family and was privy to many of their family memories.

89. Powell, *Back Over Home*, 141.
90. *Catholic Diocese of Charleston*, 76–77.
91. Narratives for the background of all of these churches can be found in Madden's diocesan history and *Catholic Diocese of Charleston*.
92. Edgar, *South Carolina*, 233, 236, 241, 242, 252, 282.
93. See Gavaghan, *Nathalie DeLage Sumter*.
94. *Catholic Diocese of Charleston*, 41.

Chapter 6

95. Heisser and White, *Patrick N. Lynch, 1817–1882*, 60, 62.
96. Ibid., 7, quoting from a letter from their son Francis to Bishop Lynch.
97. Ibid., 6–7.
98. Ibid., 8–11.
99. Ibid., 18–23.
100. Ibid., 24
101. Ibid., 28.
102. Ibid., 44.
103. *Catholic Diocese of Charleston*, 21.
104. Heisser and White, *Patrick N. Lynch, 1817–1882*, 65.
105. Ibid., 50n.50, quoting a pastoral letter issued at the conclusion of the Ninth Provincial Council of Baltimore (where Kenrick was archbishop), 1858, expressing the same laissez-faire attitude toward slavery. Suzanne Krebsbach, in her undated paper "Rome's Response to American Slavery," lists Kenrick among bishops considered actively supportive of slavery in 1840.
106. Heisser and White, *Patrick N. Lynch, 1817–1882*, 63.
107. Ibid., 171.
108. Ibid., 177–78.
109. Mitchell, *South Carolina Irish*, 81.
110. See website of the Lowcountry Hibernians, www.bplaoh.org.

Chapter 7

111. Stokes, *South Carolina Citizens in Sherman's Path*, 114.
112. *Catholic Diocese of Charleston*, 29.
113. Madden, *Catholics in South Carolina*, 101, 103–4.
114. See Madden, *Catholics in South Carolina*, 107–8, 115, 119, 123.
115. Ibid., 102.

116. Ibid., 118.
117. Ibid., 109–11.
118. *Catholic Diocese of Charleston*, 30.
119. Madden, *Catholics in South Carolina*, 101.
120. Ibid., 120.
121. Edgar, *South Carolina*, 375, 379–80, 395.
122. Ibid., 368, 370–72, 375.
123. Henry Louis Gates, "Amanpour & Co.," April 8, 2019, www.pbs.org,
124. Edgar, *South Carolina*, 387–89.
125. Ibid., 388.
126. Ibid., 392–92; West, *University of South Carolina*, 27.
127. West, *University of South Carolina*, 27.
128. Edgar, *South Carolina*, 383–85.
129. Ibid., 381.
130. Ibid., 398–400.
131. Ibid., 519.
132. Madden, *Catholics in South Carolina*, 327.
133. Joyner, *Down by the Riverside*, 170.
134. Ibid., 171.
135. Hawes, *Grace Will Lead Us Home*, 156.
136. Edgar, *South Carolina*, 382.

Chapter 8

137. *Catholic Diocese of Charleston*, 262.
138. Madden, *Catholics in South Carolina*, 104.
139. Ibid., 123.
140. *Catholic Diocese of Charleston*, 262.
141. Ibid., 91–92. Neighborhood House is described at greater length in chapter 11. Echo House, an outreach center in North Charleston, closed several years before the bicentennial celebration.
142. See the parish website, www.newstanthony.com.
143. See the Oblate website, www.oblatesisters.com.
144. Historical information about the Oblate Sisters of Providence can be found at www.oblatesisters.com. Other information here was shared by Judge Arthur McFarland in October 2019 and by the Sisters Servants of the Immaculate Heart of Mary (Scranton, Pennsylvania) and Sisters of SS. Cyril and Methodius in conversations over the years and at official gatherings.
145. Green, "There Are More Black Catholics in the U.S."
146. O'Toole, *The Faithful*, 157.

Chapter 9

147. Edgar, *South Carolina*, 408.
148. Ibid., 411.
149. Ibid., 424.
150. Ibid., 479–80.
151. Ibid., 456–67.
152. Ibid., 464–66.
153. Ibid., 471.
154. *Catholic Diocese of Charleston*, 33–36.
155. Edgar, *South Carolina*, 466.
156. Ibid., 477.
157. Ibid., 480–81; Felder, *Civil Rights in South Carolina*, 21–23.
158. Edgar, *South Carolina*, 488–89.
159. Ibid., 484.
160. Ibid., 483.
161. Ibid., 485.
162. Ibid., 502–3.
163. Ibid., 513.
164. Ibid., 515.
165. Ibid., 529.
166. Felder, *Civil Rights in South Carolina*, 78.

Chapter 10

167. There are numerous editions of the Vatican documents. The description of their content and of the spirit of the council is that of this author, who has taught the documents, their background, their content and their impact, in undergraduate and graduate courses in semester courses on ecclesiology and in adult religious education programs.

168. Among resources commenting on the permanent diaconate and the first permanent deacons ordained in the United States, the following will be found: Robert David Sullivan, "Infographic: U.S. Permanent Diaconate Marks 50 Years of Steady Growth," *America*, July 27, 2018, www.americamagazine. org; *Catholic Telegraph*, "The Permanent Diaconate: A History," August 29, 2018, www.catholictelegraph.org; Deacon Bob Yerhot, "Update on the First Permanent Deacon in the United States," *Catholic Faith and Reflections*, June 30, 2010, www.bobyerhot.org; Deacon Joseph C. Kemper Jr., Obituary, *Legacy*, June 21, 2011, www.legacy.com; *Catholic Miscellany*, "Deacon Joseph Kemper, One of SC's First Permanent Deacons, Dies," June 30, 2011,

www.themiscellany.org; and William T. Ditewig, PhD, excerpt from *Today's Deacon: Contemporary Issues and Cross-Currents*, by Alfred C. Hughes, Frederick F. Campbell and William T. Ditewig (New York: Paulist Press, 2006), 36, accessed at www.books.google.com.

169. See the works previously cited by both Carey and Cudahy for elaboration on Bishop England's ecumenical bent.

Chapter 11

170. Figures on Catholic school population are those provided by the Catholic Schools Office of the Diocese of Charleston for the 2019–2020 NCEA Data Bank Arch/Diocesan Summary Report.

171. Madden, *Catholics in South Carolina*, 264.

172. Information on the SSMN sisters is from their own bicentennial narrative; that on the MSBT sisters is from Madden, *Catholics in South Carolina*, 316.

173. Information on the history, offerings and demographics of the school are available at www.belmontabbey.edu.

174. Wikipedia, "St. Leo University," https://en.wikipedia.org.

175. Bethune, quoted in www.brainyquote.com and other online sources. South Carolina born, Bethune became noted in the late nineteenth through the mid-twentieth centuries for her establishment of schools for African American children and her civil rights activism.

Chapter 12

176. Madden, *Catholics in South Carolina*, 202, 210, 225–26, 234–35, 251.

177. *Extension*, "Miracle on Thorne Avenue," 8.

178. "Civil War Service: To Bind up the Wounds," display board at Heritage Room, May Forest, the Motherhouse of the Sisters of Charity of Our Lady of Mercy, James Island, South Carolina.

179. "The Neighborhood House," display at May Forest.

180. Information from resource materials and interview with Erika Plater, director of Our Lady of Mercy Outreach Center, Johns Island, South Carolina, September 23, 2019.

181. Information provided by Erika Plater and attested to by persons staffing the Center on September 23, 2019.

182. The author has experienced all of these as a visitor to the center when the Franciscan sisters were there and as a community member of the Sisters of SS. Cyril and Methodius and volunteer at St. Francis Center.

183. See website for Catholic Charities USA, http://www.catholiccharitiesusa.org.

184. Madden, *Catholics in South Carolina*, 292, 326.

185. See website for Catholic Charities of the Diocese of Charleston, https://charitiessc.org.

186. Information specifically about Clean of Heart can be found at https://charitiessc.org/clean-of-heart. For purposes of this section, Deacon Gabe Cuervo in Charleston; Sister Mary Fran Bassick, DC, in Hardeeville; and Michelle Borbely in Conway have provided opportunities to visit and tour their facilties over the months and several years preceding the writing of this history.

187. See Catholic Charities of the Diocese of Charleston, https://charitiessc.org, or contact jkaiser@charlestondiocese.org.

188. Cross of St. Benedict, "About the Campbell Family," http://www.crossofstbenedict.com/about-the-campbell-family.

189. Catholic Diocese of Charleston Archives, "Father Patrick Quinlan Papers," http://www/catholic-doc.org/archive1/?p=collections/finding aid&id=58q=&rootcontentid=6339; Madden, *Catholics in South Carolina*, 281, 290.

190. Madden, *Catholics in South Carolina*, 281–82.

191. Ibid., 306.

192. Knauss, "Historic Mobile Church Rediscovered."

193. Ibid.

194. Ibid.

195. Madden, *Catholics in South Carolina*, 309–312.

196. Ibid., 321.

197. McLaughlin, "Apostle of Kingstree."

Chapter 13

198. Archbishop Wilton Gregory, frontispiece note in Millies, *Joseph Bernardin*.

199. Sister Mary Lucia Skalka, "A Person First, a Cardinal Second," in Goedert, *Final Journey of Joseph Cardinal Bernardin*, 11.

200. This story was told to an audience of several hundred catechists and volunteer parish ministers in Mount Prospect, Illinois, in March 1996 by Bishop Kicanas when he was serving as an auxiliary bishop in Chicago. The author was a presenter at that conference, which was convened by Sister John Vianney Vranak, SSCM, who was active in evangelization in the archdiocese during that time.

201. See Millies, *Joseph Bernardin*, 107. Also see the eight-minute video posted by Reverend Monsignor Philip Murnion, director of the National Pastoral

Life Center, found at www.catholiccommonground.org. It includes a message from Cardinal Bernardin recorded on October 24, 1996, three weeks before he died.

202. Cf. Cardinal Joseph Bernardin and Archbishop Oscar Lipscomb, Catholic Common Ground Initiative, intro.

203. Bernardin, *Gift of Peace*, 26.

204. Millies, *Joseph Bernardin*, 108.

205. Sister Mary Brian Costello, RSM, "Laborer for the Lord," in Goedert, *Final Journey of Joseph Cardinal Bernardin*, 9.

206. Velo, "Cardinal. Eminence. You're Home," in Goedert, *Final Journey of Joseph Cardinal Bernardin*, 57–58.

207. Dr. Ellen Gaynor, "Prescription for Life," in Goedert, *Final Journey of Joseph Cardinal Bernardin*, 13.

208. Bernardin, *The Gift*, 152–53.

Chapter 14

209. Biographical information about Riley is available in numerous public sources, online and in print. The Diocese of Charleston Archives also holds copies of news reports and Riley family memorabilia.

210. Many of the facts about specific Riley awards have been drawn from the Diocese of Charleston Archives, 1015/Baker—Professional—Mayor Joe Riley, 1996–2007, file 16/1.

211. Pat Conroy, foreword to Hicks, *The Mayor*, 12.

212. Hicks, *The Mayor*, 341.

213. W. Lewis Burke and Bakari T. Sellers, "Jean Hoefer Toal: The Rise of Women in the Legal Profession," in Spruill, Littlefield and Johnson, *South Carolina Women*, 3:412–13.

214. Ibid., 415.

215. Ibid., 419–20.

216. Ibid., 421–22.

217. "Jean H. Toal," https://en.wikipedia.org.

218. Burke and Sellers, "Jean Hoefer Toal," 422–25.

219. Ibid., 425.

Chapter 15

220. Treuer, *Heartbeat of Wounded Knee*, 23–24.

221. Ibid., 27–28.

222. Ibid., 28, 56.
223. Ibid., 76.
224. Ibid., 212–13ff.
225. Dunbar-Ortiz, *Indigenous Peoples' History of the United States*, 97–98.
226. Treuer, *Heartbeat of Wounded Knee*, 28.
227. Edgar, *South Carolina*, 1, 12.
228. Ibid., 12, 30. Tribes sometimes identified with variant spellings.
229. Dunbar-Ortiz, *Indigenous Peoples' History of the United States*, 15.
230. Edgar, *South Carolina*, 39.
231. Gordon, *South Carolina and the American Revolution*, 11–12.
232. Ibid., 106–11.
233. Ibid., 177.
234. Edgar, *South Carolina*, 105.
235. Gordon, *South Carolina and the American Revolution*, 105.
236. Ibid., 65.
237. Edgar, *South Carolina*, 59, 63, 64, 70.
238. Gordon, *South Carolina and the American Revolution*, 105.
239. Huff, *Greenville*, 179.

Chapter 16

240. Mack, *Hidden History of Aiken County*, 16–17.
241. Ibid., 19–21.
242. Ibid., 116–19.
243. Ibid., 103–8, 120–22.
244. Madden, *Catholics in South Carolina*, 119, 123.
245. Ibid., 165.
246. Campbell, "Bishop England's Sisterhood," 268–69.
247. Madden, *Catholics in South Carolina*, 264.
248. Ibid., 267.
249. Muller, *Legendary Locals of Hilton Head, South Carolina*, 47.
250. Ibid., 40–42.
251. Ibid., 56.
252. Madden, *Catholics in South Carolina*, 137, 141–42.
253. Ibid., 145–46.
254. Ibid., 151–53.
255. Ibid., 154–70.
256. Ibid., 171–72.
257. Ibid., 188.
258. See U.S. News Travel, https://travel.usnews.com, August 2019.

259. Salsi, with Sims, *Columbia*, 155–56.

260. Ibid., 11.

261. Huff, *Greenville*, 333–334.

262. Fred Childs's *Performance Today* aired the story, "Chuck E Cheese and the KGB," on ETV radio, August 19, 2019. The online performance notes published by the Greenville Symphony also include the story. http://www.greenvillesymphony.org/russian-birth-american-choice.

263. See regular postings by Warner, "South Carolina Business Review." Tune in to South Carolina ETV radio broadcasts or consult Warner's Facebook® posts.

264. Hardee and McDonald, *Myrtle Beach Pavilion*, 7, 9, 10.

265. Ibid., 11, 14.

266. Ibid., 22.

267. Ibid., 7.

268. Ibid., 50.

269. *Catholic Diocese of Charleston*, 207.

270. Lee and Beard, *Rock Hill, South Carolina*, 9.

271. Ibid., 37–39, 41, 48.

272. Ibid., 50–56.

273. Ibid., 27–32, 27–38.

274. Ibid., 74.

275. Blumer, *Catawba Nation*, 36–41.

276. Ibid., 42–47, 52–53.

277. Lee and Beard, *Rock Hill, South Carolina*, 9–12; E. Fred Sanders in Blumer, *Catawba Nation*, 121.

278. Ibid., 61–63.

279. Hannah Smoot, reporter for *The Herald*, November 6, 2017, https://heraldonline.com/news/local.

Chapter 17

280. Muñoz-Vivoso, *One Church, Many Cultures* (Spring–Summer 2019).

281. Kathleen Merritt, from an e-mail to the author, August 14, 2019.

282. Madden, *Catholics in South Carolina*, 3.

283. Ibid., 2.

284. Ibid., 5.

285. Ibid., 124–25.

286. Koerner, "What Is an Irish Traveler."

287. Madden, *Catholics in South Carolina*, 360; *Catholic Diocese of Charleston*, 205.

288. Madden, *Catholics in South Carolina*, 360.

289. Blanchet, "Irish Travelers of Murphy Village."
290. Koerner, "What Is an Irish Traveler."
291. *Catholic Miscellany*, "Our Lady of La Vang Provides a Place to Call Home," December 2, 2016.
292. Office of Ethnic Ministries, "Vietnamese Catholic History," departmental page, www.charlestondiocese.org.
293. Madden, *Catholics in South Carolina*, 25–27.
294. Ibid., 125–26.

Chapter 18

295. Wikipedia, "Cardinals Created by Francis," February 22, 2014, https://en.wikipedia.org.
296. Pope Francis, *Evangelii Gaudium: The Joy of the Gospel*, 2013, www.vatican.va, §44, 47. The texts of all encyclicals and exhortations cited were accessed through the Vatican website, English-language edition. The summaries of content are those of the author of this history. Going forward the documents will be cited by Latin and English title and date, with the appropriate section numbers indicated by the symbol "§."
297. Ibid., §83.
298. Ibid., §85.
299. Pope Francis, *Gaudete et Exsultate: Rejoice and Be Glad*, 2018, §6–7.
300. Ibid., *Lumen Fidei: The Light of Faith*, 2013, §38.
301. Ibid., §17, 15.
302. Ibid., §18, 35.
303. Ibid., §35.
304. Pope Francis, *Evangelii Gaudium*, §24.
305. Ibid., §182.
306. Ibid., §179, 182.
307. Pope Francis, *Misericordiae Vultus: The Face of Mercy*, 2015, §15.
308. Kathy Schmugge, e-mail testimony to the author, September 5, 2019.
309. Pope Francis, *Evangelii Gaudium*, §86.
310. Ibid., *Laudato Si': Praised Be—On Care for Our Common Home*, 2015, §21.
311. Ibid., §49.
312. Ibid., §51.
313. Ibid., §241.
314. Pope Francis, *Amoris Laetitia: On Love in the Family*, 2016, §200–201.
315. Ibid., §271–72.
316. Dr. Michael Martocchio, e-mail testimony to the author, September 5, 2019.

317. Pope Francis, *Amoris Laetitia*, §301.
318. Ibid., §309.
319. Pope Francis, *Gaudete et Exsultate*, §85.
320. Ibid., §101.
321. Ibid., §96.
322. Deacon Jerry White, e-mail testimony to the author, September 10, 2019.
323. Pope Francis, *Christus Vivit: Christ Lives*, 2019, §78, 122.
324. Carlo Acutis, quoted in *Christus Vivit*, §106.
325. *Christus Vivit*, §286.
326. Ibid., §158.
327. Salai, *What Would Pope Francis Do?*, 55.
328. Pope Francis, *Gaudete et Exsultate*, §50.
329. Ibid.

Chapter 19

330. England, *Diurnal of the Right Rev. John England*, 9.

Chapter 20

331. Cudahy, "Bishop John England and Catholic Savannah," 5–6.
332. Madden, *Catholics in South Carolina*, 45.
333. Ibid.
334. Ibid., 46.
335. Ibid., 389–91.
336. Ibid., 391.
337. Ibid., 46.
338. GCatholic, "Catholic Dioceses in Republic of Haiti," www.gcatholic. org, updated October 2, 2019.
339. Information regarding the cathedral is based on the history posted at https://savannahcathedral.org and personal visits to the cathedral.
340. Information about the Diocese of Savannah and its parishes is readily found at www.diosav.org.
341. The story of the "Tar Heel Apostle" and the founding of the Catholic Foreign Mission Society is recounted at www.maryknollsociety.org.
342. Madden, *Catholics in South Carolina*, 84.
343. Ibid., 85.
344. Ibid., 137–38.
345. Data on Nassau's current status is found at www.archdioceseofnassau.org.

346. Geographic measures come from www.netstate.com and Georgia Encyclopedia, "Quick Facts," www.georgiaencyclopedia.org.

347. General information about the Diocese of Raleigh is available on its website, www.dioceseofraleigh.org, and its online version of *NC Catholics: The Magazine of the Catholic Church in Eastern North Carolina*. Other observations about the diocese come from the author's visits to particular areas of the state, such as Roanoke Rapids, with longer visits in Southern Pines and Pinehurst.

348. See *Saint John the Baptist Catholic Church*, blog, https://saintjohnthebaptistcc. wordpress.com.

349. St. Anthony of Padua Church recounts its story in "Our Mission and History" at www.stanthonyparish.net.

350. Wikipedia, "Francis Edward Hyland," https://en.wikipedia.org.

351. The parishes named and the city of Atlanta have been visited by the author, who is responsible for their general descriptions. Other information about the Diocese and, later, Archdiocese of Atlanta, its first bishop and its archbishops can be found on the archdiocesan website, www.archatl.com.

352. *Catholic Diocese of Charleston*, 46.

353. See Archdiocese of Atlanta, www.archatl.com.

354. Cristo Rey Atlanta Jesuit High School, "Mission and Vision Statement," www.cristoreyatlanta.org.

355. Information about Sister Mary Prema Pierick's visit was accessed from www.georgiabulletin.org, the online edition of the archdiocesan newspaper.

356. Biographical material about Archbishop Gregory is available at https:// archatl.com. Observations about the significance of Atlanta's having had three African American archbishops are from the author's encounters with the three and her general reading regarding the African American Catholic experience.

357. The self-description of Our Lady of Guadalupe Church in Cherokee, North Carolina, is cited at CardCow Vintage Postcards, www.cardcow.com.

358. Blue Ridge Music Trails of North Carolina, "St. Elizabeth of the Hill Country, Boone, NC," https://www.blueridgemusicnc.com/find-music/ location/st.-elizabeth-of-the-hill-country-boone-nc.

359. Funk, "NC Now Has Country's Biggest Catholic Parish."

360. Example taken from the bulletin of November 10, 2019, bulletins. discovermass.com, accessed from https://stmatthewcatholic.org.

BIBLIOGRAPHY

Baker, Bishop Robert J., with Tony Sands. *Cacique: A Novel of Florida's Heroic Mission History.* Indianapolis, IN: Saint Catherine of Siena Press, 2006.

Baldwin, William P., ed. *Sacred Places of the Lowcountry: Lost Photgraphs from the Historic American Buildings Survey.* Charleston, SC: The History Press, 2007.

Bass, Jack, and Jack Nelson. *The Orangeburg Massacre.* Introduction by Will D. Campbell. 2nd ed. Macon, GA: Mercer University Press, 1996.

Bernardin, Joseph Cardinal. *The Gift of Peace: Personal Reflections.* Chicago: Loyola Press, 1997.

Blanchet, Elisabeth. "The Irish Travelers of Murphy Village, SC, USA." The Accidental Photographer, 2018. www.theaccidentalphotographer. me.

Blumer, Thomas J. *Catawba Nation: Treasures in History.* Foreword by Robert P. Smith. Afterword by E. Fred Sanders. Charleston, SC: The History Press, 2007.

Buchanan, Reverend Scott James-Allen. *Catholicism in the Carolinas and Georgia, 1670–1820.* Rome: Dissertatio ad Licentiam in Facultate Historiae Ecclesiasticae, Pontificiae Universitatis Gregorianae, 1998.

Campbell, Sister M. Anne Francis, OLM. "Bishop England's Sisterhood, 1829–1929." A dissertation presented to the Faculty of the Graduate School of St. Louis University in Partial Fulfillment of the Requirements for the Degree of Doctor of Philosophy, 1968.

Carey, Patrick. *An Immigrant Bishop: John England's Adaptation of Irish Catholicism.* Yonkers, NY: U.S. Catholic Historical Society, 1982.

Catholic Diocese of Charleston, South Carolina: A History. With contributions from Reverend Scott Buchanan, with Brian Fahey et al. Charleston, SC:

Editions du Signe, with Office of the Chancery, Monsignor Martin T. Laughlin, Administrator, 2008.

Catholic Miscellany, "Our Lady of La Vang Provides a Place to Call Home," December 2, 2016.

———. "St. Anne Receives Historical Marker for Civil Rights." November 5, 2009. https://themiscellany.org/2009/11/05/st-anne-receives-historical-marker-for-civil-rights.

Catholic Theological Union, Bernardin Center for Theology and Ministry. "The Origins [of the Common Ground Initiative]." In print, along with a video segment with Most Reverend Oscar Lipscomb and Reverend Monsignor Philip J. Murnion. Catholic Common Ground Initiative. www.catholiccommonground.org.

Copeland, Ryan. *The Beauty of Beaufort*. Hilton Head, SC: Lydia Inglett Ltd. Publishing, 2017.

Cudahy, Brian J. "Bishop John England and Catholic Savannah." Paper prepared for Bishop Boland, Diocese of Savannah, date unknown.

———. *From Blackmoor Lane to Capitol Hill: An Irish Capuchin's Influence on Bishop John England of Charleston, South Carolina*. St. Bonaventure University, NY: Franciscan Institute Press, 2019. Used in manuscript edition provided by the author.

Douthat, Ross. *To Change the Church: Pope Francis and the Future of Catholicism*. New York: Simon & Shuster, 2018.

Downey, Michael, with photography by Michael Mauney. *Trappist: Living in the Land of Desire*. New York: Paulist Press, 1997.

Dunbar-Ortiz, Roxanne. *An Indigenous Peoples' History of the United States for Young People*. Adapted by Jean Mendoza and Debbie Reese. Boston: Beacon Press, 2019.

Dunsky, Martha, with illustrations by Monica Wyrick. *Fire and Forgiveness: A Nun's Truce with General Sherman*. Columbia: University of South Carolina Press, 2009.

Edgar, Walter. *South Carolina: A History*. Columbia: University of South Carolina Press, 1998.

England, John. *Diurnal of the Right Rev. John England, First Bishop of Charleston, SC, from 1820 to 1823*. N.p.: Forgotten Books, 2012. First printed in 1895 from a manuscript brought in 1891 from a convent in which Bishop England's sister had lived and preserved at Georgetown University, Washington, D.C.

Eubanks, Caroline. "Monasteries to Visit in the South." This Is My South, 2018. https://www.thisismysouth.com/monasteries-to-visit-in-the-south.

Extension. "The Miracle on Thorne Avenue: Felician Sisters in Kingstree, South Carolina" (Christmas 2011): 8.

Felder, James L. *Civil Rights in South Carolina: From Peaceful Protest to Ground-Breaking Rulings.* Charleston, SC: The History Press, 2012.

Fordham, Damon L. *Voices of Black South Carolina: Legend and Legacy.* Charleston, SC: The History Press, 2009.

Funk, Tim. "NC Now Has Country's Biggest Catholic Parish—in Charlotte." *Charlotte Observer*, April 25, 2017.

Gavaghan, Sister M. Ignatia, OLM. *Nathalie DeLage Sumter: A Dedicated Life of Faith.* Edited by W. Esmond Howell and Myrtis Ginn Osteen. Sumter, SC: Sumter County Historical Society, 1983.

Goedert, Most Reverend Raymond E., DD, with Reverend Monsignor Kenneth Velo et al., with photography by John H. White. *The Final Journey of Joseph Cardinal Bernardin.* Chicago: Loyola Press, 1997.

Gordon, John W. *South Carolina and the American Revolution.* Columbia: University of South Carolina Press, 2003.

Green, Emma. "There Are More Black Catholics in the U.S. than Members of the A.M.E. Church." *The Atlantic* (November 5, 2017). https://www.theatlantic.com/politics/archive/2017/11/black-catholics/544754.

Hardee, Lesta Sue, and Janice McDonald. *Myrtle Beach Pavilion.* Charleston, SC: Arcadia Publishing, 2010.

Hawes, Jennifer Berry. *Grace Will Lead Us Home: The Charleston Church Massacre and the Hard, Inspiring Journey to Forgiveness.* New York: St. Martin's Press, 2019.

Hazenski, Sister Susan, SSCM. "A Forensic Investigation into the Life of Bishop John England, First Bishop of the Catholic Diocese of Charleston, South Carolina." Paper prepared for Dr. Addie Lorraine Walker, SSND, Black History Studies, TS 7240, Oblate School of Theology, December 3, 2014.

Heisser, David C.R. "Bernardin, Joseph Louis." *South Carolina Encyclopedia.* University of South Carolina, 2015–16. www.scencyclopedia.org.

———. "England, John." *South Carolina Encyclopedia.* University of South Carolina, 2015–16. www.scencyclopedia.org.

Heisser, David C.R., and Stephen J. White Sr. *Patrick N. Lynch, 1817–1882: Third Catholic Bishop of Charleston.* Columbia: University of South Carolina Press, 2015.

Hicks, Brian. *The Mayor: Joe Riley and the Rise of Charleston.* Foreword by Pat Conroy. Charleston, SC: Evening Post Books, 2015.

Hill, Selden B., photographer, with songs and poems by William P. Baldwin. *The Unpainted South: Carolina's Vanishing World.* 2nd ed. Charleston, SC: Evening Post Books, 2011.

Hiltner, Stephen. "The World Is Changing. This Trappist Abbey Isn't. Can It Last?" *New York Times*, March 17, 2018. https://www.nytimes.com/2018/03/17/us/trappist-monks-mepkin-abbey/html.

Huff, Archie Vernon, Jr. *Greenville: The History of the City and County in the South Carolina Piedmont.* Columbia: University of South Carolina Press, 1995.

Jeffries, Hasan Kwame, et al. *Teaching Hard History: American Slavery.* Montgomery, AL: Southern Poverty Law Center, 2018.

Joyner, Charles. *Down by the Riverside: A South Carolina Slave Community.* Urbana: University of Illinois Press, 1984.

Kennedy, Eugene, with John H. White, photographer. *This Man Bernardin.* Chicago: Loyola Press, 1996.

Knauss, Christina. "Historic Mobile Church Rediscovered." *Catholic Miscellany*, May 28, 2015. Reprinted in the *Kingstree News*, June 15, 2015.

Koerner, Brendan. "What Is an Irish Traveler." *Slate*, September 24, 2002. https://slate.com

Krebsbach, Suzanne. "James Spencer and the Colored Catholic Congress Movement," *U.S. Catholic Historian* 35 (2017): 1–21. Online reprint, Project Muse, access provided by Catholic University of America Press.

———. "Rome's Response to American Slavery." Personal research essay provided by the author.

Lee, J. Edward, PhD, and Anne E. Beard, EdD. *Rock Hill, South Carolina: Gateway to the New South.* Charleston, SC: Arcadia Publishing, 1999.

Love Drives Us to Do This: The History of Vietnamese Catholics in South Carolina. Greenville, SC: Roman Catholic Diocese of Charleston, Office of Ethnic Ministries, 2018.

Lyon, Dr. Eugene. *Santa Elena: A Brief History of the Colony, 1566–1587.* Beaufort: Santa Elena Foundation and Institute of Archaeology and Anthropology, University of South Carolina, 1984.

Mack, Tom. *Hidden History of Aiken County.* Charleston, SC: The History Press, 2012.

Madden, Richard C. *Catholics in South Carolina: A Record.* Foreword by Joseph Cardinal Bernardin. Lanham, MD: University Press of America, 1985.

Manucy, Albert. *Menéndez: Pedro Menéndez de Avilés, Captain General of the Ocean Sea.* Sarasota, FL: Pineapple Press Inc., 1983. Reprints, 1992, 2009 by St. Augustine Historical Society.

McLaughlin, Jim. "The Apostle of Kingstree." *Catholic Miscellany*, November 15, 2011. https://themiscellany.org/2011/11/15/father-patrick-quinlan-the-Apostle-of-kingstree.

McNamara, Jo Ann Kay. *Sisters in Arms: Catholic Nuns through Two Millennia.* Cambridge, MA: Harvard University Press, 1996.

McQueeney, W. Thomas. *Holy Waters of Charleston: The Compelling Influence of Bishop John England and Father Joseph L. O'Brien.* Charleston, SC: The History Press, 2011.

———. *The Rise of Charleston: Conversations with Visionaries, Luminaries & Emissaries of the Holy City*. Charleston, SC: The History Press, 2011.

———. *Sunsets Over Charleston: More Conversations with Visionaries, Luminaries & Emissaries of the Holy City*. Charleston, SC: The History Press, 2012.

Mepkin Abbey. *Garden Guidebook*. Moncks Corner, SC: self-published, n.d.

———. *Monastery Guidebook*. Moncks Corner, SC: self-published, n.d.

Merritt, Kathleen, comp. and dev. *My Little Black Catholic History Book: History and Resources for Celebrating National Black Catholic History Month in November*. Greenville, SC: Roman Catholic Diocese of Charleston, Office of Ethnic Ministries, n.d.

Millies, Steven P. *Joseph Bernardin: Seeking Common Ground*. Collegeville, MN: Liturgical Press, 2016.

Mitchell, Arthur. *South Carolina Irish*. Charleston, SC: History Press, 2011.

Monastery of St. Clare. "Ministries." 2019. http://poorclaresc.com.

———. "Retreat House." 2019. http://poorclaresc.com.

———. "Who We Are: Our Story." 2019. http://poorclaresc.com.

Muller, Barbara, for the Heritage Library Foundation. *Legendary Locals of Hilton Head, South Carolina*. Charleston, SC: Arcadia Publishing, 2013.

Muñoz-Vivoso, Mar. *One Church, Many Cultures: The Good News of Cultural Diversity* (Spring–Summer 2019). Newsletter of the Secretariat of Cultural Diversity in the Church. www.usccb.org.

National Park Service. "Digging into the Colonial Past: Archeology and the 16th-Century Spanish Settlements at Charlestfort-Santa Elena." U.S. Department of the Interior, n.d., retrieved March 21, 2018. https://www.nps.gov/nr?twhp/wwwlps/lessons/155santaelena/155santa.

O'Brien, Joseph L. *John England, Bishop of Charleston: The Apostle to Democracy*. Foreword by Peter Guilday. New York: Edward O'Toole Company Inc., 1934.

O'Toole, James M. *The Faithful: A History of Catholics in America*. Cambridge, MA: Belknap Press of Harvard University Press, 2008.

Parker, Mary Alma. *A Comprehensive Index of Catholics of South Carolina by Richard C. Madden*. Charleston, SC: independently printed, 1990.

Perry, Lee Davis. *Historical Tours Charleston: Trace the Path of America's Heritage*. Guilford, CT: Globe Pequot, Rowman & Littlefield, 2018.

Poland, Tom. *South Carolina Country Roads: Of Train Depots, Filling Stations & Other Vanishing Charms*. Foreword by Aida Rogers. Charleston, SC: The History Press, 2018.

Pope Francis. *Amoris Laetitia: Post-Synodal Exhortation on Love in the Family*. 2016. www.vatican.va.

———. *Christus Vivit: Post-Synodal Exhortation to Young People and to the Entire People of God*. 2019. www.vatican.va.

————. *Evangelii Gaudium: Apostolic Exhortation on the Proclamation of the Gospel in Today's World*. 2013. www.vatican.va.

————. *Gaudete et Exsultate: Apostolic Exhortation on the Call to Holiness in Today's World*. 2018. www.vatican.va.

————. *Laudato Si': Encyclical Lettere on Care for Our Common Home*. 2015. www.vatican.va.

————. *Lumen Fidei: Encyclical Letter to the Bishops, Priests and Deacons, Consecrated Persons, and the Lay Faithful on Faith*. 2013. www.vatican.va.

————. *Misericordiae Vultus: Bull of Indiction of the Extraordinary Jubilee of Mercy*. 2015. www.vatican.va.

Powell, Mary Pinckney. *Back Over Home: The Heritage of the Pinckneys of Pinckney Colony—Bluffton, South Carolina*. Columbia, SC: R.L. Bryan Company, 1982. Revised 1996.

Rhyne, Nancy. *Chronicles of the South Carolina Sea Islands*. Winston-Salem. NC: John F. Blair, Publisher, 1998.

————. *Tales of the South Carolina Low Country*. Winston-Salem, NC: John F. Blair, Publisher, 1982.

Rowland, Lawrence S. *Window on the Atlantic: The Rise and Fall of Santa Elena, South Carolina's Spanish City*. Columbia: South Carolina Department of Archives and History, 1990.

Rowland, Lawrence S., Alexander Moore and George C. Rogers Jr. *The History of Beaufort County, South Carolina*. Vol. 1, *1514–1861*. Columbia: University of South Carolina Press, 1996.

Russell, His Excellency The Most Reverend John J., Bishop of Charleston. *Eighteenth Synod of the Diocese of Charleston*. Charleston, SC: Cathedral of St. John the Baptist, 1958.

Salai, Sean, SJ. *What Would Pope Francis Do?: Bringing the Good News to People in Need*. Huntington, IN: Our Sunday Visitor Inc., 2016.

Salsi, Lynn Sims, with Margaret Sims. *Columbia: History of a Southern Capital*. Charleston, SC: Arcadia Publishing, 2003.

Sisters of Charity Foundation of South Carolina, with Contributions from Women Religious in South Carolina. "The Continuing Legacy of Ministries of Catholic Women Religious in South Carolina: Five Year Report of the Collaboration for Ministry Initiative." Introduction by Mark Small and Kathy Csank. Columbia: Sisters of Charity Foundation of South Carolina, November 2009.

————. *Stronger Together: Looking Back with Gratitude and Forward with Faith—A 10 Year Woven History of the Collaboration for Ministry Initiative*. Columbia: Sisters of Charity Foundation of South Carolina, 2013.

South Carolina Institute of Archaeology and Anthropology (SCIAA). "Our History," March 21, 2018. https://santa-elena.org/history.

Spieler, Gerhard. *Beaufort, South Carolina: Pages from the Past.* Charleston, SC: The History Press, 2008.

Spruill, Marjorie Julian, Valinda W. Littlefield and Joan Marie Johnson. *South Carolina Women: Their Lives and Their Times.* Vol. 1. Athens: University of Georgia Press, 2009.

————. *South Carolina Women: Their Lives and Their Times.* Vol. 3. Athens: University of Georgia Press, 2012.

————. *South Carolina Women: Their Lives and Their Times.* Vol. 2. Athens: University of Georgia Press, 2010.

Stokes, Karen. *South Carolina Civilians in Sherman's Path: Stories of Courage amid Civil War Destruction.* Charleston, SC: The History Press, 2012.

Tisby, Jemar. *The Color of Compromise: The Truth about the American Church's Complicity in Racism.* Grand Rapids, MI: Zondervan, 2019.

Treuer, David. *The Heartbeat of Wounded Knee: Native America from 1890 to the Present.* New York: Riverhead Books, 2019.

Unsworth, Tim. "Joseph Cardinal Bernardin." *National Catholic Reporter Online.* November 22, 1996.

West, Elizabeth Cassidy. *The University of South Carolina.* Charleston, SC: Arcadia Publishing, 2003.

Willimon, Will. *Who Lynched Willie Earle?* Nashville, TN: Abingdon Press, 2017.

ABOUT THE AUTHOR

 ister Pamela Smith, SSCM, PhD, has served in the Diocese of Charleston since 2004 in a variety of educational and administrative roles. She is currently director of ecumenical and interreligious affairs for the diocese. She is the author of fifteen books. They include prose works on biblical spirituality and environmental ethics and three collections of poetry focused on the experience of racial and ethnic minorities and those living with chronic illness. The *Catholic Miscellany* has run her biweekly column since 2015. This book reflects research that has been assisted by numerous diocesan personnel and historians who live in South Carolina and have graciously shared their wisdom, and it reflects stories gleaned from travel around the tri-state area that was the original diocese.